STATE OF WAR

UNIVERSITY PRESS OF FLORIDA

Florida A&M University, Tallahassee
Florida Atlantic University, Boca Raton
Florida Gulf Coast University, Ft. Myers
Florida International University, Miami
Florida State University, Tallahassee
New College of Florida, Sarasota
University of Central Florida, Orlando
University of Florida, Gainesville
University of North Florida, Jacksonville
University of South Florida, Tampa
University of West Florida, Pensacola

STATE OF WAR

UNIVERSITY PRESS OF FLORIDA

Florida A&M University, Tallahassee
Florida Atlantic University, Boca Raton
Florida Gulf Coast University, Fort Myers
Florida International University, Miami
Florida State University, Tallahassee
New College of Florida, Sarasota
University of Central Florida, Orlando
University of Florida, Gainesville
University of North Florida, Jacksonville
University of South Florida, Tampa
University of West Florida, Pensacola

ANTHONY D. ATWOOD

STATE OF WAR

A History of World War II in Florida

UNIVERSITY PRESS OF FLORIDA
Gainesville/Tallahassee/Tampa/Boca Raton
Pensacola/Orlando/Miami/Jacksonville/Ft. Myers/Sarasota

Cover: View showing US Navy dive bombers flying over Miami during World War II. Photographed in October 1939. State Archives of Florida, Florida Memory. https://www.floridamemory.com/items/show/25729

Copyright 2025 by Anthony D. Atwood

All rights reserved
Published in the United States of America

30 29 28 27 26 25   6 5 4 3 2 1

LIBRARY OF CONGRESS CATALOGING-IN-PUBLICATION DATA

Names: Atwood, Anthony D. author

Title: State of war : a history of World War II in Florida / Anthony D. Atwood.

Description: 1. | Gainesville : University Press of Florida, [2025] | Includes bibliographical references and index. | Summary: "This book explores how World War II transformed Florida into a major hub of military industry and an important training base for ground, naval, and air forces, detailing the war's lasting impacts on the state"—Provided by publisher.

Identifiers: LCCN 2025004390 (print) | LCCN 2025004391 (ebook) | ISBN 9780813079424 hardback | ISBN 9780813081151 paperback | ISBN 9780813073941 ebook | ISBN 9780813074108 pdf

Subjects: LCSH: World War, 1939–1945—Florida | World War, 1939–1945—War work—Florida | Florida—History, Military—20th century | Florida—History

Classification: LCC D769.85.F5 A89 2025 (print) | LCC D769.85.F5 (ebook) | DDC 940.54/09759—dc23/eng/20250312

LC record available at https://lccn.loc.gov/2025004390

LC ebook record available at https://lccn.loc.gov/2025004391

The University Press of Florida is the scholarly publishing agency for the State University System of Florida, comprising Florida A&M University, Florida Atlantic University, Florida Gulf Coast University, Florida International University, Florida State University, New College of Florida, University of Central Florida, University of Florida, University of North Florida, University of South Florida, and University of West Florida.

University Press of Florida
2046 NE Waldo Road
Suite 2100
Gainesville, FL 32609
http://upress.ufl.edu

GPSR EU Authorized Representative: Mare Nostrum Group B.V., Mauritskade 21D, 1091 GC Amsterdam, The Netherlands, gpsr@mare-nostrum.co.uk

DEDICATED TO THOSE WHO SERVE,

WHO HAVE SERVED,

AND WHO WILL SERVE . . .

And to the fallen.

Lest we forget.

Major William S. Pagh (*right*) of Ormond Beach, Florida, and the gunner and crew chief of his A-20 light bomber *The Florida Gator*. Before the war, Pagh was a UF alumnus who taught high school in Ormond Beach. Soon after this photograph was taken, Pagh went into battle August 11, 1944, leading a bombing mission over seaside Utarom airfield in West Papua, New Guinea. Approaching the target his aircraft was shot down by anti-aircraft fire and cartwheeled into the sea. No remains of Pagh or his gunner Sgt. Leonard E. Zelasko of Chicago have ever been recovered. He left a widow and young daughter. Pagh is memorialized at the US Military Cemetery in Manila. Service Record #0–367251 William S. Pagh. Missing in Action Report, Feb. 12, 1945. Photo from the collection of Pagh's crew chief Sgt. Joseph S. Wray.

CONTENTS

1. The Sticks and the Hicks: Geography and Demography *1*

2. Naval Air Station Florida *19*

3. Army Airfield Florida *36*

4. Off We Go! Into the Wild Blue Yonder *50*

5. Anchors Aweigh: The Battle of the Gulf Sea Frontier *69*

6. Florida Military Academy Courses *87*

7. Bombs Away and Over the Hump *102*

8. Women, Work, Captives, and Wounded *119*

9. A Sudden End to War: Census and Remembrance *141*

Notes *161*

Bibliography *183*

Index *191*

STATE OF WAR

I

THE STICKS AND THE HICKS
Geography and Demography

Florida is the perfect example of the interplay of history and geography during World War II at the provincial level, a subject usually overlooked in the study of that conflict. Before Pearl Harbor, even before the rise of Hitler, military observers saw there was dramatic strategic potential to Florida. The peninsula offered a unique combination of *place* and *space* that determined it would host mighty armies and over two hundred fifty military installations.[1] Florida's place—its internal characteristics of gentle seashore, flatlands, abundant forests, and favorable climate—was ideal for military training in an environment that had the aspect of one big campground.

Likewise, Florida's space, its relationship to the rest of the world, made it the guardian of the most important sea lanes of the United States. Perhaps more importantly, the space Florida occupied on the planet made it the launch site for projecting aerial military power around the world. The demography of Florida likewise foreshadowed and shaped its wartime role. This chapter explores first the military geography of the peninsula, its place and space, in the context of both defensive and offensive war; second, it surveys the demographic potential of the state as revealed in the prewar 1940 census.

Florida is and always has been a maritime state. The peninsula projects into strategic waters that demand military attention. Its then-uninhabited coastline of sheltered pleasant beaches would be particularly useful in the coming war. Jacksonville, Fort Lauderdale, Miami, Key West, Tampa, and

Pensacola offered significant harbors. Such attributes and facilities ensured Florida would offer naval training of all kinds. Maps reveal Florida's importance to maritime planning. Alfred Thayer Mahan, the naval strategist and historian, identified the issues as early as 1902: "The first and most obvious light in which the sea presents itself from the political and social point of view is that of a great highway."[2] Within this context of the seas as a medium for transportation and commerce, some of the most important intersections of the great nautical highway are dominated by Florida.

Mahan's Chart of the Realm

A realm is geostrategic terminology for a region that is informed and constrained by specific geographic factors.[3] Florida is a part of the sea realm between the continents of North and South America, an expanse of ocean peppered with a clutter of island stepping-stones. The celestial mechanics of this planet's spin on its axis drives the waters of the Atlantic Ocean into the Caribbean basin through the passages flowing between the Antilles, through the Windward, Mona, and Grenada passages, and several smaller channels, traversing east to west. From the Caribbean these waters push through the Yucatán Passage to the Gulf of Mexico, swirling clockwise to generate the Gulf Stream current. Finding no other exit, the waters of the Gulf Stream then are forced back out to the open ocean via the Florida Straits, traveling west to east. Mahan, in his day, noted the increasing importance of the region.[4] Writing at the turn into the twentieth century, even before the US had begun work on the Panama Canal, the one-time president of the American Historical Association predicted the canal's completion and foretold it would confer on Florida critical new national security concerns for the US:

> Along this path a great commerce will travel, bringing the interests of the other great nations, the European nations, close along our shores, as they have never been before. With this it will not be so easy as heretofore to stand aloof from international complications. The position of the United States with reference to this route will resemble England to the Channel.[5]

Mahan's vision acknowledged the commanding geographic space of the Florida peninsula. The admiral saw intuitively that its waters were key po-

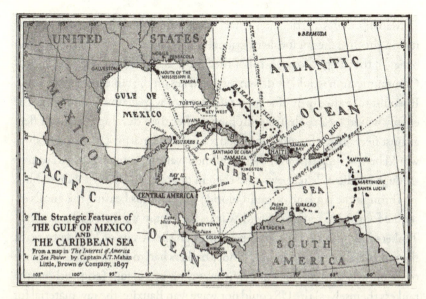

Mahan's chart of the realm. This map shows the main maritime routes in and around the Gulf of Mexico and the Caribbean Sea taken by civilian and military shipping, which highlights the strategic importance of Florida in relation to the Mississippi River, the Panama Canal, and the other peninsula sea passages to the rest of the world. Before World War I, even before the twentieth century and the opening of the Panama Canal, Admiral Alfred Thayer Mahan studied the military geography of the Caribbean Domain. He predicted that war would come to the peaceful waters of Florida and the picturesque archipelago surrounding it. When war did come, it was with a sudden and brutal vengeance. Mahan, *The Interest of America in Sea Power*.

sitions to the defense of the United States. He was specific regarding the military importance of this geography:

> At present, the United States has one frontier which is strictly continuous, by land as by water, from the coast of Maine to the Rio Grande. There are in it, by natural division, three principal parts: the Atlantic, the Gulf, and the Straits of Florida. . . . It may fairly be claimed that these three are clear, are primary, and are principal. They are very unequal in length, and, from a military standpoint, in importance; for while the peninsula of Florida does not rank very high in the industrial interests of the nation, a superior hostile fleet securely based in the Straits of Florida could effectively control intercourse by water between the two flanks.[6]

Mahan's analysis articulates what military thinkers call a "center of gravity," in this instance, a locale of critical importance to a war effort. Mahan believed that a fight for control of the Straits and neighboring Sea Lines of Communication would be driven by the stakes on the table: merchant ships. It would take the form of a *guerre de course*, a war against commerce. The enemy would seek to destroy shipping, rather than develop a battle of fleet against fleet. Three factors combined for such a scenario: a great many ships would be traveling through these confined waters, these targets had to pass through predictable narrows, and therein they would be most vulnerable.

Through the sea lanes around Florida passed ships bearing the goods essential for the US to fight World War II. Petroleum was one such material.[7] Tankers full of Texas oil had to pass through the Straits of Florida to reach the industrial eastern seaboard. Empty tankers had to return along the same route in reverse to fill up again. Without their petroleum (and without the tankers themselves) the US could not wage war. Bauxite, the raw material for refining aluminum, also passed through the narrows.[8] Aluminum had many uses for the land and naval forces of the United States. Above all, the strong and lightweight metal was essential for manufacturing the warplanes of the US air forces. Without aluminum, the US air wings would not fly. In the Western Hemisphere most of this strategic ore came from Brazil, Guyana, and Suriname (then–British and Dutch Guiana, respectively). Convoys of bauxite had to pass through the sea lanes dominated by Florida to reach the factories of North America.

All the maritime traffic of the US heartland that flowed in or out of the Mississippi River also traveled the same route. The Mississippi reaches almost to Canada and the Great Lakes. Into it pour the riparian arteries of the central United States: the Missouri, Illinois, Ohio, Tennessee, Arkansas, and Red rivers. These tributaries carry the traffic from the interior hinterlands of the continent as far reaching as Montana, Colorado, Pennsylvania, and Oklahoma. To reach the heartland, goods had to enter the Mississippi. To depart the interior, they had to exit the passes of the Mississippi. All maritime traffic coming or going had to pass through the Gulf of Mexico, before or after transiting the Florida Straits to reach the East Coast or go through the adjacent Yucatán Passage to reach the Panama Canal and the West Coast.[9] Florida commanded these chokepoints.

Mahan was not alone in seeing the predictability that war would come to these watery spaces around Florida, and that combat would focus upon the merchant ships that out of necessity had to sail through them. Contemporary British naval historian Julian Stafford Corbett seconded the fact in his 1911 maritime observations: "The most fertile areas always attracted the strongest attack.... The fertile areas were the terminals of departure and destination where trade tends to be crowded, and in a secondary degree the focal points where, owing to the conformation of the land, trade tends to converge."[10] Corbett summarized the predictability of naval warfare by borrowing from Scripture: "For wheresoever the carcass is, there will the eagles gather together."[11]

Florida's proximity to the Panama Canal engaged still other strategic concerns. All the West Coast and Pacific shipping that funneled through and emerged from the Canal—whichever way it was bound—steamed within range of Florida-based aircraft, and often within eyesight of the peninsula. The US naval historian of World War II Samuel Eliot Morison titled his work *The Two-Ocean War*. It was an apt description: the United States fought its war from the Atlantic Ocean and the Pacific Ocean. The US could not have done so without the Panama Canal.[12] It was the link to supply and communication of every kind. It connected the US war effort around the world. Writing forty years before the war, Mahan prophetically predicted: "One thing is sure: in the Caribbean Sea is the strategic key to the two great oceans, the Atlantic and Pacific, our own chief maritime frontiers."[13] The closest, largest, and strongest bastion of American power protecting this essential waterway was Florida.

The dictum of the US naval service is "To keep the sea lanes open." That is the primary mission of the Navy, and it defines the defensive role of Florida in World War II. As this global conflict spread across Europe and Asia, the United States necessarily turned first to its own defenses. Measures undertaken in Florida were part of a larger prewar program by the US to strengthen the defenses of the North American continent. In the Pacific, the forward defenses of the Continental United States (CONUS) included building the Al-Can Highway to Alaska from the "Lower-48," along with new and improved bases in Alaska and the Aleutian Islands. The defense line arced to the Hawaiian Islands, where the US fleet was moved in 1940 from San Diego to take up station in mid-ocean at Pearl Harbor. The US Philippine Islands Territory, in its exposed forward position, was reinforced with US troops and the local population was organized into a defense force.

The US Panama Canal Zone likewise received strengthened garrisons and hardened defenses.[14]

From Panama eastward ran a similar Atlantic defense line in which Florida figured prominently, with its regional appendages of Guantanamo, Cuba; Puerto Rico; and the US Virgin Islands.[15] A line of offshore outposts was to run from Brazil to Greenland. Establishing such forward defenses motivated the Administration's 1940 agreement with Britain trading arms for basing rights. In exchange for surplus warships, the US received leases to establish military bases at the British territories of Newfoundland, Bermuda, and its Caribbean territories of the Bahamas, St. Lucia, Jamaica, Trinidad, Antigua, and British Guiana.[16] The redoubts the US established in these Caribbean places were closest to the US at Florida, and the soldiers and supplies fed into these forward naval and aviation tripwire positions passed through Florida first.

As it did with defenses, Florida likewise figured in offensive considerations. Mahan knew the importance of engaging the enemy and observed that geographic conditions were part and parcel of offensive operations. "The geographic position of a country may not only favor the concentration of its forces but give the further strategic advantage of a central position and a good base for hostile operations against its probable enemies."[17] Florida's military value was more than the guardianship of vital sea routes. The peninsula was positioned to project offensive power.

Yet the military power that Florida was poised to project was not naval, but the new weapon that would become a determining factor in World War II: air forces. US military aviation had an understandable prewar interest in Florida for two reasons. The first and obvious reason is that of place: The climate and topography favored aviation development. The year-round blue skies were ideal for training up the new weapon of air forces. The peninsula was never more than a hundred fifty miles from the sea, allowing for unlimited gunnery practice. The large, empty national forests and state forests were available for bombing ranges. The flatness of the terrain invited landing fields, and any uninhabited meadow would do. Commercial aviation saw this before the war. In 1939 Florida offered six flying schools and nine prewar working airfields. Florida emerged from the war with over sixty airports, every one run by the government and operated with military precision.[18]

Developing the air arm of the US military to its full potential had long been the goal of aviation strategist and advocate General William "Billy" Mitchell. The outspoken Mitchell, who gained fame as a US Army Air Service field commander in the Great War—later renamed World War I—strongly urged the establishment of an independent air force. Such a force he envisioned would be equal to the Army and Navy.[19] Only when freed from the tactical concerns of those two services, General Mitchell theorized, could air forces be utilized for their true value as a strategic weapon and a determining military factor in modern warfare: "The influence of air power on the ability of one nation to impress its will on another in an armed conflict will be decisive."[20]

Mitchell witnessed in the Great War how armies locked in the carnage of trench warfare were unable to budge, while aircraft simply flew over them. Presuming that future warfare would repeat that model, he advocated a vast air force, commanded specifically by airmen, which would fly over the opposition and bring aerial war to the enemy's homeland with bombs. By attacking the enemy's industrial means of waging war, conflict might be ended quickly, compared to the bloodshed of ground warfare. "It is a quick way of deciding a war and really much more humane," he argued, "than the present methods of blowing people to bits by cannon projectiles or butchering them with bayonets."[21] Bombing, he believed, was how to achieve victory:

> Air Forces will attack centers of production of all kinds, means of transportation, agricultural areas, ports and shipping; not so much the people themselves. They will destroy the means of making war. . . . Today to make war we must have great metal and chemical factories that have to stay in one place, take months to build, and if destroyed, cannot be replaced in the usual length of a modern war.[22]

The surprising idea that bombing was more humane than ground warfare was one shared by other aviation thinkers in the years before World War II. The Italian aviator Giulio Douhet argued that bombing directed specifically against civilian cities was in the long run merciful, as civilian morale would quickly break and force warring nations to the peace table. In the light of such later aerial massacres as Coventry, Dresden, Tokyo, and Hiroshima, the notion of bombing being humane is one of ghastly impropriety. But it must be remembered that those horrors had not yet occurred, and Mitchell and his colleagues had no idea they would happen.[23]

Bombing "would deprive armies, air forces and navies of their means of maintenance."[24] The proposed model of waging war with airplanes instead of armies and navies included the attractive prospect of being relatively cost-free by comparison. Despite the appeal of his arguments, Mitchell's confrontational style led to his 1925 court-martial for insubordination. Even after his forced retirement, the junior officers of the Air Corps continued to believe in the offensive capability of bombing, and in the separation of the Air Corps from the Army as an independent branch of service, as was the Royal Air Force (RAF). The accidental death of the US Army Air Corps commander in September 1938 brought one of these acolytes, Lieutenant General Henry Harley "Hap" Arnold, into command of the Air Corps. Arnold oversaw the introduction into the inventory of the four-engine B-17 heavy bomber, together with congressional approval for Air Corps expansion in Florida.[25] The concurrent advent of the Dakota transport plane would make Florida a central proving ground for the assembly of a strategic bombing force, and of an airlift capacity, vital components, and core competencies of an independent air force. The second reason for airpower attraction to Florida, less obvious but equally important, was the spatial relationship of Florida to the rest of the world.

From the perspective of global travel, the technical limitations of airplanes during the war made Florida a logical starting point from which to send forth air power. First, the icy skies over the North Atlantic from the US to Europe were dangerous much of the year. Second, contemporary aircraft lacked the range to overfly the mid-Atlantic Ocean.[26] Finally, the mid-Atlantic Azores Islands of neutral Portugal were closed at the time to any but humanitarian landing and refueling.[27] Aerial refueling did not then exist. Florida offered a classic peripheral air route to reach the theaters of operation in Europe, Africa, Asia, and the Pacific. Thus, airmen could fly in stages from Florida via the Caribbean islands to South America, from there to West Africa and from thence to the fighting fronts. Such hop flights from Florida air bases developed critical strategic importance in the war. Aerial force projection from Florida rivaled training as the main wartime mission of the state. In the prewar years the groundwork would be laid for an airlift extending more than halfway around the world from its point of origin in Florida.

Another proposal of Mitchell that would manifest signs in Florida was his plan to create a "Department of National Defense," to replace the US War Department.[28] The War Department had authority over wartime matters, but it was unwieldy. In peacetime its halls were a neglected place with caretaker staff officers dressed in civilian mufti. In wartime it lurched into activity, with the Navy Department and State Department alongside. The War Department waged war zealously but inefficiently. When peace returned, the War Department squandered its strength with rapid demobilizations. Its ill-defined authority often conflicted with State Department prerogatives. Hostilities not of the nature of a declared war were handled vaguely. Mitchell proposed three branches of service—land, sea, and air—under the aegis of a new government organization each branch would always report to: a Department of National Defense.[29]

Explicit in such a reorganization of the US government was the independence of its aviation forces, modeled after the example of the Royal Air Force. Mitchell was well acquainted with the Air Marshal of the RAF, Hugh Trenchard. Trenchard similarly believed in the efficacy of strategic bombing and strongly championed air power as an independent branch of service.[30] When Roosevelt assumed the presidency, Mitchell sought him out as a private citizen and shared his concepts and concerns for the future of air power. A drive resonating within the US war effort from the start would be a technical, administrative, and managerial evolution toward an independent air force. Much of it would come to life in Florida.

An understanding of Florida's military persona, defined thus far as derived from land, sea, and air factors of place and of space, must include the demography of the state at the time: knowledge of the people and their works. The US Census of 1940 provides an essential picture of who the Floridians were, and what they were doing before the US entered the war. The census records the number of Floridians in spring 1940 at 1,897,414. The state was home to a meager 1.415 percent of the US population of 134 million. Florida by gender had 943,123 males and 954,291 females, a ratio conforming to biological norms. The population was spread out over a land mass of nearly 66,000 square miles, which meant that the land was relatively empty, with a density of only twenty-nine people per square mile. There was plenty of room for incoming soldiers and plenty of land for military activities.[31]

Racially, the census suggests that Florida was an almost classic Old South province on the eve of war. Its small population was far more mixed than most of the US, whose African American population then comprised 11 percent of the total. Florida's African American population was more than twice the national average: one in four Floridians was African American. Florida counted 1,381,986 (72.8 percent) as white and 514,198 (27.2 percent) as African American.[32] These numbers reinforce Florida's demographic alignment with the Deep South states of South Carolina, Georgia, Alabama, Mississippi, and Louisiana. Beyond race, this southern alignment perhaps explains other aspects of the state's involvement in the war. Southerners' affection for the military may help account for the very high rate of service enlistment among Floridians: almost one-quarter of a million of them donned the uniform during the war.[33]

Foreign-born Floridians had identity patterns of their own. Those whites claiming foreign birth were 69,861 men and women, or 5 percent of the total.[34] The 514,198 African American population contained 7,779 foreign-born, primarily of Bahamian, Jamaican, and Trinidadian origin.[35] Regarding the white foreign-born population, the largest group hailed from the British Isles (12,700 altogether). Another large group was homesteading snowbirds from Canada (9,482 persons). Other western European countries provided 7,764, while Russia and the Baltic States were the origin for 7,372.[36] Thus, 37,318 Floridians claimed origin from places that at the time were either at war against the Axis powers or soon would be. Conversely, those originating from Germany and Austria constituted 8,914 persons. To these may be added those from Poland, Czechoslovakia, and Hungary, another 4,147. All these points of origin in 1940 were forcibly incorporated parts of *Gross Deutschland*. Italy was the place of origin of another 5,138 persons. In 1940, therefore, 18,199 Floridians identified themselves as originating from soon-to-be enemy countries.[37] These European-born citizens of Axis origin were regularly rumored to be helping the enemy in the form of clandestine U-boat refueling sites, secret radio communications, divulging war news, and providing aid and comfort to enemy landing parties. That these stories may have contained some truth is suggested by the insertion in Florida of saboteurs in *Operation Pastorius* in 1943.[38] Florida would also become the incarceration place for thousands of enemy prisoners of war.[39] The existence of these enemy soldiers in their midst, often engaged in work connected to the US war effort, together with Florida's own subgroup who identified themselves as originating from the same place, may have fueled the persistent belief during the war that the enemy was secretly operating among them.[40]

Only 154 persons of Japanese origin lived in Florida on the eve of war.[41] One small group was the vestigial remnant of a small agricultural community created by the state in Palm Beach County known as the Yamato Colony.[42] Their fate may be illustrative of the wartime militarization of Florida. Yamato began as an experimental farm to cultivate pineapple for a cash crop using farmers brought in from Japan.[43] Blight doomed the experiment and only a handful of farmers remained, so that in 1940 only sixteen persons of Japanese birth or ancestry were counted in Palm Beach County.[44] After Pearl Harbor, the federal government seized the land and awarded it to the War Department. The acreage became part of the wartime Boca Raton Army Airfield.[45] The local community pitched in to build the base, readily taking up the employment provided by this wartime construction project, as they were doing at many other military sites across Florida.

The amazing, courageous Cuban diaspora that would transform Florida further had not yet occurred. Cuba in World War II was a staunch Ally, declaring war on Imperial Japan the day after Pearl Harbor. Guantanamo Naval Station would be augmented by four navy airship facilities on the island. The Cuban Air Force trained hundreds of US and RAF pilots. Using lend-lease subchasers supplied by the Coast Guard, the Cuban Navy proved its mettle in sinking a Nazi U-boat. A US draft board operating in Cuba processed dual nationals. The preinduction physicals and oath-of-enlistment were administrated at the US Embassy. The writer Ernest Hemingway left his finca outside Havana and put to sub-hunting in his fishing boat. The Pilar bristled with makeshift depth charges and tommy guns furnished by the FBI.

The census revealed critical aspects of employment that would directly affect Florida's role in the war. The Great Depression had hit the state hard. In 1932 the number of families on relief constituted 36 percent of the African American population, and 22 percent of the white population.[46] The 1940 Census confirms continuing poverty. The labor force comprised 402,634 white Floridians, 156,417 African American Floridians, and 465 persons of "other races," fourteen years of age and older, making a total of 559,516 "gainful workers."[47] Of those in the white labor force, 84.4 percent were categorized "at work." Those in the category of "On Public Emergency Work (WPA, etc.)" constituted 5.9 percent of the total, while those "seeking work" numbered 7.7 percent. Among African American males in the labor force, 84.3 percent were "at work." Another 5.4 percent were categorized "On Public Emergency Work (WPA, etc.)," while African American Floridians "seeking work" accounted for another 8.9 percent of the African American population.[48] That this "public emergency work" might not have been considered genuine employment is suggested by its existence as an exception to the usual category of employment. In fact, the overview of the census section reporting characteristics of the population states:

> In the interpretation of the data for persons on public emergency work, allowance must be made for the misclassification in the census returns of considerable numbers of public emergency workers.... The total number of unemployed, as usually defined, includes (1) persons seeking work and without any form of public or private employment, and (2) those on public emergency work programs established to provide jobs for the unemployed. Because of the misclassification of public emergency workers, the census total of these two groups understates the amount of unemployment.[49]

The 1940 Census has no category for unemployed per se but counts 7.4 percent of Floridians as "Seeking Work." Another 2.2 percent are categorized as "with a job," but not working at the time of the census.[50] The picture that emerges is that among the male Floridians in 1940 unemployment and underemployment was in double digits. Bringing full employment to the state, as it would, it is not surprising that the call to national defense resonated well with, and was welcomed by, the citizenry.

Another potentially martial aspect to the Florida employment picture was the female employment rate in 1940. The census counted 735,840 females fourteen and older.[51] On the brink of the US entrance into the largest war in history, only 227,238 female Floridians (31 percent) were in the labor force, while 508,552 (69 percent) were not.[52] In the event of a national emergency, many women were available for at least limited activity outside of the home. Florida on the eve of war had a labor pool of over a million persons to perform war work. Since close to half of the males of laboring age would be mustered into the military itself, this large number of unemployed female Floridians would be drawn directly into the war effort.

Armies march on their stomachs, and especially in an age of limited refrigeration and food preservation, plentiful staples were a prerequisite for total war. Florida in 1940 was blessed with the means to produce enough foodstuffs for its own, and for guests. According to the 1940 Census, agriculture provided the chief source of work in the state. Farming and fishing employed 129,293. The allied job fields of food manufacturing and food and dairy product retailing employed another 38,852. The total amounted to 168,145 persons employed in farming and food-related pursuits.[53] The primary staples were citrus, cattle, dairy, and sugar.[54] The cattle ranches, fruit groves, sugarcane fields, and truck farms of Florida were essential preconditions for the militarization to come.

The next largest industry of Florida, the category of "Personal Services," offered surprising military applications. The Personal Services industry included domestic service (73,494); hotels and lodging places (20,834); laundering and cleaning services (10,639); amusement, recreation, and related services (9,936); and miscellaneous personal services (11,644). Altogether 126,547 persons worked in occupations providing services to others.[55] Florida's hospitality staff would make a useful military adjutancy.

In addition to trained service personnel, the industry offered considerable physical plant in the form of thousands of extant rooms in hotels, motels, and apartment houses. In the present age of limited conflicts prosecuted with only the object of maintenance of the status quo, war can be approached leisurely. But in those rare cases of total war wherein the existence of the nation-state itself is at stake, time is of the essence. The existence in Florida of thousands of hotel rooms, providentially empty owing to economic conditions of the Depression, and available at the turn of a key, would be a real military asset.

Two more industries of Florida with martial attributes in 1940 were lumber and construction. Forestry, logging, sawmills, and miscellaneous wooden goods employed 30,959 persons.[56] A great deal of Florida was covered by forests of cypress, mahogany, and pine, owned and operated by the federal government, the state, and private companies. Apalachicola National Forest and Ocala National Forest were the then-largest and second-largest national forests in the US, respectively. Florida was an abundant source of lumber. Hardwood is useful for building shallow-draft vessels such as submarine chasers, minesweepers, and PT boats. Soft pine is the basic building material for any quick construction project, military or civilian. There were 43,761 people employed in the construction industry itself. In 1940 both the raw materials and the workers for an accelerated program of construction were available in Florida.[57] The heavily forested terrain of Florida was itself a wilderness readily adaptable to military bivouacs and target practice with ordnance of every kind.

One more industry of military usefulness was extant in Florida: Transport, communications, and other utilities employed significant numbers. Railroading (including repair shops), trucking, busing, lighters, and communications provided work for 45,411 persons.[58] The railroads of Florida were designed to bring people from the populous northeast of the US to Jacksonville, Miami, Tampa, and Pensacola. This rail system connected directly with Charleston, the Chesapeake, New York City, and Boston. These were the main seaports and would become the designated wartime embarkation points of the eastern seaboard. Large numbers of personnel could be brought into Florida by train and sent from Florida to these US maritime terminals for shipment overseas. Washington, DC, the nation's capital and military headquarters for the war effort, was at the midway point on this rail line, easily and quickly accessible to Florida.

While the census demonstrates Florida's rural poverty and absence of an industrial base, it also suggests the potential for wartime service as a mobilization site and force-projection platform. Florida could provide adequate food and numerous hands to assist and provide for visitors. The state's tourism infrastructure could offer living quarters to numerous visitors. Florida lumber and carpenters were available to piece together additional quick wooden accommodations, as well as smaller war vessels. The countryside was empty and available to teach and study the art of war.

Although the census of 1940 does not mention the embryonic field of aviation, Florida was ready to take off in this industry as well. For purposes of international travel by air, Florida was closer to the rest of the world than was most of the US. The peninsula was already a recognized entrepôt for air travel. Florida hosted air fairs to celebrate its aviation links, complete with flying races and aerobatic demonstrations for the public.[59] These popular and high-profile events were promoted by the state, such as the 1941 Miami Air Fair, whose organizers and guests of honor included Florida governor Spessard L. Holland and Army Air Corps generals.[60] Flight pioneers Glenn Curtiss, Amelia Earhart, Charles Lindbergh, and the Florida-born aviatrix Jacqueline Cochran all had ties to the state. The civilian air carriers of the day, Pan American, Eastern, Delta, and National airlines, all flew from Florida. The Goodyear blimp migrated to Florida during the winter.[61] Pan American

Airways in particular pursued aggressive expansion of its flights to South America, Africa, and the Orient from its headquarters in Miami. These commercial enterprises were a promising military adjunct in the event of war.

While most of Florida's population was rural and its economy agricultural, the census confirmed three urban centers. Miami boasted a population of 172,172.[62] To that may be added the populations of Miami Beach, 28,012, and Fort Lauderdale, another 17,996 more.[63] Together with the rest of Dade County, the Greater Miami population stood at 285,735 persons.[64] Tampa's population was 108,391 persons.[65] With adjacent St. Petersburg and Clearwater, it composed an urban area of 179,339 persons.[66] The city of Jacksonville had a 173,065-person population.[67] Surrounding Duval County added 37,078 more.[68] Miami, Tampa, and Jacksonville were situated around the important anchorages of Biscayne Bay, Tampa Bay, and the St. Johns River, respectively. The three coastal metropoles of Jacksonville, Greater Miami, and Tampa Bay counted a total of 675,217 Floridians. They would become enormous centers of military training. Their working harbors would facilitate shipbuilding on a tremendous scale. In Miami, Miami Beach, Palm Beach, St. Petersburg, Clearwater, and Daytona Beach, whole enclaves of the urban environment would be commandeered to serve as military barracks.

A dozen smaller municipalities existed in Florida prior to the war. Eight of them were situated along the coast: Pensacola, Panama City, Sarasota, Fort Myers, Key West, West Palm Beach, Daytona Beach, and St. Augustine. The four inland towns of Tallahassee, Gainesville, Orlando, and Sanford were the only ones of note in the interior of the state. The smaller metropolitan areas in 1940 claimed a combined population of 229,048 persons. Together with the populations of the three urban centers, they amounted to 900,000 persons, less than half the population of Florida in 1940, so that over half of all Floridians were officially rural dwellers before the war.[69] The number of Floridians truly living out in "the country" was far greater in reality. Many who were counted as urbanites lived nowhere near the urban cores. A person counted as a "city dweller" might actually reside an hour or two by automobile from the metropolitan downtown.[70]

Smaller Municipalities of Florida in 1940

In sum, Florida in 1940 was a large peninsula with a small population.[71] Its few urban areas were all harbors on the coast. Its interior was mostly undevel-

TABLE 1. Smaller Municipalities of Florida in 1940

MUNICIPALITY	POPULATION	MUNICIPALITY	POPULATION
Panama City	11,610	Pensacola	37,449
Daytona Beach	22,584	St. Augustine	12,090
Fort Myers	10,604	Sanford	10,217
Gainesville	13,757	Sarasota	11,141
Key West	12,927	Tallahassee	16,240
Orlando	36,736	West Palm Beach	33,693

Source: US Census of Florida 1940, Table 31, 124.

oped. Its natural resources were land, foodstuffs, and wood. It had unlimited access to the sea, and a working network of railroads reaching the national core. Its underemployed workforce had some specialization in tourism, and there was a budding aviation industry. The peninsula had a salient position astride some of the most important sea lanes of the day, and it was well placed to host international air routes. Florida enjoyed year-round clement weather and mostly sunny days for almost every training purpose.

The lay of the land, an appreciation of the waters and skies surrounding it, and giving a face to the inhabitants of Florida are three of the four baselines to understanding the setting of Florida at war. The final consideration is the Armed Forces themselves. The number of soldiers, sailors, airmen, and marines fielded by the United States during World War II was enormous. Serving between December 1, 1941, and August 31, 1945, were 14,903,213 men and women.[72] It was the largest *levée en masse* in American history, and one of the largest mobilizations in world history. Of those who served, 10,420,000 served in the Army (including 2,400,000 in the Army Air Corps). The Navy and Marines absorbed the rest at 3,883,520 and 599,693, respectively.[73] Fourteen percent of the whole, one-seventh of the entire US force engaged in World War II, came to Florida, which was but one of forty-eight states. The militarization of Florida can be said to have begun in 1938, and its momentum had started long before Pearl Harbor.

Once in the war Florida became an armed camp of military personnel. A total of 2,122,100 military personnel served in Florida.[74] Most striking, soldiers outnumbered civilians in Florida during the war. To be sure, most came temporarily, and at any given time the number of military personnel was fewer than civilians. But the number of Florida civilians also shrank dramatically during the war. Almost 250,000 Floridians joined the US military, more than one-eighth of the population. Their number included 51,467 African American servicemen.[75] During the war there were only 1,647,414 civilians in the state. The military presence gave the state a new identity, especially as all military members groomed alike, dressed the same, and were all sworn to government service. Still more compelling, almost all were males in the prime of life years between the ages of eighteen to forty-five. They labeled themselves "Government Issue," to be known ever after as the GIs. Their impact was enormous.

With the anonymous statement "Kilroy Was Here," they marked off their territory, scrawling this silly imprimatur across barrack walls and chow halls, artillery shells, and airplane fuselages. The joking proclamation was usually accompanied by the humorous cartoon of a hapless simpleton peeking over a fence. Kilroy was everywhere, and to his numbers may be added the uniformed civilians of the various paramilitary organizations that supported the war effort. Groups such as Merchant Mariners, the Civil Air Patrol, Coast Guard Auxiliary, Women's Air Service Pilots, Civil Defense Wardens, and the Red Cross all wore martial garb, received funding, drew rations, and sometimes were even issued weapons from the military.[76] Such persons were frequently sworn to allegiance as US civil service war workers and War Department employees.[77] They engaged in military training and activities and frequented military installations. They came under military supervision and could be construed as belonging to the military community, more so than to the civil population of Florida. It was an overwhelming influx,

more than doubling Florida's population over five years. The centrality of the state to the war was determined by the aspects of place and space that will be explored further.

Politically, Florida in 1940 was a "solid south" stronghold of the Democratic Party and the New Deal Administration.[78] The same 1940 election that returned the administration to Washington, DC, also brought fellow Democrat Holland into office as governor of Florida. Holland had fought in the Great War as an aerial gunner in the Army Air Service, and he was keen on military aviation. He would work closely with the administration and the War Department to bring military funds and programs to the state.

The election of 1940 likewise returned to office the senior US Florida senator Charles O. Andrews, another Democrat. Andrews had been a captain in the Florida National Guard. Florida's junior US senator Claude D. Pepper had served in the Student Army Training Corps during college.[79] Pepper especially held forth as a friend and supporter of the White House.[80] The political leaders of Florida were closely aligned with the administration, and in return brought home vast federal projects to their constituents. Florida would willingly adapt to wartime mobilization.[81]

2

NAVAL AIR STATION FLORIDA

The rise of the military establishment in Florida began in the late 1930s. Specifically, it can be dated to December 13, 1937, and its point of origin was on the Yangtze River west of Shanghai. That long before the attack on Pearl Harbor of December 1941, the arming of Florida began. It came from deliberate decisions of the Roosevelt Administration, Army and Navy planners, and the civic leaders of Florida as they took steps to prepare the US for war. The rise of Nazi Germany and Imperial Japanese aggression in Europe and Asia ultimately threatened the US and was paralleled by Florida's mobilization. As the world situation deteriorated into global war, Florida increasingly became a center for US military assembly. One major focus was on expanding naval activity in Florida, particularly naval aviation, in the context of the increasing international threat.

In the mid-1930s Florida had little military presence. Pensacola, the only naval station in Florida, was an antebellum Navy Yard with live oaks, Spanish moss, and broad veranda cottages whose mission was to serve as the flight school for all Navy and Marine Corps pilots. It trained about one hundred aviators annually. In South Florida a Naval Reserve training base in the Miami suburb of Opa-locka handled some aircraft activity, including occasional Navy zeppelin landings. A seventeen-man Navy radio station crew oversaw the boarded-over Key West base, and some Coast Guard station keepers manned harbor pilothouses, lighthouses, and a few sleepy Houses of Refuge. The Army Air Corps maintained a budding airstrip in North Florida at

Eglin Army Airfield, bordered by the Choctawhatchee National Forest.[1] It had been given to the Army in 1935 by the Depression-weary town of Eglin, hoping to spur a bit of prosperity. The Florida Army National Guard fielded two main units at the time: the 124th infantry regiment and the 265th Coast Artillery Regiment. These soldiers of Florida drilled at armories around the state and held annual summer encampments at Camp Foster on the St. Johns River outside Jacksonville.

When President Franklin D. Roosevelt assumed office in 1933, the US Army numbered 137,000 officers and men, and was ranked seventeenth in size among the nations of the world.[2] As war approached, the president worked to rearm and militarize the US, and during his term of office the US witnessed a nearly hundred-fold increase in soldiers under arms, along with the comparable growth of infrastructure and supply. As war clouds gathered, FDR spoke of the US as the "Arsenal of Democracy." During his presidency he fashioned it into that arsenal, fielding armies and navies of a size America has not seen since.[3] He took his position as commander in chief of the military services more seriously than any president since Lincoln.[4] Florida would figure prominently in his war plans.

Roosevelt carried Florida in every one of his four presidential elections. In the presidential election of 1940, Roosevelt won Florida by 65 percent of the vote, and he would carry Florida again in the 1944 election.[5] He was popular with Floridians, and he was personally well acquainted with the state from repeated trips there over the years, including seven visits between 1936 and 1941.[6] Each one of those visits involved train rides across the peninsula countryside and cruises at sea aboard US Navy warships either embarking from or debarking at Florida. Roosevelt was himself a competent yachtsman and a strong proponent of sea power.[7] The White House characterized his patrols aboard Navy cruisers and destroyers as "fishing holidays," and while engaged in that pastime he covered every bit of the Caribbean Sea and the Gulf, including two inspections of the Panama Canal and its military installations. His cruises informed him to the important geographic facts of the sea realm around Florida. Likewise, he knew both the demographics and the geography of the state. He saw with his own eyes the promising military attributes of prewar Florida: the large, flat, wide-open spaces of the empty peninsula with a temperate clime and a supportive, if small, population. He would soon put these military assets of Florida into play.

On December 12, 1937, the threat of war leaped suddenly into national prominence. Chaos reigned in China when the capitol city of Nanking was captured by the Imperial Japanese Army in an orgy of bloodshed. For the sake of *Dai Nippon* the Japanese Empire had invaded the creaky Chinese regime of Chiang Kai-shek.[8] The American gunboat USS *Panay (PR-5)* was on humanitarian mission on the river outside the town. In obedience to orders she was riding at anchor on the Yangtze to provide safe refuge for American Embassy citizens and friendly foreign nationals fleeing from the fighting.[9]

That day victorious Japanese aviators over Nanking went looking for targets. The pilots spotted the USS *Panay* on the river outside the city, an obvious target. Three bombers dive-bombed the ship. Nine fighters then strafed the decks in low-level passes. Three Americans and an Italian journalist onboard were killed, and most of the fifty-four-man crew were wounded, ten seriously. The sailors and civilians abandoned ship. While the Americans hid in the muddy reeds of the riverbank, the sinking US ship was boarded by Imperial Japanese Army soldiers and trashed.

By happenstance, two American newsreel cameramen who were aboard the USS *Panay* had filmed the entire attack.[10] The raw footage of the attack was secreted in film cans and, with the help of Chinese partisans, smuggled to the coast. The film was flown back to the US aboard a Pan Am clipper. It was screened by President Roosevelt before being released to the public. To avoid inflaming public opinion, FDR had thirty feet of the reel cut out. That footage showed Japanese warplanes attacking at deck level and revealed that the deck of USS *Panay* was marked clearly with large painted American flags.[11] The faces of the enemy pilots could be seen through the cockpit windshields. The film left no doubt that future hostilities were only a matter of time.[12]

The following month, on January 28, 1938, President Roosevelt addressed the American people on the subject of rearmament. He reaffirmed the US commitment to the Monroe Doctrine and spoke of national defense and the Western Hemisphere. He stressed the need to "keep any potential enemy many hundreds of miles away from our continental limits." The administration thus began its preparations for war. The 75th session of Congress responded to FDR's call to arms. At the end of the session in May, both houses passed major pieces of legislation expanding the nation's military forces. The Navy's air arm was authorized to increase to three thousand aircraft, and new warships, including an aircraft carrier, battleships, cruisers, destroyers, and submarines, were ordered. In addition, smaller vessels such as oilers, tugs, minesweepers, experimental patrol torpedo (PT) boats, and blimps were authorized.[13] The act also provided for the expansion of military facilities, including those in Florida.

To guide US naval expansion Congress created the Hepburn Board, whose recommendations profoundly impacted Florida. Admiral Arthur J. Hepburn, one of the most senior officers in the Navy, chaired the board charged with recommending improvements to national defense. Previously Admiral Hepburn had put in his papers for retirement. FDR rejected the request and issued Hepburn this final order: prepare the US for war. The Hepburn Board recommended moving the Pacific Fleet from San Diego to the forward base in mid-ocean at Pearl Harbor in Hawaii. It also called for building eighteen new bases in the Pacific and the Caribbean and expanding naval aviation. The board advised structuring the US Atlantic defense responsibilities from Canada to Panama to establish sectors of responsibility, creating a new 10th Naval District to operate from Puerto Rico, and a vastly increased Navy presence for the 7th Naval District of the US: the peninsula of Florida. Hepburn and Mahan read the same charts.

Hepburn also proposed Florida as the site for one of three large new aviation training centers proposed for the Continental United States.[14] Although naval strategy centered on the firepower of the battleship, it did not overlook the importance of naval aviation. Senior officers such as admirals Ernest J. King and William F. "Bull" Halsey Jr., for example, were qualified pilots. Navy airpower was primarily designed around smaller aircraft built to attack enemy ships: dive bombers, torpedo bombers, fighter planes, and scout planes. These operated over blue water and demanded mastery of the fine aerobatics of launch and recovery on the pitching deck of aircraft carriers at sea. The appeal of Florida above other states for such training was obvious. The Hepburn Board wanted a Navy "second to none," and this included aviation training that would generate a force of aircraft, pilots, air crews, aircraft carriers, maintenance and repair personnel, and bases that would win a world war. Florida fit those criteria better than any other locale.

As it prepared its study, the Hepburn Board toured the entire peninsula, including surveys of Miami, Fort Lauderdale, Key West, Fernandina, Banana River, and Jacksonville.[15] Jacksonville particularly interested the Hepburn Board. Its members visited the municipal airport, Eastport, Green Cove

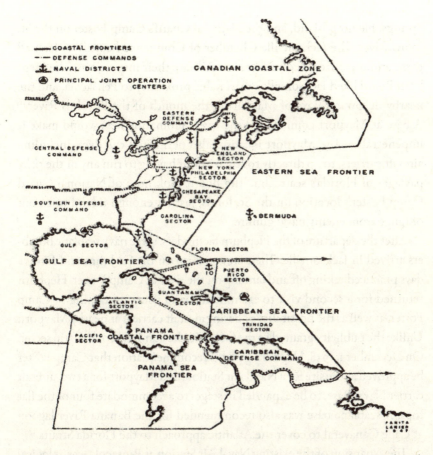

Florida at the heart of Navy Coastal Defense. Unlike the rest of the Atlantic Seaboard, the Florida peninsula was surrounded on three sides by water. It was moreover the logical and easiest place for an enemy invasion to land. As such, it was central to prewar military planning. In the runup to war the Navy built at the mouth of St. Johns River strategic Navy Station Mayport, capable of homeporting two aircraft carriers. Simultaneously, the Navy built from scratch or dramatically expanded twenty-two naval air stations, most within a few miles of the Atlantic Ocean. It did so to harden the maritime target that was Florida. The plan was to use carriers and fighter planes to stop the enemy invaders on the beaches before they could ever work their way inland. Craven and Cate, *The Army Air Forces in World War II*. Vol. I, 543.

Springs, Fleming Island, and the National Guard's Camp Foster on the St. Johns River. The Jacksonville Chamber of Commerce heartily welcomed them and organized a committee to facilitate their inspections. The Hepburn Board liked Jacksonville's reasonable proximity to Pensacola, and the nearby deepwater cove of Mayport at the mouth of the St Johns River.[16] A base at Mayport commanded the river. Submarine nets would make it impenetrable. The Mayport location also permitted the fleet, including aircraft carriers, to go directly to sea, without having to run any of the risky passages of Florida's sea realm. The Board took note of National Guard Camp Foster's location on the St. Johns, just far enough inland to be out of range from enemy naval gunfire.

After the departure of the Hepburn factfinders, three navy seaplane bombers arrived in Jacksonville. Their crews set up on the St. Johns and for five days practiced taking off and landing on the river at Camp Foster. Hepburn returned for a second visit to examine the land issues pertaining to Camp Foster, as well as the possibility of basing aircraft carriers at nearby Mayport. Unlike the publicity granted to the first visit, the admiral kept this trip secret. On December 1, 1938, Hepburn gave his recommendation that Camp Foster be approved as the site for a Naval Air Station, and Mayport for a two-aircraft carrier Naval Base, to be expanded in stages to accommodate four of the flat tops. A seaplane base was also recommended for the Banana River lagoon at Cape Canaveral to cover the Atlantic approach to the Florida Straits.[17]

The expansion of the existing Naval Air Station at Pensacola was as logical as it was predictable. Pensacola naval flight school had existed since 1913, only two years after the Navy bought its first airplane.[18] The physical plant of the long-functioning base could be readily expanded, and from a geostrategic point of view its proximity to the mouth of the Mississippi River made it a vital defense post. Hepburn's recommendation to add students, aircraft, facilities, and outlying airfields to NAS Pensacola accorded completely with Mahan's observations:

> In case of a contest for supremacy in the Caribbean, it seems evident from the depth of the south pass of the Mississippi, the nearness of New Orleans, and the advantages of the Mississippi Valley for water transit that the main effort of the country must pour down that valley, and its permanent base of operations be found there.[19]

From a prewar production of a hundred pilots a year, Pensacola would grow to graduate a thousand a month at its wartime peak.[20]

President Roosevelt visited Florida from February 14 to 28, 1939. The trip was announced by the White House as a road trip to tour the new Overseas Highway to Key West, a New Deal work project recently completed. The trip coincided with the annual Navy war games being staged that year in the Caribbean. Roosevelt announced that after visiting Key West he would observe this naval exercise. Roosevelt's participation was unprecedented. No president had ever joined the Navy for its most prominent annual exercise.[21] Roosevelt came by train to Miami, where a temporary White House was set up in the Biltmore Hotel.[22] He then motored over the new Overseas Highway to Key West in an open-top convertible. His chief of staff, Admiral William D. Leahy, accompanied him. From the back seat of his convertible, Roosevelt gave an address to his radio audience. In Key West, he and Leahy inspected the former naval station. They found yachts of the rich moored in the submarine basin and destroyer berths; squatters were living in the abandoned barracks.[23] Leahy took notes. Within a few months the civilian boats were ordered to leave. The barracks were cleared. Navy seaplanes began landing at Key West again, and before the year was out the Navy would be back in force.

After inspecting Key West, Roosevelt embarked in the cruiser USS *Houston* to join the fleet and observe the Navy war games at sea off Cuba. The exercise involved some hundred fifty ships, six hundred aircraft, and sixty thousand sailors. Roosevelt participated actively. He made gambits, suggested maneuvers, and otherwise exercised his prerogative as commander in chief. During the training he gave a statement to the press, announcing that the exercise was to test the defenses of the *entire* Western Hemisphere against outside invasion.[24] It was a surprising announcement that with a word effectively expanded the US sphere of military operations to include South America, Central America, and Canada. At the conclusion of the exercises President Roosevelt held admiral's call aboard USS *Houston*, and with the top officers of the fleet assembled in his stateroom, he only half-jested with them to watch out for Germans and Japanese.[25]

Six weeks later President Roosevelt signed into law the Hepburn recommendation creating the new Jacksonville Naval Air Training Operating Base.[26] The base was to provide primary and advanced training in all types of naval aircraft.[27] The same legislation authorized the Mayport aircraft carrier base and the Banana River Naval Air Station. Mayport was projected to grow into a Navy Operating Base, the equal to Norfolk and Brooklyn, the centers of US naval power on the East Coast at that time. The Navy's Jacksonville expansion began almost immediately. Auxiliary air stations at Jacksonville Municipal Airport, Cecil Field, and Green Cove Springs soon followed. Satellite naval air stations held groundbreakings at Lake City, Daytona Beach, DeLand, Sanford, Melbourne, Banana River, and Vero Beach.[28] Rather than oriented to operate over the peninsula or the interior Gulf of Mexico, all these new Florida Naval Air Stations (NAS) were sited to face the Atlantic, which for the Navy in times of war constituted "the front."

South Florida also drew the Navy's attention. Its proximity to the strategic Florida Straits and Caribbean demanded a strong military presence here. In the event of war with Germany, the Florida Straits could expect to be attacked, as could the waterfront city of Miami itself, the most exposed urban area of the peninsula. South Florida was, moreover, already a civilian aviation hub. In addition to the Miami Municipal Airport, the city boasted seaplane stations at Dinner Key and Watson Island on Biscayne Bay. Commercial air carriers flew from their own airport at Thirty-Sixth Street in the city.[29] In July 1939 the Navy announced it would open Naval Air Station Miami at the existing Navy Reserve Aviation Training Base in Opa-locka. Its location on the edge of the Everglades adjacent to the Miami Municipal Airport offered room to expand.

In nearby Broward County the Navy took over the rustic Merle Fogg airstrip. Renaming it NAS Fort Lauderdale, it established still another training base, with hangars, a terminal, and all the facilities for training dive bomber pilots. Those trainees numbered among others the future president George Herbert Walker Bush. The Navy opened an aircraft Ball Gunner School in Hollywood, and a Naval Facility at Port Everglades. A Naval Air Navigation School, first opened in Coconut Grove using Pan American instructors, would expand to occupy and fill the exclusive Hollywood Beach Hotel.[30]

The US Maritime Service was likewise drawn to Florida, opening a training base at St. Petersburg on September 1, 1939. The Merchant Marine Act of 1936 created the US Maritime Commission, a New Deal federal agency for priming the US shipbuilding industry to build ships. In 1938 President Roosevelt created the US Maritime Service to recruit and train crews for this new merchant marine fleet.[31] Bayboro Harbor was the location of the St. Petersburg Maritime Service Training Station. The Maritime Service was armed, uniformed, and subject to military discipline. It accepted youths as young as sixteen. Enlistments were for one year of sea duty after training, and graduates of the Civilian Conservation Corps had preference.[32] Recruits at Bayboro lived in barracks under military authority, the only racially integrated service at the time. Later the government added a Maritime Officer Candidate School to the Florida base.[33]

The Coast Guard ran the training at St. Petersburg. The first five weeks consisted of marching, swimming, first aid and hygiene, firefighting, small boat handling, knots, and gunnery. Seven additional weeks involved deck training, steering, compass and navigation, cargo handling, mooring, signaling, and more gunnery.[34] Target practice included anti-aircraft guns and the use of the top secret "Polaroid Trainer," a motion picture device invented to simulate attacks by enemy aircraft under various angles and conditions. Specialty training followed for ship engines and turbines, electricians and hull technicians, radio operators, pilots and coxswains, cooks and bakers, signalmen, and corpsmen. The five training ships at the St. Petersburg boot camp included the centerpiece of the base, the tall ship *Joseph Conrad*, the last surviving three-mast frigate in the world, with masts just under a hundred feet high.[35] Graduates won licenses in their specialties and assignment to US merchant ships. During the war, over twenty-five thousand Maritime Service personnel were trained in Florida, 10 percent of the merchant marine.[36]

The US Maritime Commission also initiated at this time what would become the premier civilian industry of the state: shipbuilding.[37] In 1940 the Tampa Shipbuilding and Engineering Company was struggling to build a few cargo ships with Maritime Commission financing. In late 1940 the business failed, with the ships only half-built. The Commission and the Reconstruction Finance Corporation approached the Tampa Chamber of Commerce for new management.[38] The company was reorganized as Tampa Shipbuilding Company (TASCO), and a leader was found in banker and civic booster George Howell. Howell, a veteran of the Great War, set about reenergizing the operation. He proved a most competent shipbuilder. By November 1941, TASCO had completed three ships. After Pearl Harbor, the War Shipping Administration would be created, headed by retired Admiral Emory S. Land, chairman of the Maritime Commission and a personal friend of President Roosevelt.[39] As the merchant marine went into emergency wartime production, shipbuilding in Florida expanded exponentially.

A sobering reminder to Florida of the drift toward war came in the summer of 1939 when the German passenger ship SS *St. Louis* steamed off its coast. The ship departed Hamburg on May 13, 1939, with nine hundred Jewish refugees seeking asylum in Cuba. When the ship reached Havana, the government refused the passengers entry. For several days negotiations went back and forth, but the Jewish passengers were not allowed to land. In June the vessel loitered at sea off Miami.[40] She was shadowed by US Coast Guard cutters at the behest of Treasury Secretary Morgenthau, who hoped the US policy of non-admittance might change. The US policy did not change, nor did the policy of Cuba. On June 17, SS *St. Louis* returned to Antwerp and disembarked its passengers. Few survived the Holocaust.[41] The incident became known as the "Voyage of the Damned," and it underscored how dangerously unstable the world was becoming, and that Florida would not escape its effects.

Less than three months later, on September 1, Germany invaded Poland. Britain and France declared war on Germany. Simultaneous to the outbreak of war, President Roosevelt promoted General George C. Marshall over numerous senior officers to be Army chief of staff, its highest-ranking officer.[42] On September 5, President Roosevelt announced the creation of the "Neutrality Patrol." He declared a two-hundred-mile buffer zone along the eastern littoral of the Western Hemisphere wherein the US would exercise command and control, keeping the seas free of belligerents and hostilities. In theory merely an extension of the Monroe Doctrine, in practice it further mobilized the US toward war. A proclamation of limited national emergency followed. Florida's military tempo ratcheted up yet another notch.[43] Air Corps bombers began patrolling the Florida coast as part of their flight plans.[44] Destroyers took up station in the Florida Straits. In October, Navy seaplanes arrived for Neutrality Patrol duty at Key West, along with several submarines. The townspeople, known as "Conchs," welcomed the return of the Navy with a military parade down Duval Street, and on November 1 Key West Naval Station was officially reopened.[45]

The following month an episode brought the war closer to home for curious Floridians. On December 14 two German merchant ships in the Gulf of Mexico, *Arauca* and *Columbus*, made a break for the Florida Straits to reach the open seas and avoid being seized by the British Navy. United States destroyers of the new Neutrality Patrol trailed them, reporting their positions in plain-language radio messages easily read by British warships in the area.[46] The HMS *Orion* cornered the *Arauca* off Fort Lauderdale. With the US destroyer USS *Philip* nearby and Army B-18s from Miami overhead, the British warship fired across the bow of the German freighter. *Arauca* fled into Port Everglades to escape capture.[47] There the German ship was quarantined by the Coast Guard. Floridians sympathetic to Britain went out to HMS *Orion* with magazines, candies, and charts of the local waters. Shots fired in US waters, the Nazi *Arauca* bottled up in Fort Lauderdale, and HMS *Orion* standing outside Port Everglades amounted to a diplomatic incident for the neutral United States. The *Arauca* and its fifty-two-man crew was left undisturbed at the harbor docks. The ship's captain and officers were allowed to move about town.[48] The US State Department expressed disapproval at the appearance of public bias shown toward Britain. The people of Fort Lauderdale good naturedly delivered several cases of beer to the crew of the *Arauca*, by way of welcoming the Germans to Florida.[49]

On May 10, 1940, the Nazi blitzkrieg swept into France.[50] Holland was overrun, Belgium collapsed, the British evacuated Dunkirk, and France surrendered. In this crisis, the new British prime minister, Winston Churchill, requested fifty surplus US Navy World War I destroyers then in mothballs. In exchange, Roosevelt asked for ninety-nine-year leases to Britain's Atlantic territories, most of them in the Caribbean. Basing rights at these would strengthen the US east coast defenses from Canada to South America.[51] On July 16 the aerial attack by Germany on Britain known as the Battle of Britain began. It marked the nadir of Allied fortunes. On September 2 the destroyers were transferred to Britain. The US got nine new bases, seven of them close to Florida.

The freshly mobilized Puerto Rican-American 65th National Guard Infantry Regiment departed San Juan's Morro Castle headquarters to reinforce the US Panama Canal Zone itself. Called to active service with the rest of the US National Guard, the polished "Borinqueneros" garrisoned island outposts across the sea realm for the Caribbean Sea Command. This was an Army Command that deferred to the Navy in nautical matters. In the dense tropical highlands of Panama, the 65th spent years honing their jungle warfare skills to perfection. When the U-boat menace was defeated, the unit

USS *Dahlgren* was one of the vintage four-pipe destroyers FDR did not trade to Britain for the Caribbean bases. Instead, Dahlgren was homeported at Key West to train sailors on the new top-secret sonar. Dahlgren also hunted U-boats and rescued the crew of the Navy K-74 blimp when it was shot down off Key Largo by the Nazi U-boat 134 on July 18, 1943. Source: US Navy History and Heritage Command. USS *Dahlgren* DD-187. Image 64538.

was redeployed overseas in 1944. With the military's customary inscrutability, the regiment was sent not to the jungle-fighting of the Pacific for which they had trained religiously. Instead, they were sent to the French Riviera from where they fought their way through the snow-covered French Alps.[52]

Another step in the US mobilization for war came two weeks later when President Roosevelt signed the conscription bill, commencing further mobilization long before the US entered the fighting. With the support of the president, the Selective Training and Service Act of 1940 was introduced in Congress. The administration's ally, Florida Senator Claude Pepper, was a principal advocate of the policy.[53] On September 16, 1940, President Roosevelt signed the draft into law. Initially conscription required men between the ages of twenty-one and thirty-five to register for service of one year.[54] After Pearl Harbor, the age range was expanded to all men from eighteen to forty-five, the time of service to last for the duration of the war and six months beyond. In the few months remaining in 1940, 18,633 men were drafted into military service. In 1941, before the attack on Pearl Harbor, 900,000 more were called to the colors. During the war years, 9,838,725 men would be drafted into the US military.[55]

One seldom-noted aspect of the program provides another metric into Florida's pervasive militarization: that was the requirement to register for service. Conscription was limited to males between the ages of eighteen and forty-five years of age. But all males from forty-five to sixty-five years of age were required to be card-carrying registrants of the Selective Service, providing regular reports to their local draft board of their whereabouts. Law required them to acknowledge in writing their obligation to serve if the age requirements were raised to include them. Insofar as this impacted Floridians it meant those between the ages of eighteen and sixty-five, some 596,161 men, over a third of the entire civilian inhabitants of Florida, formally identified themselves for military service.[56]

In December 1940 Roosevelt traveled to Florida again. From Miami on December 3 he embarked on the cruiser USS *Tuscaloosa* to inspect the new Caribbean military bases the US had acquired from Britain. While underway he steamed close to the Vichy-French Island of Martinique and dropped anchor outside of the three-mile limit. While his officers studied the island with binoculars, Roosevelt summoned the US consul general to his cabin. The consul briefed him of the situation on the Nazi-collaborating island. The Vichy-controlled Martinique posed a real threat. Soft power in the form of 268 tons of gold bullion evacuated from the French Treasury was lodged in Martinique at Fort Desaix. Hard power in the form of a battle group of the French Navy had retreated to the island along with the gold when France was overrun. The French warships included the aircraft carrier *Bearn*, armed with a hundred US-made warplanes, light cruisers *Jeanne d'Arc* and *Émile Bertin*, and several destroyers. French Admiral Georges Robert and their crews were obedient to the orders of Vichy. The French squadron posed a threat to the Panama Canal, the Mississippi passes, and Florida itself. While still at sea, the president received via Navy seaplane a four-thousand-word letter from Churchill that asserted Britain was running out of money, weapons, and time. It prompted Roosevelt to finalize plans for Lend-Lease.[57]

In Washington on January 6, 1941, he gave the nation a radio fireside chat to explain his new idea to help Great Britain while still remaining neutral. He used the famous "garden hose" simile to appeal to the American people.[58] He compared the world situation to that of a family (America) with a neighbor (Britain) whose home had caught fire. To put out the fire and save his home, the neighbor needed to borrow a garden hose:

> Suppose my neighbor's house catches fire and I have a length of garden hose four or five hundred feet away. If he can take my garden hose and connect it to his hydrant, I may help him to put out the fire. Now what do I do? I don't say to him before that operation, "Neighbor, my garden hose cost me fifteen dollars; you have to pay me fifteen dollars for it." No! What is the transaction that goes on? I don't want fifteen dollars—I want my garden hose back after the fire is over.[59]

Thus, the president justified Lend-Lease. As congressional legislation, the bill's chief sponsor was Florida's senator Claude Pepper.

President Roosevelt visited Florida again on March 22, 1941. At Fort Lauderdale he was met by presidential yacht USS *Potomac* and USS *Benson* for another "fishing trip."[60] Boarding USS *Potomac* at the pier in Port Everglades he noticed the interned German freighter *Arauca*, flying the Nazi swastika flag.[61] Roosevelt then put to sea for a week of "fishing." While at sea a classified radio message notified him the Lend-Lease Act had passed. Returning to Port Everglades March 29, USS *Potomac* again tied up near the *Arauca*, which was still flying its swastika. President Roosevelt ordered the Nazi flag struck and the vessel seized. Authorities arrested the officers and crew and jailed them at the federal courthouse in Miami.[62]

The President's executive order applied to all German ships in US ports. No less than fifty-one German ships and their crews comprised of several thousand German citizens were seized.[63] The same day Roosevelt gave his Jackson Day radio address from his USS *Potomac* stateroom at Port Everglades. The speech starkly criticized Hitler and the Nazi regime. Roosevelt's speech and orders on March 29 offered serious provocation to the Germans. Florida was again at the intersection of war.

In the months afterward Florida hosted a continuing series of visits by the top brass of the Navy, including Secretary of the Navy Frank Knox and Admiral King. They made critical inspections of the region and the new outposts being established. They examined such diverse concerns as the rail capacity of Brazil, and the suitability of the Galapagos Islands for a seaplane base. To provide a contingency haven in case the Royal Navy was forced to evacuate Britain, Naval Station Roosevelt Roads on the Atlantic coast of Puerto Rico was acquired. The outlying isle of Vieques was purchased to help defend the anchorage and serve as a gunnery range. As naval gunnery of the time required precise calibration of gun sights and range finding gear, the placid waters of the Caribbean were ideal for the purpose.[64]

Guarding the passes of the Florida sea realm—the Straits, Yucatán Channel, and the other chokepoints—was a naval priority. Navy airships were brought on this mission. With the ability to hover over the sea lanes on extended patrol, their surveillance capacity was significant. The first lighter-than-air platforms, "Type A (Rigid)" airships had metal superstructures and were called zeppelins, after the German airship inventor Ferdinand von Zeppelin. Their metal framework housed compartments of helium or hydrogen for buoyancy. The weight of the metal, however, necessitated huge helium compartments. The size of the Type-A zeppelins worked against them. Costly to build and difficult to manage in flight, the Navy had more important uses for its steel and aluminum.[65] The new "Type B (Limp)" airship, a balloon contorted by cabling into an aerodynamic shape, was the alternative. The craft went limp when deflated, hence its name "B (Limp)" or simply: "*blimp.*" A control car with radio, radar, sonar, lookouts, and weaponry was suspended beneath. Easy to build and inexpensive, blimps would be a useful guardian over the Straits of Florida. The Navy and the Goodyear Company settled on the K-ship, equipped with two Pratt-Whitney engines, four bombs, a .50 caliber machine gun, and a crew of ten. On December 4, 1939, the *Homestead Ledger* newspaper reported the Navy would seek funding for thirty-six of these airships. The *Ledger* noted the Navy's interest in building a blimp station in South Florida.[66]

In April 1941 Secretary Knox requested authorization for an airship base in Florida. The President responded with the following note:

> I approve your memorandum of April 18 in regard to additional patrol blimps and authorization for temporary stations.... I am heartily in favor of what I have been heartily in favor of all this time! (signed) F.D.R.[67]

TABLE 2. Naval Air Stations in Florida during the War

BASE	OPENED	GARRISON STRENGTH IN 1944
NAS Banana River	1940	391 officers, 2,492 enlisted, 587 civilians
NAAS Barin Field–Pensacola	1942	5,795 students. No other data.
NAAS Bronson Field–Pensacola	1942	147 officers, 1,889 enlisted, 892 students
NAAS Cecil Field–NAS Jax	1941	530 officers, 2,025 enlisted. No civilian data.
NAAS Corry Field–Pensacola	1940	210 officers, 1,610 enlisted, 423 students
NAS Daytona Beach	1942	293 officers, 1,222 enlisted, 314 civilians
NAS DeLand	1942	331 officers, 1,143 enlisted, 373 civilians
NAF Dinner Key–Miami	1942	134 officers, 607 enlisted. No civilian data.
NAAS Ellyson Field–Pensacola	1941	177 officers, 1,345 enlisted, 600 students
NAS Fort Lauderdale	1942	393 officers, 1,905 enlisted, 373 civilians
NAAS Green Cove Springs	1941	518 officers, 1,471 enlisted. No civilian data.
NAS Jacksonville	1940	1,551 officers, 1,1387 enlisted, 6,236 civilians
NAAS Jacksonville Municipal #1	1941	No data available.
NAS Key West	1940	346 officers, 1,916 enlisted, 352 civilians
NAS Lake City	1942	294 officers, 1,128 enlisted, 266 civilians
NAAS Mayport	1941	44 officers, 232 enlisted
NAS Melbourne	1942	361 officers, 1,184 enlisted, 266 civilians
NAS Miami	1940	675 officers, 7,139 enlisted, 3,136 civilians
NAS Pensacola	1915	2,628 officers, 7,559 enlisted, 8,300 civilians
NAS Richmond–Miami	1942	99 officers, 607 enlisted, 202 civilians
NAS Sanford	1942	358 officers, 1,385 enlisted, 289 civilians
NAAS Saufley Field–Pensacola	1940	210 officers, 1,145 enlisted, 458 students
NAS Vero Beach	1942	294 officers, 1,128 enlisted, 266 civilians
NAAS Whiting Field–Pensacola	1943	584 officers, 2,719 enlisted, 1,431 students

Source: Compiled from Shettle, *United States Naval Air Stations*, 23, 27, 37, 47, 57, 65, 67, 75, 79, 91, 103, 107, 113, 117, 129, 131, 139, 69, 177, 191, 197, 201, 217, and 223.

If Lakehurst, New Jersey, was the "home" of Navy airship aviation, Florida would develop into the "home away from home" for military blimps during the war. The government established the largest US airship base in the world, outside of Lakehurst, in Florida near the strategic tip of the peninsula. Authority and support for wartime airship operations from Texas to Brazil would center at the critically placed Florida airship installation overlooking the Straits and the Caribbean at NAS Richmond Field just south of Miami.

Congressional legislation and funding, the recommendations of the Navy, the attention of the commander in chief, and the welcome of the Floridians themselves were all instrumental in a dramatic expansion of naval activity, particularly of naval aviation in Florida on the eve of war. Key West was reopened, and Mayport was under construction. The triad of Navy flight schools at Pensacola, Jacksonville, and Miami was complimented by twenty more naval air stations, auxiliary stations, outlying fields, and facilities.[68] The size of this system when it reached maturity can be measured by the muster reports from 1944 of naval aviation training personnel in Florida.

At that time there was a training cadre of 10,568 officers, 53,238 enlisted men, and 20,960 civilian employees in Florida, not counting student-trainees. The training force alone numbered 85,000 personnel. To make a comparison with another educational enterprise drawn at random to demonstrate the size and impact of this wartime activity, there were more people in Florida engaged in naval aviation training in World War II than are employed today by the Florida State University System, now serving a population ten times as large. By 1944 the state of Florida was one big military academy. The course of instruction was the art of war.

3

ARMY AIRFIELD FLORIDA

The Florida peninsula was likewise a critical training base for the Army Air Corps as the war approached. The Army of the time was organized into three components: Army Ground Forces, Army Air Forces, and Army Service Forces.[1] The Army Air Forces came to Florida first. The most obvious reason for which the state was chosen to host the Air Corps was its fine flying conditions. The early welcome and appreciation that Floridians showed for aviation also contributed, as personnel in the Air Corps had heard of, and sometimes participated in, the air shows of the state. From Jacksonville and Pensacola to Key West, Floridians from the governor to common citizens were keen on bringing the military presence to the state. Military planners and strategists remained no less mindful of the state's position and potential.

The Air Corps' interest in Florida was driven by the fact that the peninsula was geographically on the front line of continental US defense. Watching the Axis powers expand from one nation to the next, the US military could not help but consider the defense of America itself. Florida was one of the first places any potential enemy invasion originating from Europe would reach, a geographic factor enough in itself to merit military interest. But there was an even greater military consideration that geography conferred on the state: thanks to its place in the world, Florida was equally well situated to be a platform from which to project US air power to the wider world. Military planners had not merely to prepare for defense but to plan for offensive operations, without which war cannot be won. The considerations of military geography, quite as much as the mostly sunny days, destined Florida to become a military base. In preparing to defend the US, and simultaneously laying the groundwork for projecting US power offensively, the two military services of the day, the Army and the Navy, came to a formal agreement over Florida. They divided the peninsula into areas of authority: the Navy operated generally along the Atlantic Ocean coast of Florida, while the Army Air Corps took the Gulf of Mexico side of the state.[2]

A shortage of pilots was an immediate concern of the Army. Florida would answer this lack. In the late 1930s the administration created the Civilian Pilot Training (CPT) Program. This New Deal program aimed to boost the US airline industry by training twenty thousand civilian pilots a year drawn from the nation's colleges and universities. At the prompting of First Lady Eleanor Roosevelt and her friend, Florida educator Mary McLeod Bethune, the program included African American colleges and women's colleges.[3] Not only was the program of flight training that was offered an egalitarian economic stimulus, but, like the Maritime Service, it assumed an underlying military dimension. The contracts each trainee signed enrolled every one of them into the Army Reserve. The Civilian Pilot Training Program thus increased the pool of potential military pilots, ipso facto.

The new commander of the Air Corps, General Arnold, looked for ways to expedite the program, as well as to militarize it further. He proposed that the civilian flight schools become government contractors and execute the program under Army oversight. The Army would provide the airplanes and curriculum. The civilian schools would provide the instructors, the training, room and board, and other facilities. The schools would receive a government hourly rate for flying hours and operating costs. Known as the "Arnold Scheme," it brought several significant flight schools and military personnel to Florida. With a CPT agreement in hand, the aviation entrepreneur, Albert I. Lodwick, relocated from Nebraska to Florida, opening the Lodwick School of Aeronautics at the Lakeland Municipal Airport and nearby Avon Park. Lodwick graduated six thousand pilots during the war.[4] Greenville Flying Academy moved from Mississippi to Ocala. Embry-Riddle, the partnership company of aviator John Paul Riddle and his financial backer Talton Higbee Embry, collaborated first with the University of Miami to open a school there, then moved to expand their business elsewhere in Florida.[5]

The expansion of Embry-Riddle is an example of the close wartime collaboration of capitalism and the military in Florida. When the Arcadia Chamber of Commerce urged the Air Corps to reopen defunct Carlstrom Field, a training airstrip from the Great War, the military approved the location and contracted Embry-Riddle to open a primary flight school there.[6] Carlstrom was rebuilt as a state-of-the-art million-dollar facility publicized as the new "West Point of the Air," giving hundreds of jobs to the surrounding community.[7] Ten miles away, Dorr Field was developed with the same energized activity. Carlstrom Riddle Aeronautical Institute welcomed its first Army cadet on March 16, 1941. Carlstrom and Dorr grew to include six more auxiliary airstrips. These eight working airfields, all within a thirty-mile radius in the center of the peninsula, were a powerhouse of Florida aviation training. Many who failed to qualify as pilots nevertheless trained successfully as bombardiers, navigators, and aviation maintenance officers.[8]

In Miami the Embry-Riddle Seaplane Flying School on Biscayne Bay operated at full capacity. Another Embry-Riddle flight school opened at Miami Municipal Airport. When the Navy annexed that entire airport in the summer of 1942, the company was required to vacate the site.[9] Riddle persuaded the Army to allow the flight school to reopen at Chapman Field south of Miami.[10] Chapman Field was yet another training airstrip left over from the Great War, its name honoring Victor E. Chapman, the first American pilot killed over France in the Great War. Chapman Field, closed to all but occasional use by Eastern Airlines and Pan American Airways as a reserve airstrip, was reopened as an Embry-Riddle CPT primary flight school. When the CPT was restructured during wartime, Chapman Field adapted to strictly military trainees of the later War Training Service, enrolling solely Army, Navy, Royal Air Force, and federalized airline pilots. Notably, Chapman Field engaged fifteen female flight instructors.[11]

Embry-Riddle also opened a major ground school at the Pan American and Miami Army Airfield complex. Mechanics, preflight, air crew, and celestial navigation were taught in partnership with the University of Miami. The campus was the former Fritz Hotel, known as the Aviation Building, on the edge of the flight line.[12] The school was open to civilians, male and female, to learn hangar work. The grounds were strewn with fighters, bombers, and cargo planes in various stages of assembly and overhaul. Army and Navy trainees were housed on the upper floors, and when those spaces filled, in a nearby bowling alley, in private homes, and in thrown-together wooden bungalows nicknamed "shacks," on the grounds of the university itself. They roomed with RAF cadets taking preflight instruction and navigation courses. Riddle flight schools graduated 2,241 of the British pilots, among them Desmond Leslie, nephew of Winston Churchill.[13]

Florida's Embry-Riddle flight schools expanded to Clewiston, Daytona Beach, and even Tennessee, and ultimately gained international status. The institution was contracted by Brazil to train Brazilian, Bolivian, and Cuban fliers. In São Paulo they would eventually operate the Escola Técnica de Aviação (Technical Aviation School), providing training to hundreds of Allied airmen from South America.[14] These ventures further expanded Florida's premier role in military aviation and its growing international status.

However energetic and useful such civilian enterprises, they were eclipsed by the Army Air Corps itself. The same 1939 Congress that approved naval expansion authorized the Four Base Plan to establish four new major Army Air Corps bases. Each of the four quadrants of continental United States had one. They were intended to specialize in heavy bomber aviation. The "Southeast Air Base" was an economic plum that would have military jurisdiction over all the southern states from Virginia south and from the Mississippi River east. Under the Four Base Plan, the continental aviation forces would be restructured into four numbered air forces, one per base.[15]

Besides the other southern states, several Florida municipalities competed for the Southeast Air Base. Tampa made the most promising bid. The community's welcome had pleased the Air Corps authorities in hosting the aviation war games between March 14 and 29, 1938. For the exercise, the Tampa Chamber of Commerce Aviation Committee had secured facilities for thirty-three Air Corps planes, as well as lodgings for three hundred Air Corps personnel for training that included dogfights, bombing runs, and a mock aerial attack on Jacksonville. The exercise underlined the potential Tampa and the rest of Florida held for Air Corps activity.

When Congress passed the Four Base Plan, the Hillsborough County Commission offered the War Department a perpetual gift of thirty-five hundred acres at the southern end of Tampa Bay's Intercity Peninsula. The Air Corps accepted. Soon after, President Roosevelt approved a plan of the Florida WPA administrator to use WPA funding for the construction.[16] General Arnold personally flew the plans to town on December 5, 1939.[17] Although infested with rattlesnakes and palmetto scrub, the site possessed strategic potential. Located on important Tampa Bay, it commanded the Gulf of Mexico and was within range of the sea passages of the Caribbean. The Florida peninsula itself shielded the base from Atlantic Ocean enemy aircraft carrier-borne air attack.[18] No less than the weather, such considerations inspired the Air Corps. Flyboys soon swarmed to Florida.

The concentration of air power in Florida came as the Air Corps sought independence as a branch of service separate from the Army and coequal with the Army and Navy. This idea propounded by General Mitchell resonated throughout the Air Corps. With the coming of war, the Air Corps would redesignate itself the Army Air Forces (AAF), and the war would provide it the opportunity to demonstrate its independence. When the US entered the war, FDR moved to bind his military commanders into an efficient team, christening his top military leaders the Joint Chiefs of Staff (JCS).

Notwithstanding his jovial public persona, President Roosevelt was no respecter of persons, especially not of those under his rule as commander in chief. Generals and admirals unwilling or unable to execute his orders were shunted into career dead-ends, while those he favored he advanced. One was General Marshall, promoted to Army Chief of Staff over two dozen senior generals. The chief of naval operations at the time of the Pearl Harbor disaster was soon reassigned to diplomatic duty. His replacement was crusty Admiral King, who was reported to shave with a blow torch. Together with the new Army chief of staff, General Marshall, and Admiral Leahy, a close friend of the president serving as its chairman, they made up the Joint Chiefs of Staff. The president appointed Arnold, technically only a three-star general, to membership in this exclusive original JCS, despite his secondary rank of lieutenant general. Elevated as such, Arnold wielded much the same power as if he were the four-star head of an independent branch of service.[19]

Arnold believed in strategic bombardment and found in Florida a place to test this activity.[20] The Air Corps had settled on the Boeing B-17, a four-engine long-range bomber, as its main weapon for bombing. The B-17 aircraft would soon assume mythic proportions in the lexicon of air power. The plane was strong, dependable, and had the range to project air power great distances. Armed with as many as thirteen machine guns, it won the nickname "Flying Fortress." By 1940 the Army Air Corps had a hundred fifty of these heavy bombers. Tampa would be home for many of them. The Third Air Force was activated at Tampa in December 1940. Its mission was the air defense of the Southeastern District of the US: Louisiana, Arkansas, Tennessee, Virginia, North Carolina, South Carolina, Mississippi, Alabama, Georgia, and Florida. The Gulf of Mexico fell also in its area of responsibility. The Third Air Force remained in Tampa throughout the war.[21]

The base was formally dedicated on April 16, 1941, as MacDill Field in memory of Col. Leslie MacDill, an Army pilot killed in a flying accident a few years previously. The popular base commander of Osage Native American heritage, Brigadier General Clarence L. Tinker, flew in the first B-17 bomber.[22] Senator Pepper gave the keynote address.[23] On May 16, 1941, the 29th Bomb Group began arriving. It typified the Air Corps units coming to Florida, consisting of about fifty aircraft organized in four squadrons.

MacDill Field was primarily for training bombing units, with Third Bomber Command its principal tenant. Across town, Third Fighter Command established itself at Tampa's city airport, Drew Field Municipal Airport. Located at the northern end of the intercity peninsula, the Army annexed the airport and shortened its name to Drew Field.[24] The Army built a six-mile military highway, Dale Mabry Boulevard, for the express purpose of connecting the two bases. Dale Mabry was a Tallahassee native and pilot who served under Billy Mitchell in the Great War and gave his life in the 1922 crash of the Army blimp *Roma*. From MacDill Field and Drew Field, and Hillsborough Army Airfield a few miles north, the Third Air Force spread across the state. St. Petersburg, Bradenton, Venice, Sarasota, Fort Myers, Naples, Punta Gorda, Immokalee, Sebring, Bartow, Lakeland, Brooksville, Bushnell, Cross City, Dunnellon, Kissimmee, Leesburg, Gainesville, Montbrook, Zephyrhills, and Panama City all hosted Army airfields for bomber and fighter plane training.[25]

The government also established Air Corps fighter plane training facilities at the state capital. On May 8, 1941, the Air Corps took over Tallahassee's Dale Mabry Airport. With the blessings of Governor Holland, P-39 Airacobras, P-40 Warhawks, and P-51 Mustangs populated the sky over Tallahassee for the next five years. Flybys over the state capitol building were routine. Nearby Eglin Army Airfield grew exponentially when Congress transferred Choctawhatchee National Forest's 341,000 acres to the base. Renamed Eglin Military Reservation and comprising over 640 square miles, it encompassed an area more than half the size of Rhode Island.[26] It was the largest base in the Army Air Corps inventory and remains one of the largest air bases in the world.[27] Similarly, the Air Corps commandeered Orlando Municipal Airport in Central Florida. Reopened as the Orlando Air Base in December 1940, it became the center for fighter plane activities.[28] The AAF School of Applied Tactics for fighter plane training operated there, in conjunction with nearby Pinecastle Army Airfield.[29] In South Florida, the government established Morrison Army Airfield in West Palm Beach and Miami Army Airfield.[30] By December 1941 the Air Corps had no less than forty Army airfields up and running, or in various stages of construction.[31]

The tremendous burst of aviation training was not the only aspect of Air Corps activity in Florida. The War Department and the Administration were concurrently pondering how to defend the Western Hemisphere if it was attacked. The geographic feature of the Atlantic Narrows between western Africa and Brazil was a primary concern. The French possessions in Morocco, Algeria, and French West Africa all faced this Atlantic Ocean passage. Because of the collaboration between Germany and Vichy France, US planners feared that France would introduce the *Wehrmacht* into those African territories. From there the Axis armies could cross the Atlantic and work their way up the coast of South America to attack the US Panama Canal and America itself. If the Panama Canal was the strategic lynchpin, then geographically it was also the Achilles' heel of the US defenses. Destroying the canal did not require an invader to overcome its thousands of defenders. A single dive bomber, a salvo of accurate naval gunfire, or even a satchel charge damaging one lock mechanism could close the canal. Especially after its feat of steaming unnoticed four thousand miles from the Sea of Japan to attack Pearl Harbor, the Imperial Japanese Navy was believed fully capable of conducting such an amphibious attack. If a Japanese raid such as this were executed in cooperation with the contemplated advance of its German ally up the coast of South America, strategic planners foresaw disastrous consequences. Were the Vichy-French Navy task force riding at anchor in Martinique to join in, the picture was bleaker still. Mexico remained a question mark.[32]

An attack on the US was not a far-fetched scenario at the time. Britain was struggling to survive. If Britain fell, the US could expect to be attacked next by Germany. Strategically, the Atlantic Narrows offered an enemy the obvious line of approach. Argentina was openly pro-Axis. Most of South America and Central America would have watched from the sidelines, their support based pragmatically on whichever side appeared stronger. The later US alliance with Brazil did not exist at that time. In the event of an attack from this direction, planners recognized Florida as being central to the national defense. For such a defense, Washington inaugurated a series of Army commands to compliment the naval districts. The military strategy involved other countries, and creating the outlying defenses made for touchy diplomacy, as the US introduced armed guards and erected defenses at airstrips on foreign soil where permission to even land was a revocable permission of the host nation. The British and Dutch territories welcomed the insertion of US Army garrisons. The matter was more delicate elsewhere. Spanish American states requested weapons as a quid pro quo, a difficult request since the US itself was moving to full mobilization, and Washington had earmarked any spare weapons for Britain and Russia. Particularly difficult were the Antillean islands of Martinique and Guadalupe, and French Guiana on the mainland. Obedient to Vichy France, they remained stiffly neutral toward the US.[33]

If Florida figured centrally in defensive operations, it played an equally important strategic role in offensive planning. The Florida-Brazil coastal corridor offered a logical path of advance for striking at the Axis powers.[34] As the US sought to supply Britain and the Soviet Union, the path from Florida was even more critically important. The shortest route to Europe had significant disadvantages. Pioneered by Lindbergh in his famous flight of 1927, this "North Atlantic Route," extended from the US to the British Isles, with refueling stops in Montreal and Newfoundland.[35] It was a relatively short 2,700 miles, and specially fitted four-engine planes could fly it nonstop. But weather conditions made the route dangerous half of the year, and often impossible.[36] Aviators contended with rain, hail, sleet, snow, and gale-force winds. If storms forced down an aircraft into the rough seas below, hypothermia and drowning was the likely result, along with the complete loss of the aircraft itself. Florida presented an alternative.

Military geography suggested a safer route to both Europe and Asia by flying south by southeast from Florida. Florida-based aircraft could fly safely all year long across the Caribbean to Brazil, then across the Atlantic Narrows to Africa. From Africa, airplanes could fly north to the Mediterranean and Europe, or fly easterly across Africa to the British base in Egypt. From there planes could deliver war materials to Russia via Iran. Just so, they could continue to British-held India, and from there to the Far East and the Pa-

Florida at the Center of Army Defense Planning. In June 1940 the sudden surrender of France presented the US Army with a stark military reality. England was on the ropes struggling to survive. Hitler and his then-ally Stalin could combine their millions of soldiers in French West Africa and from there convoy at will across the Atlantic Narrows. This force could then blitzkrieg its way up the Caribbean with no one to stop them, and many to welcome them as deliverers. The gentle and pleasant beaches of Florida is where their invasion would come ashore. Only the Nazi dictator's decision to betray his friend Stalin and instead go east against Russia precluded the possibility. Conn et al., *Guarding the United States and Its Outposts*, 39.

cific.[37] While the Florida-based departure solved critical issues, it posed other problems, however. First was distance. The route from Florida to Asia was nearly twelve thousand miles, and for most of the way it lacked anything but the most primitive air transportation infrastructure. Second, it required seasoned pilots. Florida offered a ready-made solution to the latter issue.[38]

Florida's legendary Pan American Airways fliers had piloted its powerful "Clipper Ship" seaplanes around the world. Almost no other US pilots possessed the practical experience of transcontinental flying. Washington took advantage of the circumstance. In 1940 the New Deal's Airport Development Program (ADP), under the US Civil Aeronautics Administration, commissioned Pan American to pioneer a route to Asia.[39] With ADP funding, the Miami-based airline created what would become a critical air route of the war. It started in Florida and took advantage of the new leases at the British colonies in the Western Hemisphere to create airstrips reaching to South America.[40] In addition to the major stops at Puerto Rico and Trinidad, auxiliary landing fields were laid in Cuba, Haiti, the Dominican Republic, British Guiana, and Venezuela. While these auxiliary locations were not directly part of the new route, the airfields were built to satisfy the safety concern of providing places for emergency landings in the event of aircraft malfunction. In reality, the military potential of these additional airstrips complemented the new worldwide force-projection system being extended from Florida.

Known as the South Atlantic Route, and sometimes as the Southeastern Route, the Pan Am subsidiary, *Panair do Brasil*, initiated or improved airfields along the coast of South America as far as Recife and the offshore Brazilian islands of Fernando de Noronha.[41] On the African side of the Atlantic Narrows, Pan Am worked with British authorities to carve out a string of simple landing fields from the British colonies of Gambia and Sierra Leone to Egypt and the Middle East. Ostensibly an enterprise to improve the US civilian airline industry, the Pan Am project involved working in concert with the US military authorities. Whatever the benefit to the civilian air carriers, the results significantly enhanced the American ability to project hard military air power overseas. The Pan Am project also strengthened the emerging friendship between Brazil and the United States, while undercutting Nazi influence in the region. On August 31, 1941, a pair of Army pilots left Florida to test-fly the route in a B-24 bomber.[42] Two weeks later the flight reached Basra, Iraq. The bomber then retraced the route back to Miami. Their flight underlined the significance of the flight going two ways. Thus, Florida served as both the point of origin and the destination of this first international air route of the war.

Mobilization for war brought international aviators to Florida. Lend-Lease was initially interested in flying warplanes and shipping supplies to Britain, using the merchant marine and the newly created Army Air Ferrying Command to facilitate. The Act, howsomever, also provided for training foreigners to use American equipment, allowing the president to employ the US military "to instruct others in matters of defense vital to the security of the United States."[43] "Others" included the Royal Air Force. Britain needed pilots desperately. After a meeting with the Royal Air Force delegation, General Arnold proposed enrolling the British flight cadets in the civilian

American flight schools.[44] The US Army would lend the British two hundred sixty primary training planes, and two hundred eighty-five advanced training planes. Calling itself the British Flying Training Schools (BFTS), the program enrolled British cadets at Civilian Pilot Training schools for a twenty-week course in primary, basic, and advanced flight training.[45] As with the already existing civilian-contract flight schooling program, the BFTS operated under Army Air Corps oversight. Arnold offered the facilities in Lakeland, Arcadia, and Miami for this purpose.

In the summer of 1941, British airmen began arriving in Florida. Royal Air Force pilot-candidates first crossed the Atlantic by ship to Canada. They then traveled in civilian clothes by train across the neutral US to Florida, a four-day journey. Upon reaching their flight school they were enrolled as civilians. Albeit low-key, there was nothing unmilitary about BFTS. Once in Florida, the RAF cadets changed back into uniform and joined the American cadets already in khaki. The schools were run as military training schools. RAF officers supervised their own contingents.[46] The first ninety RAF cadets enrolled in the Lakeland flight school on June 9. The town gave them a warm welcome, feting them with simple banquets and unlimited orange juice. Soon they were on the flight line, and in the skies overhead. At the graduation ceremony of the first class on August 16, Governor Holland appeared personally to present the RAF cadets with their pilot certificates.[47] "We think of you as eagles going out to fight for the right," he lauded them.[48]

The RAF aviation training, especially of the pilot-cadets, fell under the auspices of the Army Air Corps. Some of the RAF students received Navy instruction in navigation courses, but for the most part the BFTS operated within the portfolio of the Air Corps.[49] The RAF's existence as an independent branch of service lent validation-by-association to their counterparts of the Army Air Corps in its campaign for autonomy. The British contracted directly with aviation entrepreneur Riddle for Clewiston air school. The land for the airfield was purchased in July by Riddle, and Lend-Lease funds paid for the construction. The Clewiston Flight School rose from cow pastures and sugar cane fields in record time. Within a few months the Riddle-McKay Aero College at Clewiston was in operation as a British Flight Training School.[50]

In September 1940, another major step in the US mobilization came with the call-up of the National Guard. The Florida National Guard was activated and ordered to report for a year of active service at the new National Guard base of Camp Blanding. Earlier, in approving the Navy takeover of Camp Foster, the secretary of war simultaneously approved a municipal bond sale to provide the Florida Guard $400,000 for a new training camp. In facilitating the transfer of Camp Foster and the bond sale, the Jacksonville Chamber of Commerce stipulated that the new National Guard camp be located within an hour's drive of the city. The Guard chose a forest near Starke, initially acquiring thirty thousand acres. WPA labor, reservists, contract workers, and convicts from nearby Raiford State Prison threw Camp Blanding together. Water and sewer systems were established, and Florida Power and Light Company strung electricity.[51] The camp was named for Lt. General Albert H. Blanding, the senior officer of the Florida Guard, who was then completing his final tour of duty as President Roosevelt's appointed chief of the National Guard.[52] After Pearl Harbor the Regular Army assumed authority, and the camp grew to over a hundred fifty thousand acres. Based on population alone, it would become the fourth largest "city" in the state.[53]

Among the National Guard units activated in the prewar mobilization was the 31st National Guard Division, known as the "Dixie Rifles." The Division consisted of guardsmen from Florida, Alabama, Mississippi, and Louisiana. The 124th Infantry Regiment of Florida, one of its units, was ordered to muster at Camp Blanding in November.[54] Camp Blanding was soon swarming with thousands of young riflemen, and the woods rang with the drawl of the Deep South. The Dixie Rifles set up pup-tent camps and went on twenty-mile hikes; they hunted each other in mock-battle situations and took potshots at the wildlife. Florida's 124th Infantry Regiment was only the first to train at Camp Blanding. By the end of World War II, this base in an obscure corner of the state would become the largest Army basic training camp in the United States.[55]

Once the Florida National Guard was federalized, Governor Holland and the state legislature were without a military force of their own. In April 1941 they created the Florida Defense Force. This "home guard" consisted of several thousand volunteers armed and equipped by the state. The Florida Defense Force served as bodyguards and escorts for leading officials assisting the war effort. They were uniformed, carried weapons, and were paid by the state.

On May 27, 1941, President Roosevelt went on the radio to proclaim a state of unlimited national emergency confronting the United States. He stated to the listening nation in no uncertain terms that the United States was increasingly threatened by the Axis powers. In proclaiming this unprecedented executive decree, Roosevelt emphasized the geographic factors influencing his concern. Referring to the map, he noted how Axis forces were fully capable of crossing the Atlantic Narrows and how their air and sea forces directly menaced the United States.

> They [the Axis] also have the armed power at any moment to occupy Spain and Portugal; and that threat extends not only to French North Africa and the western end of the Mediterranean, but it extends also to the Atlantic fortress of Dakar, and to the island outposts of the New World—the Azores and Cape Verde Islands. The Cape Verde Islands are only seven hours' distance from Brazil by bomber or troop-carrying planes. They dominate shipping routes to and from the South Atlantic. The war is approaching the brink of the Western Hemisphere itself. It is coming very close to home.[56]

His sober observation was that if Britain fell, the United States could expect to be attacked next. "Control or occupation by Nazi forces of any of the islands of the Atlantic would jeopardize the immediate safety of portions of North and South America, and of the island possessions of the United States, and, therefore, the ultimate safety of the continental United States itself."[57] Roosevelt stressed the conclusion he had reached, emphasizing that the circumstances "directly endanger the freedom of the Atlantic and our own American physical safety. Anyone with an atlas, anyone with a reasonable knowledge of the sudden striking force of modern war, knows that it is stupid to wait until a probable enemy has gained a foothold from which to attack."[58] Implicit in his reasoning was the fact that the Florida peninsula was the first US landfall an enemy invasion from the east would encounter. The president exhorted the US military, naval, air, and civilian defenses to prepare themselves for just this possibility.

By autumn 1941 Florida had reached a conventional state of readiness. The Florida National Guard was federalized. The 124th Florida Infantry Regiment was in the field on maneuvers in the forests of Camp Blanding with the rest of the Dixie Rifles. The 265th Florida Coast Artillery Regiment was at target practice in Texas. At post office induction stations in Tampa, Miami, Tallahassee, and Jacksonville, conscripts were raising their right hands to be sworn in and report for training. The newly created Florida Defense Force mustered at armories and county courthouses around the state. Twenty naval air stations were under construction in Florida. Thirty-seven new Army airfields were being built.[59] Formations of bombers and fighter planes were regular features in the Florida skies. The civilian flying schools of Florida were sending up their own flights of Army reservists, Navy cadets, Royal Air Force trainees, and WASPs. Carpenters were building barracks and classrooms at construction sites across the state. Three top-secret military schools teaching the new cutting-edge Navy technology of sonar, Army radio signaling, and the Air Corps technology of radar were being established at Key West, Hobe Sound, and Boca Raton, respectively. Navy destroyers and cruisers of the neutrality patrol steamed offshore. Military mobilization in Florida was apparent to all. Nationwide the efforts of the administration and the War Department had raised the Army to a strength of 1.5 million, from a force numbering 189,839 men at the end of 1939.[60]

Then unexpectedly, the war arrived, not from Europe, but from the Pacific. At 8 a.m. on Sunday morning, December 7, 1941, the Japanese suddenly and devastatingly attacked Pearl Harbor. Eighteen American ships, including eight battleships, were sunk or severely damaged at their moorings, with scarcely a shot fired in their defense. One hundred eighty-eight aircraft were destroyed, and 2,403 Americans were killed. The war had come, and with a vengeance.[61] The way the war began was the first of two great surprises to the United States in World War II. At about 2:30 p.m. Florida radio stations began interrupting their usual broadcasts with the first news of the catastrophe. The initial reports were soon followed by public service announcements ordering servicemen to return to their stations and report for duty. Florida would be one of the first places to trade blows with the enemy.

4

OFF WE GO!

Into the Wild Blue Yonder

The war began disastrously for the United States. The same day Hawaii was attacked, the Imperial Japanese military struck across the Pacific.[1] The Army Air Forces in the Philippines were destroyed on the ground. The US garrisons at Peking and Shanghai awoke to find themselves prisoners. The US island of Guam was overrun, and Wake Island was attacked. British Malaya and the Dutch East Indies were similarly invaded. Adolf Hitler declared war on the United States four days after Pearl Harbor. Japanese Imperial forces invaded the Philippines and thirteen thousand US soldiers and sixty-five thousand Filipino Allies were cornered in the Bataan peninsula. By March, British Singapore had fallen, the US-British-Dutch-Australian fleet was annihilated, and the US forces on Bataan and Corregidor Island were under siege.[2] The US fought back, and much of its response began with aviation strikes from Florida bases. In Florida much of the Air Corps infrastructure of airfields, airplanes, pilots, and crews was already concentrated.

The first and best-known US air operation at this early period, the Doolittle Raid, was trained in Florida. After Pearl Harbor, President Roosevelt insisted that the home islands of Japan be bombed as soon as possible.[3] Yet the distance to Japan was too far for even the longest-range American bombers to reach. In theory the US aircraft carriers could bring airplanes close enough, but aircraft carriers carried only smaller aircraft with limited range and firepower. None of the large bomber aircraft had ever taken off from a carrier. Worse, in getting close enough to strike, the US fleet would face the Imperial Japanese Navy at the height of its military strength. The risk to the remaining US Navy was great. The chance of success was small. Still, Roosevelt persisted.[4]

By January the War Department had a solution, and Florida was the centerpiece. The plan was simple enough. Longer-range US Air Corps bombers would be loaded aboard an aircraft carrier. The carrier would steam to within range of Japan and launch the bombers. The planes would fly over Japan, drop their bombs, and fly on to China and land safely at Chinese airfields. Simple. But audacious to the extreme. No bomber pilots had ever flown off an aircraft carrier.[5] The government selected Eglin Army Airfield for the training base.[6] The Panhandle facility provided an optimum location. Its vast, uninhabited spaces included gunnery and bombing ranges, airstrips to practice the short takeoffs all day and night, and no civilians to watch.[7] The Gulf substituted for the Pacific. On February 27 B-25s and volunteer crews began arriving at Eglin.

For the next month the airmen trained in Florida with the mission commander, Lt. Col. Jimmy Doolittle. They began launching at 7 a.m. and trained at short takeoffs until 10 p.m.[8] As the Doolittle Raiders grew proficient, the length of the runway was shortened, and shortened again. The raiders practiced flying long distances at wave-top level over the Gulf of Mexico to avoid visual and radar detection. They rose to execute their bombing runs and a climbing escape, then descended again and flew hours more at low altitude, returning to Eglin at the end of the day.[9] In the third week of March the entire group flew the length of the Florida Gulf Coast. After the shortest takeoff yet, the bombers flew at wave-top height from Eglin to Fort Myers. Then they turned west and crossed the Gulf of Mexico, still at wave height. Over Texas they gained altitude and simulated their bombing run. Then they descended and flew back to Florida at an altitude of fifty feet. It was their final exam, and all passed.[10] On March 24 they departed Florida for Alameda Navy Base in California.

On April 18 the Doolittle Raiders launched their mission from the aircraft carrier USS *Hornet* off the coast of Japan. Because USS *Hornet* was spotted by enemy picket boats, they were forced to take off at extreme range. All sixteen bombers did so successfully. They bombed Tokyo, Yokohama, Kobe, and Nagoya. The raid came suddenly and seemingly from out of nowhere.

Although they experienced great difficulty in reaching China, most of the raiders did so safely. Two of the aircrews were captured. Though their payload of bombs was too small to cause significant damage, the raid demonstrated the vulnerability of the Japanese homeland to US arms. The Japanese military lost face in failing to protect their emperor.[11] It marked a profound morale-boosting psychological victory for the US.[12] When Roosevelt announced the raid to the world, he teased that the raiders had come from the new secret base at "Shangri-La."[13] Above all, the raid encouraged the Allies to fight on.

While the Doolittle Raiders were training at Eglin, other flight crews assembled in Florida to project US airpower into the war. These raids departed by way of the South Atlantic Route to the Far East. The expeditions were known as "Aquila Force," "Project X," and "HALPRO." Aquila Force went first, flying a scratch force of the available bombers in Florida. The government ordered the Aquila Force to fly to China by way of the South Atlantic Route, and from China make a bombing attack on Japan from the west, in coordination with the Doolittle Raid coming from the east.[14] Aquila Force consisted of a dozen B-17 bombers, one B-24 Liberator, and a few C-47 cargo planes. The haste of the operation was indicated by the cargo planes eliminating seats with strapped fifty-gallon drums of aviation gasoline in their place.[15] The initial wartime confusion led the State Department to require Aquila Force to apply for visas for all the countries they would fly over—Brazil, Liberia, Nigeria, Egypt, Arabia, India, and China.[16] The aircraft launched into the war from Palm Beach's Morrison Field.

Just as the Doolittle Raid required great daring to fly off the pitching deck of an aircraft carrier, the raiders traveling the South Atlantic Route faced challenges of their own. The logistics were daunting. At the time, only the B-17, B-24, and powerful C-47 cargo planes had the range to make the journey. The fuel tanks of the average B-17 had a capacity of 1,700 gallons, giving it a range of 1,850 nautical miles, without a bombload. The range of the empty B-24 was slightly better at 2,000 nautical miles.[17] The first leg of the South Atlantic Route from Florida to Puerto Rico was approximately 1,000 miles. Washington had prepared brand new Borinquen Army Airfield on the west coast of the island to facilitate just such traffic. The next hop from Puerto Rico to British-controlled Trinidad was an easy 632 miles.

From Trinidad to Atkinson Airfield, British Guiana, the distance was 350 miles, and from Atkinson Field to Belém, Brazil, was 862 miles. Flights from Trinidad could overfly Atkinson, making a nonstop flight to Belém of 1,200 miles. The next hop from Belém to Natal was 960 miles. At Natal the Flyboys came face to face with the narrows of the Atlantic Ocean.

The Narrows may perhaps be a euphemistic name for this body of water. From Brazil to the Dakar Bulge of the west coast of Africa meant flying twelve hours over 1,800 miles of blue water. Unless one departed Brazil at daybreak, at least part of the flight would be in nighttime darkness. Deviation of a few degrees south or north from the course, a common effect of headwinds and tailwinds, could result in missing Africa altogether and flying straight into the sea when the fuel was exhausted. If one missed the landfall, there was precious little fuel remaining to retrace the flight.

Allied airfields were waiting across the narrows at the British colonies of Sierra Leone and Gambia. But the B-17 and the B-24 were the only military aircraft that could cover the distance. For single-engine and twin-engine planes (unless specially equipped with extra fuel tanks) it was impossible to reach Africa. It proved an endurance test even for the B-17s and B-24s. For inexperienced pilots and navigators with the bare minimum of training, it was a white-knuckled flight experience sometimes finished with a landing on fumes alone.[18]

In Africa the route was far from refined. Miami Pan Am's subsidiary, Atlantic Airways Ltd., had built outright or improved on the colonial airstrips at Bathurst in Gambia, Freetown in Sierra Leone, and Accra in Gold Coast. The pro-US nation of Liberia granted landing rights at Hastings Field.[19] Pan Am pioneered bare airstrips across the waist of Africa at Kano and Maiduguri in Nigeria, Fort Lamy in French Equatorial Africa (a place nominally Free-French), and El Geneina, El Fasher, El Obeid, and Khartoum in Anglo-Egyptian Sudan. From Khartoum pilots followed the Nile north to Cairo, then east to Iran, India, and the Orient.[20]

Aquila Force left Florida with Col. Caleb Haynes leading the way at the controls of the B-24. Beside him was a briefcase with a million dollars provided by the War Department.[21] The planes departed singly and in pairs so as not to overburden the infrastructure along the way. At one stop, the Americans used cash to bribe the local sheik to guard the aircraft from his own tribesmen while the aircrews slept. In Karachi, British constables tried to impound the airplanes for their own army; they were deterred only when the American aircrews displayed loaded Tommy guns.[22] Several planes were

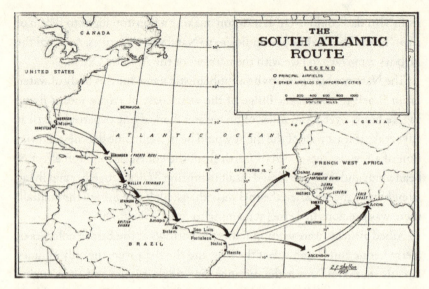

The South Atlantic Route from core to periphery. The Florida air bridge pioneered by Pan Am first hopped across the Caribbean islands, landing for fuel and sleep at the new US bases FDR had gotten in exchange from Britain for fifty aging US destroyers. Then it was on to Brazil on the mainland of South America. Over Amazonian rainforests and stops at Belém and Natal; until at last the fliers faced the daunting Atlantic Ocean crossing to Africa. The stubby-pencil navigation calculus of the times was rudimentary. A one-degree miscalculation in crossing the Atlantic to Africa made the chance of missing Africa altogether and splashing with empty tanks into the vast ocean a very real and very deadly gamble. Only after "Wide-Awake Airstrip" was carved out of Ascension Island did the odds improve. Craven and Cate, *History of the Army Air Corps in World War II*. Vol. VII, 228.

left behind at Caribbean, African, or Asian airstrips for lack of fuel or parts. Still, most of the aircraft of Aquila Force reached India in early April.

The Aquila Force of air power projected from Florida assembled in northeast India at Assam. At the time US Lieutenant General Joseph "Vinegar Joe" Stilwell and his Chinese troops were being overrun in the attempt to stop the Japanese invasion of Burma.[23] Haynes personally flew to the assistance of the American general. Landing in a clearing, the Aquila Force commander found Stilwell in the midst of the retreat.[24] "Vinegar Joe" refused to be flown to India, preferring famously to walk to safety leading his staff.[25] When Haynes returned to Assam, he received orders to fly aviation gas from India to China.[26] With China now cut off from all directions except the air, this flight initiated the airlift over the Himalaya Mountains. The feat would become known as "Flying the Hump," and this airlift would become a primary war mission for Florida.

The second of the Florida-based air strikes aimed to relieve the Philippines. "Project X" was a much larger mission than Aquila. It included seventy heavy bombers to reinforce the US forces fighting on Bataan. Much better organized, it reflected the maturing plans of using Florida in the air offensive. The strategic approach exploited the peninsula for the express purpose of systematically launching American air forces into the war. The process accomplished several military goals. By launching from Florida, more military hardware and personnel were introduced into the state, making it that much more defensible against invasion. The missions increased US presence at the outposts along the way, as well, further forestalling the possibility of the enemy gaining a beachhead in the Western Hemisphere. Above all, it provided the most practical way to get at the enemy. Although the South Atlantic Route was hardly in good shape for serious air traffic, the exigencies of the situation in the Pacific demanded urgent action.

On December 19 the first six B-24 Liberator bombers of Project X arrived at MacDill Field.[27] Over the next six weeks, sixty more B-17 bombers joined them.[28] Neither planes nor crews were prepared to fly halfway around the world using the most primitive air route of the day. Extraneous weight consumed precious fuel and made the planes harder to fly. As with the aviators of Aquila Force, the pilots and crews of Project X had only vague notions of the geography they had to cover. None were trained in flying without radio contacts, homing beacons, or landmarks. None were experienced in unassisted takeoffs and landings at mud-drenched airstrips, navigation by the stars, or night landings.[29]

But unlike the "fly-by-the-seat-of-the-pants" urgency of Aquila Force, Project X paused for rigorous training. Pan Am pilots experienced in transatlantic flights were brought to MacDill to provide instruction. While arriving bombers were methodically stripped of excess weight, the crews attended classroom instruction on what to expect along the route. They studied primitive briefing books, sometimes no more than tourism brochures. Their training included information about stopping points, refueling arrangements, weather, local inhabitants, health conditions, food, shelter, and safety conditions in route. Pilots, navigators, and radiomen were given training in how to find their way

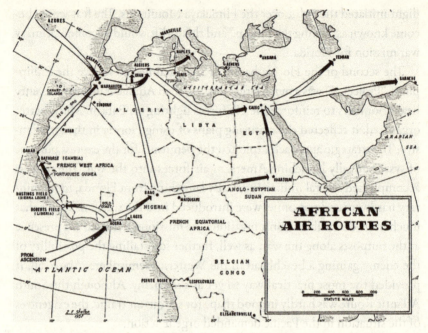

The route to the war across Africa. Once they reached Africa, fliers over the South Atlantic Air Bridge faced more challenges. The airstrips across the African continent were primitive at best. Crash landings were routine, and crashes themselves not uncommon. The landing strips had no stocks of the simplest nuts and bolts, let alone critical airplane parts or even potable water. Amenities were few to none. The local inhabitants were indifferent or hostile. Yet over jungles and sand storms the flyboys pressed on to Arabia. Craven and Cate, *The Army Air Forces in World War II*. Vol. VII, 229.

across the Amazon, the Atlantic, and the Sahara they were to cross. In the wake of Aquila Force the first planes of Project X took off: destination Karachi.[30]

The effort came too late. By the time the aircraft of Project X reached India, Bataan had been overrun and Corregidor Island was under siege. A few Project X bombers managed to make their way to Australia. In Australia the planes of Project X formed the nucleus of the newly created 5th Air Force.[31] Although only a handful, the arrival of the bombers coincided with the arrival in Australia of US General MacArthur following his escape from the Philippines. The B-17s lent credence to the defeated American general's brave vow: "I shall return." His exhortation to continue resistance boosted the morale of the Americans as well as the threatened Allied population of Australia, cheered to see US Flying Fortresses arriving after a journey of eighteen thousand miles beginning in Florida.[32]

Others of the Project X aircraft remained in India. Combined with the Aquila Force, they made up the core of the new 10th Air Force. Four of the Project X bombers crashed into the ocean during the Atlantic passage, one went down over the Amazon, and two were parked permanently in Africa and cannibalized for spare parts by succeeding flights.[33] Yet, for all those failures, the bombers had flown two-thirds of the way around the world and taken the war from Florida to the enemy.

The third early air strike from Florida was also launched with the inten-

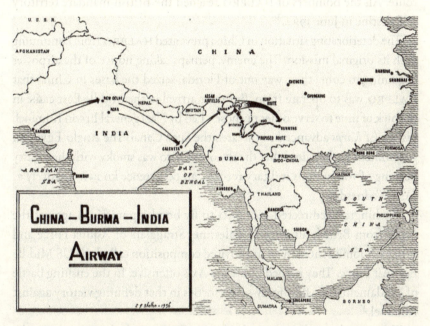

China-Burma-India and over the Hump. Once the Middle East was behind them the huge subcontinent of India stretched before them. More thousands of miles of propellor time had to be traversed crossing the rugged subcontinent to the highlands of Assam. There the final and most formidable challenge rose to block the aviators' way: the tallest objects on earth, the Himalaya Mountains. From the abrupt takeoff climbing a dangerous three hundred feet per minute, flying over these ice-covered, gale-swept peaks required steady nerves . . . and good luck. With their penchant for nicknames the GIs dubbed the Himalayas the "Hump." Studded with the wrecks of over sixteen hundred unlucky aircraft that went down trying to fly over these mountains, they called their flight path the "Aluminum Trail." The reward for reaching the end of the warpath was to turn around and fly another eighteen thousand miles going back the same way. This longest air bridge of all time, thirty-six thousand miles roundtrip, began and ended in Florida. Craven and Cate, *The Army Air Forces in World War II*. Vol. VII, 231.

tion of bombing Japan from Chinese bases. Codenamed HALPRO, the secret operation began at Fort Myers.[34] The codename referred to its commander, Col. Harry E. Halverson. For the mission the Army appropriated civilian Page Field and renamed it Fort Myers Army Airfield.[35] Twenty-three B-24D Liberator bombers and hand-picked crews secretly assembled there. The bombers launched from Morrison Field beginning on May 20, 1942, in three synchronized groups with a two-day timed interval between each group. The Florida commanders of the South Atlantic Route were learning to feed aircraft through a pipeline while avoiding overwhelming the facilities on the route. All the bombers of HALPRO reached the British-mandate territory of Palestine in June 1942.[36]

The deteriorating situation in China prevented HALPRO from continuing with its original mission. The enemy, perhaps taking notice of the airpower beginning to come their way out of Florida, seized the bases in China that HALPRO was to operate from. But their arrival in the Middle East came in the nick of time to serve other purposes. Led by Nazi general Erwin Rommel, his *Afrika Korps* advanced to threaten the Suez Canal. The Anglo-Egyptian government so despaired that the sky over Cairo was smoky with their hasty burning of voluminous military records, an occurrence known derisively as "Ash Wednesday."

Washington redirected HALPRO to fly bombing missions against the Nazis from British airstrips in Palestine. Stragglers of Aquila Force and Project X joined them in an improvised composition called the US Middle East Air Force. They helped blunt the Axis offensive. In the ensuing battle of El Alamein, they flew forty-seven sorties in that defining victory against Rommel.[37]

These aerial expeditions taught the Air Corps much about operating the air bridge from Florida. Florida might be the home base for all these fliers, but the state's role hardly ended with crew training and the like. All the departing aircraft, pilots, and aircrews were kept track of and accounted for on situation boards in Florida. Morrison Army Air Base in West Palm Beach was designated the Aerial Port of Embarkation for the South Atlantic Route. Its first job was to properly establish the overseas airfields with bulldozer-graded runways overlaid with the new interlocking perforated steel planking "Marston Mats." Control towers, radio shacks, hangar facilities, barracks, and chow halls were built. Orders were issued assigning engineers, controllers, technicians, mechanics, and guards for every stop along the way. Logistic systems for fuel, lubricants, parts, communications, security, and health were set up. Miami Army Airfield was assigned to handle air cargo over the route, and liaison with the contract carriers of Pan American, Eastern, and National airlines.[38] Aquila Force, Project X, and HALPRO pioneered the vital aerial transportation system from Florida that would supply US military operations throughout the war, especially in the emerging theater of operations that would come to be known as China-Burma-India (CBI).

One major activity from Florida begun at this time to supplement the CBI airlift was the Stilwell Road project. General Stilwell, the theater commander, was skeptical of the ability of aviation to supply China from India. He called for the construction of a road to be built from Allied India to China.[39] The road was meant to traverse the jungle highlands of Burma and connect with the old Burma Road the Japanese had cut. When complete, the road would enable truck convoys to supply China easier, and in larger volume. The problem was that the road had to pass through some of the worst terrain on earth. Known as the Stilwell Road, for its main advocate, or as the Ledo Road, for its point of origin in India, or simply the Burma Road, the road was one of the unsung feats of the war. Florida troops were instrumental in building it.

One of the first units assigned to build the road was the 45th Engineer General Services Regiment, composed entirely of African American soldiers, many of them Floridians. The unit was one of the first activated at Camp Blanding. After training at Camp Blanding, the unit was deployed to Burma in June 1942. The twelve hundred soldiers of the 45th Engineer Regiment spent the next three years in-country. Their leadership and expertise directed the many local laborers hewing the road through the mountainous jungle with switchback after switchback. The African American GIs from Florida contended with steep mountains, dense jungles, and sweltering heat. Besides the monsoon, malaria, and cobras, the soldiers faced Japanese ambushes and raiding parties. Late in the war the road finally reached China. The first truckload of supplies arrived there in spring of 1945, to complement the air bridge.[40]

By June 1942 over four hundred military aircraft had been launched into the war via the air route from Florida.[41] Airplanes arriving in Florida to start on combat expeditions were joined by Lend-Lease aircraft destined for US Allies abroad. Many of these aircraft were flown from the factories to the

Florida embarkation points by female pilots. Because of the demand for and shortage of male pilots, women began flying airplanes in large numbers. Organized into the wartime Women's Air Service Pilots (WASP) program, over a thousand female pilots participated.[42]

Helping wherever needed, the WASPs brought warplanes to their trainees at bases across Florida. They flew charters for the nationalized civilian air carriers. WASPs served as flight instructors, and contract pilots towing sleeves for aerial target practice. Throughout the war, female pilots made up a visible part of Florida's aerial landscape. Thirty-nine WASPs gave their lives.[43]

It is perhaps time to touch upon the human cost of the war to America. It is impossible to gauge this price merely from archival material. First must be established the baseline number of Americans killed in World War II. The number is often rounded down. Such authorities as British writer John Keegan, and John Lewis Gaddis quote 292,000 killed:

> The United States waged separate wars simultaneously—against the Japanese in the Pacific and the Germans in Europe—but suffered remarkably few casualties: just under 300,000 Americans died in all combat theaters.[44]

But that is not the whole story.

The authority for the numbers of US war dead is the Congressional Research Service of the United States, and an examination of how we count our losses is necessary. The Congressional Research Service gives US World War II "Battle Deaths" at 291,557 killed, the basis of the "under 300,000" observation quoted above.[45] Yet, the same tabulation also counts 113,842 "Other Deaths" in the same war.[46] This figure includes those who donned the uniform, reported for duty, and during their wartime service lost their lives other than falling in battle. They were killed while training for combat, on their way to combat, on their way from combat, and as the result of wounds, injuries, illness, and diseases contracted while in uniform under military jurisdiction during the war. The combined battle deaths and other deaths amount to 405,399 lives lost, a much larger number.[47]

Nor is this the total number of US war dead. The US Maritime Service was a uniformed service under arms and military law in World War II. Some 6,100 merchant mariners lost their lives in World War II.[48] If their war dead are included, then roughly 411,499 US military personnel died in World

War II. However droll this tabulation may be, it is the real loss of life that America experienced in World War II.

Another aspect of the war to consider is the number of those who while in service suffered what is categorized as "Wounds Not Mortal." The number of US wounded in World War II is tabulated at 670,846 personnel.[49] This number, in association with the real number of dead, 411,499 persons, adds up to 1,082,245 casualties.[50] The real bottom line is over 1 million of the 14,903,213 persons who served were either killed or wounded, a metric giving a better understanding of the seriousness of the event.

Two examples may suffice.

Alexander Ramsey Nininger was born on October 20, 1918. His nickname was "Sandy." He grew up in Fort Lauderdale. His father ran a furniture store; his mother was a seamstress. Sandy was the child of a broken home, his parents divorced soon after he was born.[51] His mother never learned of his fate until long after his sacrifice. Sandy had a yen for adventure matched by a bent toward scholastics and the arts. He secured an appointment to the United States Military Academy at West Point and entered the Academy in 1937. He was proficient in track and field. He was on the debate team and

Nininger of Florida was the first Medal of Honor recipient of World War II. Florida Veterans Homes, Florida Veterans Affairs, and other state facilities, as well as monuments and memorials at the United States Military Academy are named in his memory. Photo courtesy of the State Archives of Florida, Florida Memory.

chaired the lecture club. He served as cadet sergeant for L Company of the 3rd Battalion of Cadets. His class yearbook indicates he was interested in theater, books, painting, and music. Nininger graduated with the class of 1941 and simultaneously was commissioned an Army 2nd lieutenant. He was assigned to the US Army Philippine Division.

At the time the Philippine Islands were a US territory, scheduled to be granted their full independence by the United States on July 4, 1946. Yet in 1940 the threat of war pervaded the Pacific. The provisional Philippine commonwealth government of President Manuel L. Quezon hired retired US Army General Douglas MacArthur to serve as its field marshal and train up the Philippine Defense Force. Much of MacArthur's Army career had been in the Far East. He was fond of the Philippines and its people. He and his wife and young son took up residence in Manila. But in July 1941 MacArthur was recalled by FDR to active duty in the American Army. He assumed command of both the US garrison troops and the new Philippine Defense Force.

That same month Lieutenant Sandy Nininger reported for duty with the American forces in the archipelago. Nininger was posted to the Philippine Scouts. These were a cavalry regiment of Philippine soldiers enlisted into the US Army and usually, though not always, led by Americans officers.[52] Accompanied by his victrola, classical music recordings, and books, Nininger might have cut a quizzical figure to his rough Filipino troopers. But little time for amusement remained anywhere in the world.

On December 7, 1941, the Japanese Imperial Fleet appeared off Oahu, savaging the US Navy and bringing global war. The Imperial Japanese Army soon landed on the north coast of Luzon, and the Philippines became a theater of war. Nininger and the Philippine Scouts engaged the enemy. The rugged mountainous jungles of northern Luzon witnessed the horsemen of the Philippine Scouts fighting against Imperial Japanese Army tanks, just as mounted Polish lancers fought against the steel Panzers of the *blitzkrieg* on the other side of the world. Heroically. Hopelessly. The written word of his Medal of Honor citation reflects his bravery in battle:

> For conspicuous gallantry and intrepidity above and beyond the call of duty in action with the enemy near Abucay, Bataan, Philippine Islands, on 12 January 1942. This officer, though assigned to another company not then engaged in combat, voluntarily attached himself to Company

K, same regiment, while that unit was being attacked by enemy force superior in firepower. Enemy snipers in trees and foxholes had stopped a counterattack to regain part of position. In hand-to-hand fighting which followed, 2d Lt. Nininger repeatedly forced his way to and into the hostile position. Though exposed to heavy enemy fire, he continued to attack with rifle and hand grenades and succeeded in destroying several enemy groups in foxholes and enemy snipers. Although wounded 3 times, he continued his attacks until he was killed after pushing alone far within the enemy position. When his body was found after recapture of the position, 1 enemy officer and 2 enemy soldiers lay dead around him.

Nininger was the first American recipient of the Medal of Honor in World War II. He was twenty-two.

Dorothy Evelyn Blackwelder was born on July 20, 1924. The catastrophe of total war has never been confined to the spear side of humanity. The distaff half of humanity is equally afflicted. It may be observed that the triumph of humanity in the natural kingdom has been due to the unlimited partnership between humans, male and female. The extremely long time from gestation to maturity of the human young approaches ten years at the very least; whereas in the animal kingdom creatures may be able to fend for themselves in as

Dorothy Evelyn Blackwelder, HA1/C, US Navy WAVES, from St. Paul's Catholic High School, Yearbook 1944, Daytona Beach, FL.

little as a day. So, the unrestricted welcome of womenkind for mankind, in contrast to the seasonal strictures governing the animal kingdom, is astonishing. This is even more so since up until the medical advances of modern times, childbirth events have claimed the lives (and today continue to claim in parts of the planet) of up to 20 percent of mothers. This casualty rate is higher than Gettysburg, or Verdun.

Of such sober reflections Dorothy Blackwelder of Daytona Beach presumably thought little. Her father Benjamin was a truck farmer, her mother, Percy Mae, a housewife. She went to school in Volusia County, the scene of the Rawlings novel about backwater America, and applied herself to earning a high school diploma, a signal accomplishment of those days. She was interested in nursing, basketball, and was the YWCA club treasurer. Blackwelder graduated from St. Paul's Catholic High School in Daytona Beach, Florida, in the summer of 1942. Her three brothers, Everitte, Earl, and Harvey, were all serving in the military overseas.

September 2, 1943, she raised her right hand, swore the oath to defend the Constitution, signed her name, and joined the Navy Reserve Women's Reserve, better known as the WAVES (Women Accepted for Volunteer Emergency Service).[53] She was sent to boot camp at Hunter College, NYC. She was an apprentice, "striking," a naval term, to achieve promotion to the naval rating of hospital corpsman. Corpsmen were the medics of the Navy. She was promoted to hospital apprentice 1st class on December 5, 1943.[54]

At New York's Grand Central Station on December 15, 1943, Blackwelder boarded Atlantic Coastline Train #91, the Tamiami West Coast Champion. She was bound for Christmas leave with her family in Florida. Her parents prepared for her return.

The train left New York at 11:45 a.m., with scheduled stops in Baltimore, Washington, and Richmond. The final stop was to be in St. Petersburg, FL, at 4:15 p.m. the following afternoon.[55] The train was full of military personnel. There was a snowstorm over North Carolina. Shortly after midnight outside of Lumberton, NC, the train slipped off the rails. The last four cars came to rest on the northbound tracks. The derailed train posted signal lanterns.

Coming from the opposite direction at 1:30 a.m. in twelve-degree weather was northbound Train #8, the Tamiami East Coast Champion from Miami. Amid the snow storm, Northbound #8 failed to see the signal lanterns indicating the derailment ahead. Train #8 struck Train #91 at eighty miles per hour, destroying the four passenger cars.[56] Seventy-nine passengers were killed, including Blackwelder.

Her body was shipped home by train to her family.[57] The cause of death was listed as "crushed face, body, and extremities." HA1st Class Blackwelder, USNR, rests in Greenwood Cemetery in Daytona Beach. The students of the class of 1944 dedicated a page of St. Paul's yearbook to her, with a prayer said to be her favorite. She was nineteen. Her nickname was "Dottie."

The class of 1944 gave tribute to Blackwelder's memory by dedicating the following prayer, "Mother at Your Feet Is Kneeling":

Mother at your feet is kneeling
   One who loves you, 'tis your child,
Who has sighed so oft to see you,
   Bless me Mother, bless your child.

Dearest Mother, tell my Jesus
   How I love him, fond and true;
And, oh Mary, dearest Mother,
   Tell Him I belong to you.

Mary, oh my dearest Mother,
   May it e'er to me be given,
As on earth I fondly love thee,
   So to love thee still in heaven.

Such case studies repeated over four hundred thousand times may convey the seriousness of the war.

The importance of the air power projected from Florida led to continuous improvement and care for the route by the US military. The Army Air Ferrying Command was renamed Air Transport Command, with designated headquarters at Morrison Field in West Palm Beach. Three subordinate commands were parsed out along the way: Caribbean Wing in Florida, South Atlantic Wing in Brazil, and Africa-Middle East Wing at Sierra Leone. A general officer directed airlift operations in each sector.[58] Many of the major war councils of the Allies, including the overseas conferences at Casablanca, Cairo, and Tehran, as well as many meetings in the United States, were facilitated by the Florida route. The oldest of the air routes, and throughout 1942 the most important, stretched from Florida across the South Atlantic to Africa and the Middle East, and from thence all the way to China.[59]

In July 1942 a small but critical construction project made the South Atlantic Route fully operational as an Allied air bridge: the completion of the runway on the British-held Ascension Island in the middle of the Atlantic Narrows. The airstrip was nicknamed Wideawake Airfield because flocks of terns congregated on its flightline. The birds were a peculiar aviation danger. Aircraft landing at and lifting off from Ascension were forced to plow through a multitude of birds as they came and went. But the danger was surpassed by the military significance of the island. Ascension Island is 1,437 miles from Brazil, and 1,357 miles to Accra, Ghana. With Ascension Island as a refueling point, those distances were possible for twin-engine medium B-25s and B-26s bombers, and even single-engine fighter planes. The homing beacon on Ascension further assisted navigating the narrows and opened the South Atlantic Route to most aircraft in the AAF inventory.[60]

The Pan Am engineers and Army Air Corps advisers who initially planned the South Atlantic Route from Florida had no idea it would bear such a vast airlift of daily cargo flights, across two-thirds of the Great Circle of the Earth and over the tallest mountains in the world. But that was the result. Among those who took the route was President Roosevelt himself on his final visit to Florida. His trip included what may be called the First Flight of Air Force One.[61]

January 3, 1943, Roosevelt called a small press conference to the White House to review the recent US invasions of Morocco and Algeria. Roosevelt confided to the press that his concerns over the war were such that he was going to Hyde Park for a few days to think things through. He invited the press to see him off at the train station a matter of blocks away. The flattered reporters accompanied FDR, where he boarded the *Ferdinand Magellan* presidential train car and waved a cheery bon voyage as the locomotive pulled away on its northward journey.[62]

Unknown to the press and the rest of the world, the train came to a halt that night at Fort Meade, Maryland. Then it jolted back to life and began moving again. But this time it was heading south to Florida. The presidential train had executive right-of-way and made no stops along the way, passing through the Miami train station without pause two days later. Ten miles out of town the train came to a halt alongside Dixie Highway, near the stately Vizcaya mansion. Government cars were waiting beside the road. Secret Service agents whisked the president and the Joint Chiefs of Staff to the cars, and a short drive through Coconut Grove to the seaside Dinner Key Naval Air Station, home to amphibious flying boats. Two federalized Pan Am clippers were waiting, their crews all federalized military personnel. "Mr. Jones and his private party" went aboard. The majestic clipper ships taxied over Biscayne Bay and rose into the sky bearing the president and his entourage over the Caribbean realm.[63]

That night the top-secret seaplanes and their passengers arrived at Trinidad, now home to a US base. The next day the travelers flew on to Belém and Natal, Brazil, and then across the Atlantic Narrows to Africa. US fighter planes from Ascension Island flew escort. In Africa the cruiser USS *Memphis* met the group on the Gambia River. The commander and his generals switched to an Army C-54 cargo plane and flew north over the Atlas Mountains to Casablanca, Morocco.

There FDR was met by none other than British Prime Minister Winston Churchill, and the two leaders convened the Casablanca Conference, the first of many such transatlantic war meetings. At one point Roosevelt was taken aboard a Jeep to inspect the front. He made a standing drive-by inspection of thousands of assembled soldiers. "Gosh," exclaimed one amazed sergeant, "It's the Old Man himself!" FDR dined with his GIs in the field on Spam, green beans, and coffee.[64] The Army Band gave a command performance of "Deep in the Heart of Texas."

After the conference FDR returned to Florida by seaplane over the same South Atlantic Route, landing on Biscayne Bay once more at Dinner Key. The presidential train was again waiting his return. Back in Washington, the president grinned sheepishly to the press. Perhaps he smiled inwardly, as well. FDR was not a simple man. He was the only president to hunt for sharks from the deck of US destroyers. This public figure was a victim of polio who refused to ever allow his crippled physical condition to be photographed.[65] He was a chain-smoker who relished a dry martini and a salty joke, and he was a past master at politics, statecraft, and the art of war. Dying as he did while in service may have entitled him to the Purple Heart.

Florida as a major aerial staging area threw together a great variety of Army aviators, some of whom played compelling roles later in the war.

Among them were several serving in the new 97th Bomb Group, assigned to training at Sarasota Army Airfield.[66] Its B-17 pilots included the young captain Paul Tibbets. Tibbets had grown up in Hialeah and learned to fly there before dropping out of UF Medical School to join the service. In Sarasota he made friends with Capt. Thomas Ferebee, a navigator, and Lt. Theodore "Dutch" Van Kirk, a bombardier. These three officers would serve together and become the nucleus of the crew of the B-29 bomber *Enola Gay*. Tibbets would name the bomber for his mother, who lived in the Shenandoah neighborhood of Miami. Later in the war they would become part of something called the Manhattan Project. *Enola Gay* would deliver the "Little Boy" on target.[67]

5

ANCHORS AWEIGH

The Battle of the Gulf Sea Frontier

As Admiral Mahan had foreseen, the war came to Florida, quickly and viciously. Germany declared war on the United States four days after the Pearl Harbor attack, and within a week the first U-boats sailed to attack the eastern seaboard of the United States.[1] Three weeks later the submarines reached their areas of operation. Florida was among the destinations and became one of the few places in the continental United States to see active combat. The sea battle occurred within sight of the beaches of Florida and in the surrounding waters of the Florida Straits, the Gulf, and the Caribbean Sea.[2]

Only supplies could prevent the fall of England and the Soviet Union: food, fuel, aircraft, cannons, rifles, and bullets. The US merchant marine set course to cross the Atlantic. The German Navy wisely fought to prevent the ships from reaching the open sea in the first place. For that purpose, they came here to close the sea lanes of the Gulf Sea Frontier. A sea battle of Homeric proportions ensued.

On February 19 German submarines arrived off Florida and began their campaign against Allied shipping. That day, a German U-boat torpedoed the tanker SS *Pan Massachusetts*. The tanker had just exited the Florida Straits northward bound for New York with ninety thousand barrels of oil.[3] Twenty miles off Cape Canaveral two torpedoes turned the ship into an inferno. Twenty crewmembers died as she sank in three hundred feet of water. The tanker sank within sight of NAS Banana River, the new seaplane base being built near Cape Canaveral to prevent just such attacks.[4] The spectacle horrified crowds watching from the beach. The sinking of the tanker SS *Cities Service Empire* four days later repeated the disaster of the *Pan Massachusetts*. The U-boat simply remained on station and waited for the next target to appear. Another fourteen sailors were killed.

As more submarines arrived, the U-boats launched successive waves of attacks down the coast of Florida. Four tankers were sunk in four days. The first week in May the battle grew in intensity. Merchant ships were attacked every day. Twelve were sunk; two more of them tankers. Another two tankers and a freighter were damaged by torpedoes and only managed to limp into harbor. On May 6 five ships were sunk in a single day.[5]

The waters around Florida were the *schwerpunkt*, the natural center of gravity where a sea battle would develop, much as Admiral Mahan had observed:

> A cross-roads is essentially a central position, facilitating action in as many directions as there are roads. Those familiar with works on the art of land war will recognize the analogies. The value becomes yet more marked if, by the lay of the land, the road to be followed becomes very narrow; as at the Straits of Gibraltar, the English Channel, and in a less degree the Florida Strait.[6]

Knowing the terrain, or rather, the seascape, is central to understanding the sea battle off Florida. The Yucatán Passage and the Florida Straits both saw extensive combat. The deepwater Yucatán Passage, seven hundred fifty fathoms at its shallowest, is shaped like the waist of an hourglass. Although the passage itself is short, the shoal water shallows of the Campeche Bank extending due north from the Yucatán Peninsula serve to accentuate the narrows. Ships have little room to maneuver before entering the slot. The hundred-thirty-five-mile-wide strait was a battlefield where thirty ships were attacked and sunk in the approaches that funnel shipping through the passage itself.

The Florida Straits represents a lengthy stretch of confined waters, one not always apparent on ordinary maps. The Bahamas Islands that define the eastern end of the Straits act practically as a stopper to the channel. Although the islands themselves are only inconsequential land masses rising slightly above sea level, they mark a much larger mass of submerged limestone shoals known collectively as the Bahamas Banks.[7] The name of the Bahamas itself derives from the Spanish word for shallows: *baja mar*. These flats are nowhere more than a few fathoms deep.

A fundamental difference between maps and charts is that charts indicate the depth of the water depicted. A simple but vital fact that charts convey is depth between one fathom and two fathoms of water. A man standing over six feet tall can walk safely across water a single fathom deep, be it for one mile or twenty. In two fathoms of water the same individual will surely drown unless he can swim. Charts are of good value in plotting naval warfare.

The Bahamas Banks confine shipping to the coastline of Florida, along which flows the mighty Gulf Stream current. In wartime, shipping would normally fan out before entering or after exiting narrows such as the Florida Straits, but the Bahamas Banks restrict access to the open sea and force shipping to hug the Florida coast.[8] Not until the banks recede opposite Fort Pierce can vessels strike for the open seas. The net effect of the Bahamas Banks, in combination with the Straits, is to double the length of the confined passage shipping is forced to take. The waters of the passage itself are quite deep: four hundred fathoms off Port St. Lucie, five hundred fathoms off Cape Florida, and over nine hundred fathoms between Key West and Havana. Such depths were ideal for lurking U-boats. The sea lane a veritable shooting gallery for submarines. Thirty-eight ships were to be sunk in the Florida Straits.

Another geographic feature makes the space even more advantageous for the attacker. Only two passages cut through the Bahamas Banks from the Atlantic Ocean to the coastal waters of Florida. The Northwest Providence Channel lies between the island groups of Grand Bahama and Andros. The Old Bahama Channel flows between the Banks and the north coast of Cuba. Both these channels are winding and narrow, but hundreds of fathoms deep. They lead away from the destination of any surface vessel heading either north to the US eastern core, or south to the Panama Canal. In wartime there would be no reason for ships to use either passage except to make for the safety of the open sea. Any surface vessel plying the Old Bahama Channel or the Northwest Providence Channel would be in extreme peril, exposed and far from any assistance. A fetching target.

On the other hand, U-boats in the Atlantic wishing to enter the hunting grounds of the Gulf Sea Frontier could simply dive deep, negotiate the preferred twisting channel unseen, and slip unnoticed into the Florida Straits. No submarine deployed at random into the war zone without orders to take up station within a specific grid sector of the battle space. Each was assigned to an area perceived by U-boat Command to offer the best chance to cause maximum damage, death, and destruction. In this regard, the Nazis simply repeated naval history. The treasure galleons of the Spanish Main were at the mercy of pirates in these confined waters. During World War II the U-boats hunted these same spaces assiduously.

As Mahan predicted, the mouth of the Mississippi River was central to the battle.[9] For the obvious reason that so many targets came and went via the great river, U-boats concentrated there. Twenty-five ships were sunk within sight of Louisiana, and one U-boat even laid mines at the entrance to the Father of Waters. As elsewhere, the attacks followed a pattern. The U-boat never revealed its presence in advance and did not scruple to confine hostilities to identified belligerents. They attacked anything coming within their periscope crosshairs.[10] The successful torpedo hit its target within a minute or two. Seldom did the U-boat linger over the kill. The *U-bootfahren* were brave, not suicidal. Their mission after sinking one ship was to sink another, and then another. To do so they had to save themselves by leaving the area.

The undersea topography of the west coast of Florida served to limit combat there to only seven ships sunk.[11] The long land mass of the Florida peninsula acts as a rampart against the Atlantic. Sheltered by the lee of the peninsula in the relatively calm waters of the Gulf Coast the sand and silt has accumulated for ages, giving west Florida a wide band of smooth flat shallows. The usual U-boat in theater, the workhorse VIIC, displaced 769 tons when surfaced, and 871 tons submerged. The VIIC was 67 meters (about 220 feet) long, 6.2 meters (20.34 feet) wide, with a 4.74-meter (about 15.5 feet) draft.[12] It was not so small an object to hide, and not difficult to detect under the right conditions. From the sky, foreign objects in calm shallow water stand out, especially on a sunny day against a level sandy background.

The topography of Florida's Gulf Coast favored the weapons of antisubmarine warfare. Sonar operates best in shallow waters. The deeper the water, the weaker the signal, and the less certain the return impulse. Similarly, against a smooth and uniform seabed, detection is easier. Radar operates by sending sound waves over the surface of the ocean. If the rays hit a

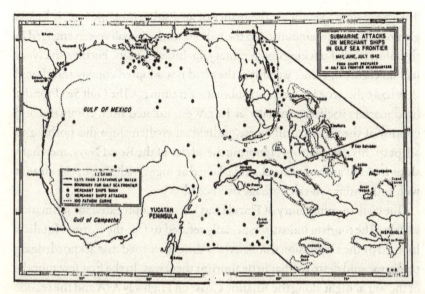

Battlefield of the Gulf Sea Frontier. Each of the ninety-eight dots on the chart represents a ship sunk by the Nazi U-boats. It was a huge loss in lives and ships. At the mouth of the Mississippi River alone seventeen ships were sunk. Enterprising U-boats even laid mines to seal the entrance. The attack on Florida and the Gulf Sea Frontier was aggressive, determined, and fully demonstrative of Nazi logic. US oil came then from Texas. The sinking of a tanker was a grim "two-for": the loss of both the precious ship and its precious fuel. Equally dire was the sinking of ships loaded with bauxite, without which aluminum aircraft could not be manufactured. The ships of every nationality were fair game. Nazi U-boats even landed Nazi saboteurs at night on the Ponte Vedra Beach near Jacksonville. The sea battle was existential. US Navy, War Diary of the Gulf Sea Frontier Headquarters, Quarterly Summary Report May, June, July 1942. Situation chart, August 1942.

foreign object on the water, a return bounces back, signaling it. The calmer the sea-state, the better the capability to detect foreign objects afloat on its surface. Shallow water is generally calmer. But alas, no such technology was initially employed in any systemic response to the U-boat attack.

The US Navy was surprised, overwhelmed, and nearly defeated by the relentless and implacable war the U-boats waged. Altogether a hundred twelve ships were attacked in the Gulf Sea Frontier in a first few months. The great majority of them were sunk. It was a naval disaster.[13]

Before Pearl Harbor the Navy planned for battles of big ships on the open sea, and its strategists only adapted reluctantly to the war they now faced.

They were slow to embrace the reality of anti-submarine warfare. It lacked glamour. The battle amounted to the tedious work of small vessels engaged in the monotony of tracking down solitary, invisible U-boats. Further, the Navy had no classes of escort warships; they had not adopted convoy travel; and they had otherwise ignored anti-submarine training.[14] The Gulf Sea Frontier headquarters itself was initially at Key West, isolated from command and control of the region. Still worse, individual civilian ships did nothing to adapt to this ugly wartime. Ignoring the advice of the Royal Navy, merchant ships traveled as they pleased, undarkened at night, radioing in the clear at will, and tossing tell-tale garbage overboard.

The civilian community of Florida was likewise unprepared for submarine attacks. The tourism industry especially refused to face the storm. Hoteliers hit hard by the Depression dismissed the danger, worried that acknowledging the war would destroy what little tourism there was. In the first few months of the war at night along the Atlantic Coast on Highway A1A and the seaside towns, lights from beachfront hotels and motels nicely silhouetted passing freighters.[15] Twenty-nine ships were sunk in May, and five more damaged.

In June 1942 the Gulf Sea Frontier lost more ships than had been sunk worldwide in any month of 1940–41.[16] Army Chief of Staff General Marshall demanded attention from the Navy. In June he wrote Admiral King: "The losses off our Atlantic seaboard and in the Caribbean now threaten our entire war effort.... Of the 74 ships allocated to the Army for July by the War Shipping Administration, 17 percent have already been sunk. Twenty-two percent of the bauxite fleet has already been destroyed.... Tanker sinkings have been 3.5 percent per month of tonnage in use."[17]

Censorship, both official and self-imposed, prevailed across Florida. The case of the Mexican tanker *Potrero del Llano* serves as an example. The *Potrero del Llano* was transiting the Florida Straits bound for New York with six thousand tons of petroleum. As she cleared Key Largo, traveling north toward Key Biscayne on the morning of May 14, she came into the sights of U-boat *U-564*. The sub's torpedoes set the ship on fire, and thirteen crewmen were killed outright. The rest abandoned ship. Blazing from stem to stern, the crewless ship drifted north with the Gulf Stream past the most populated region of Florida: Miami, Miami Beach, and Fort Lauderdale. Clouds of black smoke boiled skyward. Thick black crude oil and dead sailors washed ashore. Thousands witnessed the sinking tanker, and many photographed it.

Survivors were brought to Miami. *Potrero del Llano* went down at dusk. It was vivid proof that the United States was under attack, and a news story of international scope. Yet reporting was minimal.[18]

Besides sinking ships, the U-boats fostered espionage. In a notable incident on the night of June 16, 1942, the *U-584* surfaced off Ponte Vedra Beach near Jacksonville. Four Nazi saboteurs came ashore bearing explosives, civilian clothes, and US cash. The four were Edward John Kerling, Hermann Otto Neubauer, Werner Thiel, and Herbert Haupt. Their mission was to infiltrate and destroy. All spoke English, had lived in the United States before the war, and were familiar with America and its customs.[19] After landing, they buried their rubber raft, hiked to Jacksonville Beach, and in the morning caught a bus to Jacksonville. There they split up, boarding trains for the US interior. Armed with paper lists of the names and addresses of secret agents and safe houses, written in invisible ink, they planned to rendezvous in Cincinnati on the Fourth of July and begin destroying such targets as the locks on the Ohio River, the water system for New York City, and the Newark train station. It was an ambitious plan, to be accomplished in concert with another group of four saboteurs landed a few nights earlier on Long Island, New York.[20]

Fortunately for the United States, the enemy team on Long Island was discovered soon after landing.[21] The ringleader, George John Dasch, and fellow-spy Ernst P. Burger sought out the FBI and confessed. All eight saboteurs were apprehended. They were taken in custody to Washington. President Roosevelt regarded the matter with great seriousness and invoked the Articles of War to order trial by a military tribunal, the first such tribunal since the assassination of President Lincoln. Seven general officers assembled in the Justice Building in Washington to try the case.[22] The federal government preferred four charges against the eight spies: violating the Law of War; violating Article 81 of the Articles of War, defining the offense of corresponding with or giving intelligence to the enemy; violating Article 82 of the Articles of War, defining the offense of spying; and conspiracy to commit the offenses alleged in the first three charges.

The tribunal convened July 2, and all eight were soon convicted and sentenced to death. The Supreme Court, on July 31, in *Ex Parte Quirin* sustained the conviction. On August 8, 1942, the White House issued the following news release:

The President approved the judgment of the Military Commission that all of the prisoners were guilty and that they be given the death sentence by electrocution. However, there was a unanimous recommendation by the Commission, concurred in by the Attorney General and the Judge Advocate General of the Army, that the sentence of two of the prisoners be commuted to life imprisonment because of their assistance to the Government of the United States in the apprehension and conviction of the others. The commutation directed by the President in the case of Burger was to confinement at hard labor for life. In the case of Dasch, the sentence was commuted by the President to confinement at hard labor for thirty years. The electrocutions began at noon today. Six of the prisoners were electrocuted. The other two were confined to prison. The records in all eight cases will be sealed until the end of the war.[23]

The six dead spies, including all four who landed in Florida, were buried in numbered graves without names in Anacostia potter's field across the river from downtown Washington, DC.

By summer the military, government officials, and ordinary Floridians were mobilizing into a series of specific strategies to fight the Nazi submarine attacks. To harden the defenses of the peninsula, the Coast Guard created a unique unit for Florida's 1,197-mile coast: the Mounted Patrol. To cover this enormous stretch of coastline, including almost seven hundred miles of beach, the Coast Guard put its guardsmen on horseback.[24] The Army Remount Service provided the horses for this new Coast Guard cavalry. The Guard enlisted volunteers from among cowboys, jockeys, rodeo riders, and polo players.[25] These mounted sentries rode the coast day and night. Ad hoc cavalry sailors, with rifles and the new walkie-talkies slung across their backs, became a routine sight along the once-serene shoreline of the Sunshine State. Soon dogs from the Military Canine Corps joined the patrols.[26] The tiny islands of the realm, such as Fort Jefferson, the Swan Islands, and the Corn Islands also got Coast Guard sentries, seaplanes, and wireless radio sets.

The State Civil Defense Agency erected coastal watchtowers up and down the beaches of Florida. Built of donated telephone poles and plywood, these towers averaged fifty feet in height. The Florida Defense Force organized a volunteer force of lifeguards, housewives, students, and the elderly to man these watchtowers. Among the hundreds of volunteers was the author Marjorie Kinnan Rawlings.[27] With sun helmets and binoculars, coastwatchers scanned the sea for enemy U-boats. The attacks had galvanized the public, civic leaders, and military authorities. They reached for whatever means was available to defend Florida.[28]

The threat also brought response from the surging military aviation training program of the state. Army and Navy pilot and aircrew trainees learned to fly on anti-submarine warfare (ASW) air patrols crisscrossing the Gulf Sea Frontier. Civilian aviation joined them. With all private air flights in Florida outlawed for the duration of the war, the Air Corps organized the Civil Air Patrol (CAP), a volunteer association of private airplane pilots assisting the military.[29] The first two squadrons were established to defend New York and the New Jersey Shore. Civil Air Patrol Squadron Three defended Florida.[30] Fuel, facilities, and uniforms with CAP insignia were provided by the military. Pilots and mechanics drew daily pay of seven and five dollars, respectively. A pilot who was a popular newspaper comic strip cartoonist drew up a squadron emblem of a small Piper Cub airplane gamely carrying a bomb larger than itself. The CAP flew their own planes from Army Airfields across the peninsula, patrolling the coast at low level. They scanned the seas for signs of the enemy, Allied ships in distress, dead bodies, oil slicks, and debris; the flotsam and jetsam of sea war.[31]

Navy blimps were also deployed against the submarines.[32] Armed with radar (and later towed sonar), radio, and even homing pigeons for times of radio silence, depth bombs, machine guns, and a crew of ten, they were well suited for aerial surveillance. Rather than waste time and steel on expensive rigid airships, the Navy and Goodyear commenced a crash production run of a hundred fifty blimps for service up and down the US coasts. Powered by Pratt and Whitney twin-engine propellors, blimps came to roost at coastal bases on the Atlantic, Pacific, and the Caribbean. At NAS Richmond, south of Miami, government contractors scraped and graded an immense landing mat on the edge of the Everglades. While an army of civilian workers built three huge wooden hangars, airships arrived from the Akron plant to activate Zeppelin Patrol (ZP) Squadron 21, with charge over the Florida Straits and Yucatán Passage. NAS Richmond was at midpoint of the Florida Straits

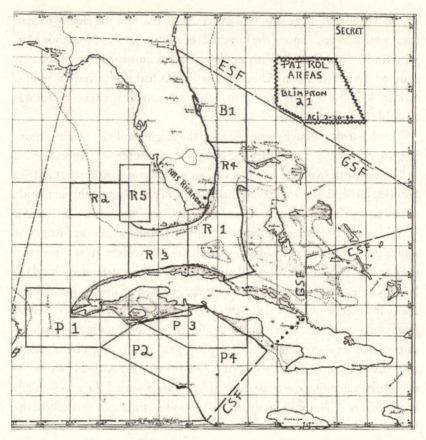

Blimp patrol sectors over the Florida Straits. Navy airships were everyday routine sights in the blue skies over Florida. Ten-man crews with binoculars and small arms manned King-ships armed with four 500-pound depth bombs; .50 caliber machine guns; and radar, sonar, and carrier pigeons for times of radio silence. Painted with silver nitrate to increase buoyancy and blend in with the clouds to escape detection, the nearly invisible airships watched like shepherds over crucial convoys, while like hawks they hunted for subs from coastal bases at Brownsville, Texas; Houma, Louisiana; and Richmond Field, where Zoo Miami is today. In the anti-submarine war the auxiliary Navy bases on the coast at NAS Banana River and Key West were augmented by naval facilities in Cuba, Jamaica, Trinidad, and Brazil. One doughty airship squadron crossed the Atlantic Narrows to fly support for the battles in Italy and the D-day invasion. US Navy, War Diary of Naval Air Station Richmond, February 20, 1944, Situation Report, Sector Map.

hosting the largest such squadron in the Navy, with twenty blimps. ZP-21 had outlying fields at the north end of the Straits at NAS Banana River, and at the south end of the Straits at NAS Key West's Meacham Field.

With the concurrence of the Cuban government, forward stations were set up at San Julián and the Isle of Pines to patrol the Yucatán approaches. At NAS Houma, Louisiana, another hangar was built, and ZP-22 activated to patrol the Gulf. Another such unit, ZP-23, was stood up on Jamaica to cover the Panama Canal.[33] All these units operated under the command of Airship Wing Two, headquartered at NAS Richmond. Military blimps, their rubberized canvas envelope spray painted with shiny silver nitrate dope to reflect heat, maintain buoyancy, and blend in with the sky, were a common sight floating over Florida and the Caribbean for the duration of the war.[34]

Most critical of all, small craft came into play against the German subs. Admiral Mahan had warned: "there should be a local flotilla of small torpedo-vessels, which by their activity should make life a burden for an outside enemy."[35] He accurately characterized this decisive element of the sea battle:

> Such a flotilla, owing to the smallness of the components, and to the simplicity of their organization and functions, is to be found the best sphere for naval volunteers; the duties could be learned with comparative ease, and the whole system is susceptible of rapid development.[36]

Florida's civilian small boaters were enrolled by the Coast Guard into the so-called Corsair Fleet. Officially named the Coastal Picket Patrol, they were nicknamed the "Hooligan Navy." The Coast Guard was not picky, accepting practically any boat "capable of going to sea in good weather for a period of at least 48 hours at cruising speeds."[37] Yachts, shrimp boats, and small craft were signed on; their owners were given the honorary rank of chief bosun's mate. Pickup crews were assembled from whomever claimed nautical experience; college men, beachcombers, and even ex-bootleggers.[38] The Coast Guard organized the force as the Coast Guard Auxiliary. Vessels were assigned picket stations. Uniforms, binoculars, a few sidearms, and gray deck paint were scrounged up and distributed. The vessels were put to work as picket boats guarding the harbors and patrolling the waterways of the peninsula.

They were joined in Florida waters by the new warships of the Navy's crash program to build small wooden combatants. Known as the "Splinter Fleet" because of their hardwood construction, a hundred-ten-foot submarine chaser could be built in sixty days. Hundreds of them were built, many in Florida. The "Subchaser" rode so low in the water they were often invisible to the U-boat periscope. They were simple to operate. Armed to the teeth with cannons, machine guns, and depth charges, the three officers and twenty-four-man crews needed only quick military training before putting to sea.[39]

The Navy also transferred the Gulf Sea Frontier headquarters from isolated Key West to the mainland city of Miami. It commandeered the entire downtown DuPont Building for headquarters. The mezzanine between the second and third floors was removed to provide a thirty-foot-tall situation room, complete with radio room, telex, and gigantic charts of the Caribbean. Navy yeomen and WAVES plotted the courses of friendly vessels, shuffled toy ships about with pool cues, and noted the location of enemy contacts night and day. Experienced at anti-submarine warfare from his earlier duty as the initial officer in charge of Iceland, Rear Admiral James L. Kauffman assumed command.[40]

The Navy established a major anti-submarine warfare school to train seamen for the battle. It took over Biscayne Bay for training exercises and preempted downtown hotels to serve as barracks for the student-draftees. The Navy nicknamed its people "Gobs." "Gobbies" swarmed about the town. The Port of Miami was annexed to become the Navy's Submarine Chaser Training Center (SCTC), opening March 16, 1942, using dockside warehouses for classrooms.[41] The sailors called themselves the "Donald Duck Navy" in recognition of the unit logo provided by Walt Disney Studio artists of a swashbuckling Donald Duck armed with a cutlass, depth charges on his back, and a stethoscope about his neck.[42]

Yet nothing comical characterized the exhibit the school's commanding officer installed to welcome new seamen: a bloodstained lifeboat riddled with bullet holes.[43] The lifeboat had been found adrift and brought to the school. Trainees were marched to the site for a fiery lecture about how the survivors in the boat had been slaughtered.[44] The sailors graduated to man the thousand new Navy subchasers, patrol craft, and destroyer escorts putting to sea up and down the East Coast to fight the U-boats. By 1944 the Navy deployed twenty-five thousand officers and fifty-seven thousand sailors to the Splinter Fleet from the Florida Subchaser Training School.[45]

All these efforts finally influenced the battle in the waters around Florida. The large numbers of suitable warships now being launched into the theater armed with the anti-submarine weapons of depth charges, sonar, and radar, together with the air patrols now overhead, both airships and fixed wing, military and civilian, dramatically restricted the U-boats previous freedom of operation. Even the darkened lighthouses of the Florida coast contained radio rooms applying the newly developed art of triangulation. Triangulation amounted to the ascertaining the position of a U-boat from the strength of the radio messages it transmitted. It required three listening stations to pick up the same radio signal. Calculations could then deduce the origin of the signal, hence getting a fix on the enemy sub location. The lighthouses at Key Biscayne, Hobe Sound, and Bimini, crammed with radio gear, were one top-secret set of triangulation outposts known as Stations X, Y, and Z.

Concurrently, the targets of the U-boats began traveling in convoys under the command of the Gulf Sea Frontier Headquarters. Every civilian skipper who had refused to sail in convoy was now either dead or convinced of the need to sail in groups under naval jurisdiction. They adopted steaming on evasive zig-zag courses, riding darkened at night, maintaining radio silence, trash control, and subordinating themselves to Navy discipline. Navy Armed Guards were assigned to every merchant ship, and all were equipped with deck guns of some kind. Minefields were sown at the approaches to Key West, providing a safe anchorage for convoys to assemble before transiting the Straits under escort.[46]

June 11, 1942, marked the shifting tide. That day the U-boat *U-157* torpedoed the tanker SS *Hagan* off the north coast of Cuba. The next day an Army B-18 sighted the U-boat. It dropped four depth bombs and forced the submarine to dive. The contact brought more aircraft to the scene, together with naval vessels from Key West and Miami. Ships and planes combed the Straits between Havana and Key West. On June 13 the Coast Guard cutter *Thetis* spotted a periscope rising above the water and dropped a pattern of depth charges. They hit the mark. Only scraps of clothing and a pipe fragment stamped "Made in Germany" were recovered.[47] Finally an enemy U-boat had been sunk.

By the end of 1943 the Gulf Sea Frontier had achieved a *mare clausum*. Enemy efforts to keep up the offensive failed. On May 13 the *U-176* attacked a

TABLE 3. Sea Battle of the Gulf Sea Frontier, 1942

	VESSEL	DATE	TYPE	ACTION
1	*Pan Massachusetts*	Feb. 19	Tanker	Sunk off Cape Canaveral
2	*Republic*	Feb. 22	Tanker	Sunk off Hobe Sound
3	*Cities Service Empire*	Feb. 22	Tanker	Sunk off Cape Canaveral
4	*W.D. Anderson*	Feb. 23	Tanker	Sunk off Hobe Sound
5	*Halo*	March 11	Tanker	Damaged in Gulf of Mexico
6	*Colabee*	March 13	Freighter	Damaged north of Cuba
7	*Esparta*	April 9	Freighter	Sunk off Fernandina Beach
8	*Gulfamerica*	April 10	Tanker	Sunk off Jacksonville
9	*Leslie*	April 13	Freighter	Sunk off Cape Canaveral
10	*Korsholm*	April 13	Freighter	Sunk off Cape Canaveral
11	*Federal*	April 30	Tanker	Sunk north of Cuba
12	*La Paz*	May 1	Freighter	Damaged off Cape Canaveral
13	*Worden*	May 1	Freighter	Sunk off Cape Canaveral
14	*Sama*	May 3	Freighter	Sunk off Fort Lauderdale
15	*Ocean Venus*	May 3	Freighter	Sunk off Cape Canaveral
16	*Laertes*	May 3	Freighter	Sunk off Cape Canaveral
17	*Norlindo*	May 4	Freighter	Sunk NW of Dry Tortugas
18	*Eclipse*	May 4	Tanker	Damaged off Delray Beach
19	*Munger T. Ball*	May 5	Tanker	Sunk NW of Dry Tortugas
20	*Joseph M. Cudahy*	May 5	Tanker	Sunk NW of Dry Tortugas
21	*Delisle*	May 5	Tanker	Damaged off Hobe Sound
22	*Alcoa Puritan*	May 6	Freighter	Sunk in Gulf of Mexico
23	*Java Arrow*	May 6	Tanker	Sunk off Fort Pierce
24	*Amazone*	May 6	Freighter	Sunk off Port St. Lucie
25	*Halsey*	May 6	Tanker	Sunk off Port St. Lucie
26	*Green Island*	May 6	Freighter	Sunk south of Cuba
27	*Empire Buffalo*	May 6	Freighter	Sunk south of Cuba
28	*Ohioan*	May 8	Freighter	Sunk off Delray Beach
29	*Ontario*	May 8	Freighter	Sunk in Gulf of Mexico
30	*Torny*	May 8	Freighter	Sunk in Gulf of Mexico
31	*Lubrafol*	May 9	Tanker	Sunk off Boca Raton

	VESSEL	DATE	TYPE	ACTION
32	*Calgarolite*	May 9	Freighter	Sunk south of Cuba
33	*Gulfprince*	May 11	Tanker	Damaged in Gulf of Mexico
34	*Virginia*	May 12	Tanker	Sunk in Gulf of Mexico
35	*David McKelvy*	May 13	Tanker	Sunk in Gulf of Mexico
36	*Gulfpenn*	May 13	Tanker	Sunk in Gulf of Mexico
37	*Amapala*	May 14	Freighter	Sunk in Gulf of Mexico
38	*Eastern Sun*	May 14	Tanker	Undamaged-Gulf of Mexico
39	*Potrero del Llano*	May 14	Tanker	Sunk off Miami
40	*Comayagua*	May 14	Freighter	Sunk south of Cuba
41	*Gulfoil*	May 16	Tanker	Sunk in Gulf of Mexico
42	*Sun*	May 16	Tanker	Damaged in Gulf of Mexico
43	*William C. McTarnahan*	May 16	Tanker	Damaged in Gulf of Mexico
44	*Mercury Sun*	May 18	Tanker	Sunk south of Cuba
45	*William J. Salman*	May 18	Freighter	Sunk south of Cuba
46	*Ogontz*	May 19	Freighter	Sunk north of Yucatán
47	*Heredia*	May 19	Freighter	Sunk in Gulf of Mexico
48	*Halo*	May 20	Tanker	Sunk in Gulf of Mexico
49	*George Calvert*	May 20	Freighter	Sunk in Yucatán Passage
50	*E.P. Theriault*	May 21	Freighter	Damaged in Florida Straits
51	*Clare*	May 21	Freighter	Sunk south of Cuba
52	*Faja de Oro*	May 21	Tanker	Sunk Dry Tortugas
53	*Elizabeth*	May 21	Freighter	Sunk south of Cuba
54	*Samuel Q. Brown*	May 23	Tanker	Sunk south of Cuba
55	*Hector*	May 24	Freighter	Sunk south of Cuba
56	*Atenas*	May 26	Freighter	Damaged in Gulf of Mexico
57	*Carrabulle*	May 26	Tanker	Sunk in Gulf of Mexico
58	*Mentor*	May 28	Freighter	Sunk in Gulf of Mexico
59	*Cacalilao*	May 31	Tanker	Damaged in Gulf of Mexico
60	*Hampton Roads*	June 1	Freighter	Sunk in Yucatán Passage
61	*Knoxville City*	June 2	Freighter	Sunk south of Cuba

TABLE 3. *continued*

	VESSEL	DATE	TYPE	ACTION
62	*Domino*	June 2	Freighter	Undamaged-Gulf of Mexico
63	*M.F. Elliott*	June 3	Freighter	Sunk off Key West
64	*Nidarnes*	June 4	Freighter	Sunk south of Cuba
65	*Velma Lykes*	June 5	Freighter	Sunk in Yucatán Passage
66	*Castilla*	June 7	Freighter	Sunk south of Cuba
67	*Hermis*	June 7	Freighter	Sunk east of Key West
68	*Rosenborg*	June 8	Freighter	Sunk south of Cuba
69	*Suwied*	June 8	Freighter	Sunk south of Cuba
70	*Merrimack*	June 10	Freighter	Sunk in Yucatán Passage
71	*Hagan*	June 11	Tanker	Sunk north of Cuba
72	*Sheherazade*	June 11	Tanker	Sunk in Gulf of Mexico
73	*Cities Service Toledo*	June 12	Tanker	Sunk in Gulf of Mexico
74	*San Blas*	June 16	Freighter	Sunk in Gulf of Mexico
75	*Managua*	June 16	Freighter	Sunk south of Key West
76	*Rawleigh Warner*	June 22	Tanker	Sunk in Gulf of Mexico
77	*Maj. Gen. Henry Gibbins*	June 23	Transport	Sunk in Gulf of Mexico
78	*Edward Luckenbach*	July 2	Freighter	Sunk in Gulf of Mexico
79	*Lalita*	July 6	Freighter	Sunk in Yucatán Passage
80	*Umtata*	July 7	Freighter	Sunk off Miami
81	*Paul H. Harwood*	July 7	Tanker	Damaged in Gulf of Mexico
82	*J.A. Moffett Jr.*	July 8	Tanker	Damaged off Lower Matecumbe Key
83	*Nicholas Cuneo*	July 9	Freighter	Sunk SW of Key West
84	*Benjamin Brewster*	July 9	Tanker	Sunk in Gulf of Mexico
85	*R.W. Gallagher*	July 13	Tanker	Sunk in Gulf of Mexico
86	*Andrew Jackson*	July 13	Freighter	Sunk off Havana
87	*Pennsylvania Sun*	July 15	Tanker	Sunk SW of Dry Tortugas
88	*Gertrude*	July 16	Small craft	Sunk in Gulf of Mexico
89	*Baja California*	July 19	Freighter	Sunk NE of Dry Tortugas
90	*Port Antonio*	July 19	Freighter	Sunk SW of Dry Tortugas

	VESSEL	DATE	TYPE	ACTION
91	*William C. Bryant*	July 21	Freighter	Damaged off Key West
92	*Onondaga*	July 23	Freighter	Sunk north of Cuba
93	*Robert E. Lee*	July 30	Liner	Sunk in Gulf of Mexico
94	*Santiago de Cuba*	Aug. 12	Freighter	Sunk off Key West
95	*Manzanillo*	Aug. 12	Freighter	Sunk off Key West
96	*R.M. Parker Jr.*	Aug. 13	Tanker	Sunk in Gulf of Mexico

convoy off Cuba. She sank two vessels but quickly paid the price. Subchasers, destroyers, aircraft, blimps, and small craft converged on the site. Members of the gallant Cuban Navy aboard the new subchaser *C-13* attacked with depth charges. The *U-176* went down with all hands lost. The Navy Subchaser School in Miami honored the *C-13* Cuban crew: the crew was piped aboard the station, and the flags of the two allies were exchanged in a ceremony on Biscayne Bay. A few months later another U-boat was sunk, this time in the Gulf.[48]

The offensive petered out. The night of July 18, 1943, the Navy K-74 blimp from NAS Richmond went up on a routine patrol of the Florida Straits. Its radar revealed a U-boat surfaced and angling to attack a pair of merchant ships who were transiting the passage.[49] The blimp strafed and bombed the enemy, the *U-134*. The U-boat's anti-aircraft guns shot down the airship, but not before its bombs had mortally damaged the enemy U-boat.[50] Vainly endeavoring to escape, the U-boat was hunted as far as Cape Ferrol. There she was sunk by the RAF with all hands lost.

The sea battle off Florida was a victory for the United States, but the battle was long and costly. Enemy submarines attacked over a hundred merchant ships in the Gulf Sea Frontier. Almost all were sunk, with the loss of the ships, their cargoes, and fifteen hundred lives. Most of the United States interior did not experience the U-boat attacks. The Eastern Seaboard states were hit by the full attack of the U-boats, but for them the fight was only along their one coast facing the sea. Only the Florida peninsula experienced

TABLE 4. Sea Battle of the Gulf Sea Frontier, 1943

	SHIP	DATE	TYPE	ACTION
98	*Olancho*	March 11	Freighter	Sunk in Gulf of Mexico
99	*Lysefjord*	April 2	Freighter	Sunk west of Havana
100	*Gulf State*	April 2	Tanker	Sunk in Florida Straits
101	*Nickeliner*	May 13	Tanker	Sunk north of Cuba
102	*Mambi*	May 13	Tanker	Sunk north of Cuba
103	*Touchet*	Dec. 3	Tanker	Sunk in Gulf of Mexico

the battle all around it on three sides: east, west, and south—a front twelve hundred miles long.

All too often, venturesome civilians and the mounted patrols were drawn by eerie nighttime flames or telltale smoke to the beaches of the battlefield. The grim tableaux of war; miles and miles of beaches fouled with gooey black fuel oil churned by the sea and gritty beach sand into a tar coating countless dead seabirds and fish. The horses and dogs stepped warily amid the wreckage. The larger lumps were corpses washed ashore covered in the thick goo, sometimes bloated to bursting, sometimes fricasseed. At the water's edge more bodies washed gently to and fro with the waves. Upon these unfortunate cadavers the crabs feasted. Florida's population was directly exposed to the war and militarized far more than most of the United States. It was on a war footing from end to end. Florida was the seat of war.

6

FLORIDA MILITARY ACADEMY COURSES

With the declaration of war, the US Army Ground Forces reported to Florida in great numbers to take advantage of the training opportunities the peninsula offered. Three bases at Camp Blanding in North Florida, Camp Gordon Johnston in the Panhandle, and Fort Pierce in South Florida trained over a million ground soldiers, graduating many with a specialty in amphibious warfare, which the war demanded, and for which training Florida was the ideal place. Camp Blanding was absorbed by the Regular Army and gave basic training to hundreds of thousands of volunteers and draftees, teaching them how to camp, march, and shoot; transforming them into riflemen, machine gunners, and cannoneers.[1]

Camp Gordon Johnston on the Gulf of Mexico south of Tallahassee taught soldiers how to go from ship to shore, not via water taxis from luxurious cruise ships, but in the heat of battle. The training was focused on teaching the soldiers how to survive in one piece going from pitching open boats into mortal danger. This base also trained the officers and crews of Army Transport Service how to service the invasions from the sea.

At the Fort Pierce Naval Amphibious Training Base sailors and soldiers learned how to pilot the doughty little landing crafts executing ship to shore operations. Fort Pierce also generated the commandos, scouts and raiders, rangers, and frogmen who enabled the invasions with secrecy and sabotage.[2] There is an intimate connection between command of the sea and control of the shore. All the elements of the military ensemble needed to teach the art and science of seaborne invasions required to conquer the enemy were orchestrated in Florida. Florida was to become one of the most important Army training grounds in the entire country.

The US could only win the war by bringing troops to bear on the battlefield: putting boots on the ground. The main allies of the United States—Britain, the Soviet Union, and China—were all hard-pressed by Nazi Germany and Imperial Japan. The United States had to go to the "World Island" made up of Africa, Europe, and Asia, and it had to go in overwhelming force. Aviation forces could wound the enemy, and naval forces could engage the enemy offshore, but only land forces could conquer the enemy, and the land forces were needed in great numbers.

Twelve full infantry divisions trained in Florida.[3] Each was organized into three regiments. The regiment was broken down into battalions, and the battalions into rifle companies.[4] The weapon of the individual soldier was the new M1 Garand rifle, a semiautomatic (self-loading) weapon that fired a clip of eight rounds.[5] It was the first such semiautomatic rifle issued in mass to the soldiers of any nation. It gave the US rifleman a great advantage in fire power. Enemy soldiers were armed with bolt-action rifles requiring manual operation of the bolt for each shot. By contrast, the M1 rifle fired more rapidly, and was comparably accurate and dependable on the battlefield. The weapon weighed ten pounds and issued with it was either a sixteen-inch or a ten-inch bayonet. Every soldier had a utilitarian pot-shaped steel helmet with a net or fabric cover allowing for shrubbery to camouflage it.

Officers, sergeants, military police, runners, and drivers carried the government-issue .45 caliber pistol, a sidearm with notable close-range stopping power. The Browning automatic rifle (BAR), Thompson submachine gun, M1 carbine, bazookas, and hand grenades were all widely issued and available.[6] The field uniform was brown or olive drab; the soldiers wore brogan shoes with canvas leggings. The private soldier's pay was thirty dollars per month. These GIs poured into Florida by the thousands.

Their other weapons included machine guns, mortars, and, as the technology progressed, flamethrowers. Each regiment included a field artillery battalion, and the standard fieldpiece was the 105mm howitzer with a range of 11,200 meters. Guns were towed by a truck or a jeep, might be mounted on a tractor, or manhandled into position by soldiers. Each division also had an independent artillery battalion armed with the larger 155mm howitzer,

TABLE 5. Infantry Divisions Trained at Camp Blanding

UNIT	NICKNAME	CAMPAIGNS	CASUALTIES [a]
31st Infantry Division (National Guard)	Dixie Rifles	New Guinea, Philippines, Western Pacific	KIA 340 WIA 1,391 DOW 74
43rd Infantry Division (National Guard)	Winged Victory	Northern Solomon Is. New Guinea, Philippines	KIA 1,128 WIA 4,887 DOW 278
1st Infantry Division	Big Red One	Algeria, Tunisia, Sicily, D-day, Northern France, Rhineland, Ardennes, Central Europe	KIA 3,616 WIA 15,208 DOW 664
29th Infantry Division (National Guard)	Blue and Gray Division	D-day, Northern France, Rhineland, Central Europe	KIA 3,887 WIA 15,541 DOW 899
30th Infantry Division (National Guard)	Old Hickory	Normandy, Northern France, Rhineland, Ardennes, Central Europe	KIA 3,003 WIA 13,376 DOW 513
36th Infantry Division (National Guard)	Texas Division	Naples, Rome, Anzio, Southern France, Rhineland, Ardennes, Central Europe	KIA 3,131 WIA 13,191 DOW 506
63rd Infantry Division	Blood and Fire	Rhineland, Central Europe	KIA 861 WIA 3,326 DOW 113
66th Infantry Division	Black Panthers	Northern France	KIA 795 WIA 636 DOW 5
79th Infantry Division	The Cross of Lorraine	Normandy, Northern France, Rhineland, Ardennes, Central Europe	KIA 2,476 WIA 10,971 DOW 467

Note: a. "KIA" indicates "killed in action." "WIA" indicates "wounded in action." "DOW" indicates "died of wounds."

Source: Compiled from *The Army Almanac*, 651–84.

capable of dropping explosives on targets 14,600 meters away.[7] Men armed with such weapons arrived in Florida in droves. An engineer battalion with specialized construction and destruction talents, and a medical battalion, accompanied each division. The division headquarters contained a signals company equipped with radios, a quartermaster company with trucks, military police, and a musical band. At full strength a US Army division and its attached elements numbered close to twenty thousand soldiers. Camp Blanding held maneuvers on a grand scale, with aggressor forces and defenders contending against each other. At night the forest campground was lit by the eerie glow of flares and tracer bullets arcing through the night.

Many of the units were raised elsewhere and came to Camp Blanding for war games, practicing for battle while they waited to go overseas.[8] Other units were activated on the spot at Camp Blanding. Volunteers and draftees from across Florida and the rest of the Southeast US reported to Camp Blanding straight from civilian life. They were stripped of their civilian belongings and herded through physical examinations and inoculations. Their heads were shaved, and their military kit dumped in their arms. They were assembled into recruit companies under the supervision of Drill Sergeants. For the next thirteen weeks they learned the basics of soldiering: rigorously long marches to build up stamina, field bivouacs to toughen them, and target practice to learn riflery.

They were taught a healthy obedience for the authority of wartime discipline. The object of the training was not to break their spirit, but rather to break their individuality and forge the pieces into a group that would act together as a team to win in the face of war. The recruits lived roughly, slept sparingly, and exerted themselves greatly amid the enforced privations of the field. The rights and privileges of the buck private were few.

In addition to the numbered infantry divisions, many specialized combat units trained at Camp Blanding. The 508th Parachute Regiment was activated there. Known as the "Red Devils," these paratroopers fought at D-day, in Operation Market Garden, and the Battle of the Bulge. The 156th Regiment of Military Police served in North Africa and then provided security for the "Red Ball Express" supply truck convoy system across Europe. They also processed thousands of German prisoners of war. The 6th Cavalry (mechanized) Regiment was activated at Camp Blanding and answered to General George Patton Jr., serving through 281 continuous days of combat.[9]

Camp Blanding was Army Headquarters in Florida, and a major replacement training center. Army Ground Forces policy was to keep its original units intact, but as the war wore on these were depleted by casualties. Reinforcements were required to keep the line of battle up to strength. Rather than activate more units, fresh soldiers were trained at Camp Blanding and then forwarded to units already overseas to join them as replacements. With their penchant for acronyms the GIs named it a "Repl-Depo," a replacement depot of major proportions. The base also served as the Army reception center for soldiers returning from overseas for reassignment either to another war theater or to duty stateside. Because of the seriousness of World War II, soldiers were enlisted for the duration. It was the processing center for soldiers being discharged, primarily for wounds. The camp hosted so many soldiers in 1943 and 1944 that based on its population it was statistically the fourth largest city in Florida.[10] The combat arms—infantry, armor, and artillery—more than 825,000 soldiers, received all or part of their training at Camp Blanding. They amounted to 10 percent of the 8,020,000 soldiers of the Army Ground Forces in World War II.[11] More soldiers trained at Camp Carrabelle Army Amphibious Training Center, the second major Army base in Florida. The base opened on the Florida Gulf Coast in the autumn of 1942, thanks to its military geography. Army Amphibious Command began life at Cape Cod, Massachusetts, but the site proved incompatible with wintertime training. The New England seas were too rough and too cold. The coastline was too rough for invasion practice. The dense populations on the East Coast also compromised security. Florida filled the need. Its calm waters, long placid beaches, and absence of a civilian population made it a perfect schoolyard for the seaborne invasions critical to winning the war.[12]

Planners studied various locations in the state, choosing Carrabelle for its twenty miles of contiguous beachfront, sheltered by the offshore barrier of St. George and Dog islands. It offered privacy, warm waters, and easy beaches long enough to land an entire division at once. The Gulf Coast location was close enough to the eastern seaboard to suit the US strategy of "Germany First." Another bonus quality recommended the site: The inland terrain approximated the arduous jungles of the Pacific. It was a swamp infested with snakes, wild boars, scorpions, and mosquitoes.[13]

The camp was soon renamed Camp Gordon Johnston in honor of Army Medal of Honor recipient Col. Gordon Johnston (1874–1934).[14] Landing craft for mock invasions assembled on the beaches and in adjacent Apalachicola Bay.[15] Hitting the beaches was the specialty practiced there. Ten thousand acres at Carrabelle were purchased outright by the War Department, and another hundred fifty thousand acres were leased from the St. Joe Paper Company.[16] Unlike Camp Blanding, Camp Gordon Johnston was not built as the result of the planned and premeditated buildup of the US military. It was set up in haste once the fighting began. Field latrines and canvas pup tents were about all the camp had to offer.[17] The soldiers gave it a name of their own: "Hell-By-The-Sea."[18]

The first instructors transferred from Cape Cod arrived under the command of Brig. General Keating in September 1942: the 2nd Engineer Amphibian Brigade, four hundred officers and seven thousand enlisted men.[19] Their mission was to train the infantry who would come next. The engineers hacked the camp out of the wilderness. Tall wooden towers were erected and hung with Jacob's ladder netting overlooking the shores to simulate ship debarking into small boats. Rifle ranges and obstacle courses were laid out. In early November the 38th Infantry Division arrived for training.[20] Landing craft at Carrabelle were in short supply. Some came from Cape Cod lashed down on flatbed cars and sent by train.[21] Other landing craft reached the camp by a more circuitous route: a journey that demonstrated the can-do attitude of the soldiers and showed the spirit of the times.

Army engineers from Camp Gordon Johnston were sent to Norfolk, Virginia, to bring back mechanized landing craft.[22] These were motorized open barges, with a ramp and a small, armored wheelhouse mounted aft. They were built to be driven as close to shore as possible. When the vessel grounded, the ramp was lowered to allow the sixty troops inside to storm ashore. At Norfolk, the Camp Gordon Johnston engineers took charge of twenty LCMs, three soldiers to each.[23] In a flotilla they headed south along the Atlantic seaboard, destination Carrabelle.[24] They followed the East Coast to Florida's Indian River. At Port Saint Lucie they entered the Saint Lucie River. Halfway across the interior of the state they came to Lake Okeechobee. Striking across Lake Okeechobee in their convoy of landing craft, the soldiers picked up the Caloosahatchee River on the western shore of the lake. They piloted their LCMs the length of the Caloosahatchee River, emerging into the Gulf of Mexico at Fort Myers. From there they steered north up the Gulf coast of Florida, eventually reaching the Carrabelle beaches. It was a nautical feat, a journey of fifteen hundred miles in open boats.[25]

Camp Gordon Johnston itself developed a reputation all its own. General Omar Bradley remembered the camp in his memoirs:

> Camp Gordon Johnston was the most miserable Army installation I had seen since my days in Yuma, Arizona, ages past. It had been hacked out of palmetto scrub along a bleak stretch of beach.... Every training exercise was a numbing experience. The man who selected that site would have been court-martialed for stupidity.[26]

The Camp mission statement epitomized how warlike Florida had become:

> The instruction was to emphasize loading and unloading landing craft quickly and quietly by day and night; boat discipline and control of landing craft; organization and control of troops during loading and unloading operations; tactical operation, and supply of combat teams, including the seizure of the beachhead and the advance inland to the objective. Crossing beach obstacles and defensive works; clearing the beach of obstacles, demolitions, etc., and the subsequent beach organization to support operations; resupply; night operations; development of an effective intelligence to amphibious operations, including the employment of intelligence agencies and scouts of all units; development of signal communications peculiar to amphibious operations; using smoke screens; the use of chemicals for contamination purposes; decontamination; air-ground support; anti-aircraft defense; swimming; camouflage; knife and bayonet fighting; judo; infiltration; battle firing; firing automatic weapons from landing craft; and combat in cities.[27]

The war the GI Army fought was one of invasions of foreign shores, often in the face of the enemy. Armadas had to assemble suddenly offshore at a specific place and time, arriving stealthily and in secret. The nature of the shoreline and the whereabouts of the enemy were unknown factors. While warships and aircraft pulverized the shore with gunnery, bombing, and strafing, the soldiers of the transport ships clambered down into small craft alongside. The stubby open boats then lumbered to the shore loaded with soldiers, under whatever sea-state prevailed. As close to the water's edge as possible the boats dropped their ramps, and the soldiers disgorged. Sometimes they landed dry-shod on empty beaches.

But often they stepped into the face of hell: water over their heads, overpowering undertow, barbed wire entanglements, razor-sharp shoals, and murderous enemy fire. As they struggled ashore, friendly fire from the ships had to cease at exactly the right moment, or the ships guns would be killing their own men. Meanwhile, the landing craft returned to the ships to take on another load of troops and repeat the process. It was organized chaos, dangerous and difficult under the best of circumstances.

Camp Gordon Johnston provided realistic amphibious training. Soldiers trained for the daunting invasions of Sicily, Italy, and France in the European Theater of Operations, and the equally tough invasions of New Guinea, the Philippines, and other islands of the Pacific Theater.[28] Assault troops and beach masters learned the craft of conquering overseas enemies on Florida's sunny shores.[29] In typical training, a wave of landing craft loaded with troops closed in from the sea on a specific beach, of which there were five at Camp Gordon Johnston. Barrage balloons were deployed overhead while landing craft hit the beach. Each beach covered five hundred yards strewn with realistic obstacles and was capable of handling a hundred twenty-five men (a standard rifle company) every forty minutes. The landing craft ground themselves on the sands of the beach. The soldiers sloshed ashore. They were hurried every step of the way by umpires. The waterline was considered the most dangerous place in a landing. The soldiers were pushed to get off the beach and press inland. Minutes behind them came the next wave of assault troops.

Scrambling in from the beach the soldiers encountered the infiltration course. Each course was a hundred fifty yards wide and a hundred yards long, designed to expose the soldier to the noise, confusion, and danger of the battlefield.[30] Soldiers crawled the length of the course under or through barbed wire, obstacles, logs, stumps, and shell holes. The course was "traversed by the interlocking fire of six machine guns the trajectory of which cleared the ground by thirty inches." Everything about the training was meant to be as real as possible. The deadly machine guns fired live ammunition.[31]

Once past the infiltration course, the soldiers crashed into a simulated

TABLE 6. Infantry Divisions Trained at Camp Gordon Johnston

UNIT	NICKNAME	CAMPAIGNS [a]	CASUALTIES [b]
38th Infantry Division	Cyclone Division	New Guinea, Luzon, Leyte	KIA 645 WIA 2,814 DOW 139
28th Infantry Division	Keystone Division	Normandy, Northern France, Rhineland, Ardennes, Central Europe	KIA 2,316 WIA 9,609 DOW 367
4th Infantry Division	Ivy Division	D-day, Normandy, Northern France, Rhineland, Ardennes, Central Europe	KIA 4,097 WIA 17,371 DOW 757

Notes: a. Table 6 shows where each division saw action. b. "KIA" indicates "killed in action." "WIA" indicates "wounded in action." "DOW" indicates "died of wounds."

Source: Compiled from *The Army Almanac*, 651–84.

Nazi town named "Schicklgruber Haven."[32] The military had turned the abandoned logging village of Harbeson City into a European town for the practice of urban combat. The soldiers were exposed to the street fighting they would face in the shattered towns of Europe. They learned such useful combat skills as scaling walls with and without ropes, fighting from rooftops, using grenades at close quarters, and recognizing and disarming booby traps. House-to-house searches and urban fighting in the bombed-out village used live ammunition. Additional training included target practice from moving jeeps to simulate firing from landing crafts.[33]

The training also included swimming classes at three sites: the Carrabelle River, Wakulla Springs, and the Gulf seashore.[34] Three entire divisions went through the course, practicing day and night.[35] Among them was the 4th Infantry Division, being brought to a high state of readiness to serve as an invasion spearhead.[36] The experience of Private Bert Davis was typical of the rough-and-ready regimen:

> Almost upon arrival, I saw a notice on the bulletin board regarding the need for volunteers (a dirty word) for a project involving swimmers. As I had been a Red Cross swimming instructor, I stuck my neck out

and volunteered. Much to my surprise, the next day I was ordered to report to battalion headquarters at "X"-Hour, with a towel and a packed lunch. For the next six weeks, this was my daily routine. I, along with the other volunteers, assembled at a nearby lake to give lessons in swimming to novices and/or non-swimmers.

The lake, inhabited with alligators, had a sandy beach at one end with two piers extending out into the water. The first day there, we just stood on the beach while the engineers built a tower for armed guards to stand and shoot at the alligators. We then began to give swimming lessons to truckloads of GIs and officers scheduled to arrive with light field packs, fatigues, and shoes. The troops were marched out one pier, ordered into the water, and then to remove their shoes and tie laces, then hang the shoes around their neck and swim to the other pier. We had numerous near drownings but did not lose a single person.

I recall one day a group of officers of many ranks arrived. The ranking officer was a non-swimmer and had brought his staff along to assist him in covering the distance from pier to pier. We instructors, on and off duty, had to form a line in the water between the piers and in front of the alligators. In mid-November our swimming detail ended and we returned to our units to prepare for amphibious training. My last thought was, *No more peanut butter and jelly sandwiches for lunch*.[37]

The 4th Division culminated its training with the entire division staging a landing on Thanksgiving Day, 1943. Then they departed for the war. On D-day, June 6, 1944, the 4th Division's soldiers were the first American infantrymen to hit the beach—apart from the Army Rangers who had been trained at Fort Pierce.[38]

At Camp Gordon Johnston the Army also began assembling naval equipment in anticipation of amphibious landings. The Army acquired an armada of seagoing vessels. These included 35 troopships, 16 cargo ships, 55 inter-island freighters, 2 cable-laying ships, a communications ship, 36 floating, self-propelled warehouses, and 23 hospital ships. Smaller vessels included 510 barges, 104 small tankers, and 746 tugs. This fleet came under the command of the Army Transport Service, and much of it collected at the Apalachicola Bay estuary of Camp Gordon Johnston.[39] By mid-1943 the camp was a major staging port for the ATS fleet.

The Army drew heavily on the graduates of nearby St. Petersburg Merchant Marine Training Center to man these vessels. Many of the officers for the Army's vessels came from the St. Petersburg Maritime Service Officer Candidate School. The ten-week OCS there graduated 614 deck officers and 512 engine officers in 1943. The graduates, commissioned as junior Marine officers in the Army Transport Service, went to Jackson Square in New Orleans for advanced instruction at the US Maritime Service Upgrade School on Lake Pontchartrain.[40] The graduates were designated third mates in the Army Transport Service, ostensibly to be assigned to merchant marine ships.[41] The needs of the Army, however, came first.

In February 1944 the entire graduating class of the Maritime Service Upgrade School, four hundred junior Marine officers who had just completed six months of training there and at St. Petersburg, were assembled in a drill hall.[42] They were asked to volunteer for the US Army. Volunteers would be given direct appointments as 2nd lieutenants in the Army with assignment to the Army Transport Service. Those who refused would have their Maritime Service commissions revoked and be drafted into the Army as privates and assigned to the same duty, at one-third the pay and no rank. All volunteered for the first option.[43]

The former Maritime officers were sent to Camp Gordon Johnston to learn their new duties. Organized into platoons of forty men each and given a six-week Army officer training course, they were assigned to specialized Army Harbor Craft Companies. These units, unlike any other in the Army, contained tugboats, barges, cranes, and small craft. Harbor Craft Companies comprised fifty officers and two hundred fifty enlisted men each.[44] These units facilitated seaborne invasions, utilizing war-devastated ports and harbors and repairing them. Once proficient, they shipped out around the world to manage invasions. Many of the tugboats, barges, skiffs, scows, and lighters that would join them were built in Florida during the great shipbuilding activity that seized the peninsula.

A third major Florida base dedicated to invasion training was Fort Pierce Naval Amphibious Training Base. Fort Pierce trained commandos and landing craft skippers, without whom the seaborne landings could not take place.[45] In early 1942 the initial joint Army-Navy Amphibious Command for training Scouts and Raiders began at Chesapeake Bay in Maryland, but the winter seas prevented year-round training there. The military scouted for a suitable location and found it at Fort Pierce.[46] The long barrier islands of North Hutchinson and South Hutchinson Island sheltered the Indian River beaches, and Sebastian Inlet between the islands gave controlled access to the Atlantic. There were miles of sweet empty beaches, and Indian River provided a calm maritime staging area. The government claimed the nineteen-thousand-acre site and annexed miles of the Florida coast. The Naval Amphibious Training Base opened formally on January 26, 1943.[47]

Like Camp Blanding and Camp Gordon Johnston, Fort Pierce also lacked amenities. The base made do with pine shacks for classroom and training facilities. Tent cities housed the troops. The newly created JANET (Joint Army/Navy Experimental Testing) Board set up shop at the base, taking over North Hutchinson Island for a research and testing facility.[48] Commando training of combined teams of Army and Navy volunteers known as "Scouts and Raiders" began immediately. The Scouts and Raiders trained to infiltrate by water wherever there was coastline that could be penetrated. The twelve-week course covered swimming and small boat handling, photographic interpretation, hand-to-hand combat, camouflage, survival techniques, signaling, and radio operations. A lightweight and collapsible rubber raft was created by Goodyear specifically for their use.[49]

One unit created at Fort Pierce was Special Service Unit #1, established in July 1943 and later renamed the 7th Amphibious Scouts.[50] Their mission was to go ashore ahead of the assault forces marking channels for the incoming landing craft, taking soundings, blowing up beach obstacles, and communicating between those coming ashore and the warships engaged at shore bombardment. The 7th Amphibious Scouts served in more than forty such landings throughout the Pacific during the war.[51] Other Scouts and Raiders from Fort Pierce deployed to the China-Burma-India Theater to prepare for the inevitable invasion of Japan.[52] Disguised as Chinese coolies operating from sampans, they infiltrated the Japanese-held coast of China. They surveyed the coast, studied the enemy, and set up covert stations to facilitate the invasion when it was to be launched.[53]

United States Army Rangers also came to Fort Pierce for training.[54] A wartime experiment of General Marshall, the Rangers sought to be self-sufficient light infantry shock troops operating independently, harking back to the colonial rangers of the Revolutionary era. In September 1943 the 2nd Battalion of Army Rangers came to Fort Pierce. The unit, commanded by

Col. James E. Rudder, went through the Scouts and Raiders School at Fort Pierce. After training in Florida, they shipped out to Scotland, where they practiced mountain climbing. This unit had the assignment to storm the heights of Pointe du Hoc, one of the most dangerous missions of the D-day invasion of Normandy.[55]

Navy commandos trained in Florida for D-day included Naval Beach Battalions and Navy Combat Demolition Units.[56] In June 1943, the combat demolition program began at Fort Pierce.[57] Six-man teams trained to neutralize obstacles on the beaches. The enemy had embedded barriers of steel girders and cement, often booby-trapped, offshore. The demolition teams were to dynamite the obstacles before the landing forces reached them. Replicated obstacles were strewn along the Fort Pierce beaches, and the swimmers practiced the dangerous art of blowing them up at close range while under live fire.[58]

Thirty-one such teams from Fort Pierce participated in the D-day invasion. The morning of June 6, 1944, the teams hit the beaches at 0630 hours. Their rubber boats full of explosives offered tempting targets. Some team members had to stand on each other's shoulders under fire in chest-deep water to place their charges. Casualties of ninety-one killed and wounded at Omaha Beach ranked over 50 percent of the men engaged. The 2nd Ranger Battalion, the 6th and 7th Naval Beach Battalions, and the Navy demolition units were only the advance elements of the largest of the seaborne invasions.[59]

All three of the infantry divisions, over sixty thousand soldiers making up the American contingent of Allied landing force on D-day (the 1st Infantry Division, 29th Infantry Division, and 4th Infantry Division), had previously trained in Florida.[60] The D-day invasion spearhead contained a high percentage of troops who had received training in Florida.

Fort Pierce also developed the Underwater Demolition Teams for covert warfare.[61] Lieutenant Commander Draper L. Kauffman led them. Kauffman was an Annapolis graduate who upon graduation from the Navy Academy was denied a commission because of his poor eyesight. When the war broke out, he volunteered as an ambulance driver in France, and later joined the Royal Navy as a bomb disposal expert. After Pearl Harbor Kauffman rejoined the US Navy and was readily promoted for his skill with explosives. He was ordered to create the UDT and chose Fort Pierce for the purpose.[62] They pioneered such swimming devices as flexible rubber fins, face masks, oxygen bottles, and mini-subs. These champion swimmers were known as the "Naked Warriors," and nicknamed "frogmen." Their method of rapid seaborne extraction by PT boat involved grasping an arm ring extended by the craft as it sped past. About thirty-five hundred frogmen trained at Fort Pierce.[63] The rigorous training was capped by "Hell Week," involving extreme challenges such as carrying telephone poles over their heads to learn group dynamics, discipline, and endurance.[64]

The Fort Pierce Attack Boat School was a major component at the Fort Pierce base teaching sailors how to operate landing craft. Over thirty thousand sailors received instruction to operate landing craft (attack boats) on the Indian River.[65] They learned how to stow their landing craft aboard transport ships, and how to deploy them offshore when the time came. They practiced maneuvering their small craft alongside troop transports and holding them steady while troops climbed down into them. They trained at bringing their landing craft inshore, reading the buoys and the signals of the beach masters, and coming as close as possible to the shore. The difference between landing troops in three feet of water, or six feet of water, was life and death. The school taught how to operate the rocket launchers, cannon, and machine guns; some of the landing craft were armed for pummeling the shoreline with firepower immediately in advance of a disputed landing.

The Fort Pierce base gave instructions at operating all the various landing craft. There were several classes of ships whose bows swung open like gate leaves to disgorge troops and tools of war. Somewhat smaller were Landing Craft for Tanks, and the most widely used Landing Craft Vehicle, Personnel, known as the Higgins Boat. Named after Lumberman Andrew Higgins and produced in thousands at his New Orleans factory, these were landing craft equipped with a drawbridge ramp in the bow. Upon reaching as close to shore as possible the ramp went down, and the GIs charged ashore.[66]

Second-generation landing craft at the Fort Pierce base included the DUKW, and the LVT (Landing Vehicle, Tracked) of Florida-inventor Donald Roebling.[67] Roebling designed the LVT at Dunedin, Florida, and perfected it in the Everglades.[68] Known as the Alligator, or the Amtrac, this landing craft could cover sixty miles of open sea, and was equipped with tank-like caterpillar treads that engaged on reaching the shore.[69] The "Alligator" could crawl over offshore reefs, and was unstoppable by beach obstacles. Protected by chassis armor, the Alligator was prized by the US Marines who stormed the atolls of the Pacific.[70] Altogether, a hundred ten thousand soldiers and sailors trained at Fort Pierce, making it during the war a major Florida city.[71]

The topography of Florida was essential for invasion training. Not only was the peninsula ideal for field bivouacs, but its shelving sandy beachfront was the best-suited place on the North American continent for the amphibious training needed. The beaches of the West Coast of the US are narrow, rocky, and obstructed by mountain ranges running down to the shoreline. The seas themselves are cold, falling off quickly into deep waters with strong and difficult currents. Basic training for invasions there was impractical. On the East Coast of the US, the North Atlantic Ocean renders much of its shoreline similarly unsuitable. Where there were spacious, hospitable beaches there were usually curious civilian populations, undesirable witnesses to military activity. That left temperate, unpopulated Florida.

The seriousness of the mission demanded precisely executed invasions. The British geostrategist and colleague of Admiral Mahan, Col. C. E. Callwell, devoted considerable study to the tactical difficulties of amphibious warfare. His appreciation of the dangers they faced was realistic: "If the attacking army is prepared to accept heavy loss, it may succeed. But the operation is not one to be ventured on with a light heart, or one to be undertaken without counting the cost and without accepting risk of disaster."[72]

Of the twelve infantry divisions who trained in Florida, nine of them, three out of four, were sent to the African-Mediterranean-Middle Eastern and European Theater of Operations, fulfilling the US strategy of "Europe First." Florida's rail links to the East Coast embarkation centers facilitated their departure aboard Army troop transport ships and merchant marine convoys. Florida's elementary school for war taught the Army the basics of soldiering, how to storm enemy shores, and how to dig in and hold them. It trained the Maritime Service officers and crews who supported the invasions and exploited them. It taught the Navy landing craft coxswains and boat crews who brought the troops and cargo onto the beaches. The frogmen and commandos who led the way honed their skills in Florida as they sharpened their knives. Their mission of invasion and conquest was learned in Florida. It was realistic training delivered with urgency. The war was at its peak.

7

BOMBS AWAY AND OVER THE HUMP

It was Florida's destiny to become the launchpad for aerial force projection worldwide. Two activities pertaining to aviation combined to fine-tune the state's wartime mission. Florida was a major host to the deadly art of massed aerial bombardment taught to great numbers of students. The Army Third Air Force routinely carpeted the peninsula and uncomplaining Gulf of Mexico with bombs. Literally. Upon graduation these air warriors departed for the front. Equally important, with combat theaters around the world, a new weapon of war, the airlift, emerged as a central mission of Florida. This was especially true of the critical, often overlooked China-Burma-India Theater. Flyboys came to Florida to learn their craft and take the war overseas.

On March 1, 1943, General Arnold insisted to the secretary of war: "The No. 1 job of an air force is bombardment."[1] Florida was the center for developing this capability with fleets of B-17 and B-24 bombers, and with even greater numbers of the newer Martin B-26 Marauder twin-engine medium bomber. The B-26 was first flown in November 1940, and after Pearl Harbor it went into crash production. As quickly as the B-26s came off the Martin assembly lines in Maryland and Oklahoma they went straight to the Air Corps in Florida. MacDill Field was the primary training base for the new bomber. Most of the B-26 bomber groups the US fielded in World War II were activated and fully trained in Florida.[2] Pilots, navigators, radiomen, gunners, bombardiers, and mechanics all trained at MacDill Field and its many auxiliary airfields across the peninsula.[3]

A shaky start to the new B-26 training program in 1942 seemed like training for disaster. The B-26 had difficult characteristics for inexperienced pilots to fly. Most dangerously, the plane tended to stall out. The plane had to be flown at exact airspeeds, and if the final approach before landing was not kept at the relatively high speed of a hundred fifty miles per hour, the engines tended to fail.[4] Engine failure right after takeoff was also common. MacDill Field in Tampa was surrounded on three sides by water, and the bombers regularly splashed in. "One a day in Tampa Bay," was an unwelcome joke at MacDill.[5] In a thirty-day period, fifteen bombers crashed into Tampa Bay. It generated other B-26 nicknames, such as the "widow maker," and the "flying prostitute," a sobriquet referring to the plane's short wingspan that gave it no "visible means of support."[6]

These difficulties prompted the Air Corps to assign the now-famous Jimmy Doolittle to solve the problem. Back from his spectacular bombing raid on Japan and promoted to brigadier general, he came to MacDill Field to investigate that summer.[7] The problem, he determined, lay less in the aircraft itself than in inadequate pilot training.[8] He modified training to correspond to the plane's requirements. Pilots under instruction were coached in the idiosyncrasies of the B-26, while the plane itself was modified with a longer wingspan and larger fin and rudder.[9]

Nine of the twelve operational B-26 bomb groups that fought in World War II were activated and trained in Florida. All served in the European Theater, and many flew as part of the Eighth Bomber Command (later renamed the 8th Air Force). Together with the Florida-trained B-17 Flying Fortresses and B-24 Liberators, the B-26 bomb groups made up over 20 percent of the "Mighty Eighth."[10] That command, at top strength, fielded two thousand bombers, a thousand fighter planes, and over two hundred thousand American personnel. It was half the size of the entire Air Force of today. The Eighth suffered twenty-six thousand killed and twenty-one thousand wounded: half of the Air Corps casualties in the war. It also boasted 261 fighter pilot aces and 305 gunner aces in the Eighth Air Force. Thirty-one of the fighter aces had fifteen or more aircraft confirmed victories.[11]

Every time a squadron was activated the entire unit assembled in ranks on the flight line tarmac: pilots, bombardiers, machine gunners, radiomen, ground crews, and maintenance personnel. During the war years these impressive ceremonies were a regular part of Florida's landscape. The commanders and local civilian officials gave speeches. The ceremonies included flags,

TABLE 7. B-26 Marauder Bomb Groups Activated and Trained in Florida

COMMAND	SQUADRONS	ACTIVATED, MACDILL	BASES/THEATERS/AWARDS
21st Bomb Group	313th, 314th, 315th, 398th	June 17, 1942	Third Air Force Trainer Cadre
320th Bomb Group	441st, 442nd, 443rd, 444th	June 23, 1942	North Africa, Sicily, Italy, France Distinguished Unit Commendation for the Battle of Siegfried Line
322nd Bomb Group	449th, 450th, 451st, 452nd	July 17, 1942	England, France, Germany Distinguished Unit Commendation for the Battle of D-day
323rd Bomb Group	453rd, 454th, 455th, 456th	August 21, 1942	England, France, Germany Distinguished Unit Commendation for the Battle of Bastogne
344th Bomb Group	494th, 495th, 496th, 497th	September 8, 1942	England, France, Belgium, Germany Distinguished Unit Commendation for the Battle of Northern France
386th Bomb Group	552nd, 553rd, 554th, 555th	December 1, 1942	England, France, Belgium Distinguished Unit Commendation for the European Theater of Operations
387th Bomb Group	556th, 557th, 558th, 559th	December 1, 1942	England, France, Holland Distinguished Unit Commendation for the Battle of the Bulge
391st Bomb Group	572nd, 573rd, 574th, 575th	January 21, 1943	England, France, Belgium Distinguished Unit Commendation for the Battle of the Bulge
394th Bomb Group	584th, 585th, 586th, 587th	March 5, 1943	England, France, Holland Distinguished Unit Commendation for the Battle of D-day
397th Bomb Group	596th, 597th, 598th, 599th	April 20, 1943	England, France, Holland Distinguished Unit Commendation for the Battle of the Bulge

Source: Compiled from Maurer, *Air Force Combat Units of World War II*, 70, 199–200, 202–3, 203–4, 222, 273, 274, 278, 281–2, 283, 81–82, 154, 156–58, 162–63, 166–67, 168–69, 338, 354–55, 101–2, 160–61, 168–69.

Army Air Forces Kiowa Tribal Member Gus Palmer, waist gunner, and aerial photographer Horace Poolaw pose in traditional war bonnets in front of their B-17 at MacDill in 1944. Photo by Horace Poolaw.

military bands, bugles, and salutes. The civilian community poured onto the base to witness the event. Under their eyes, the airmen paraded the flight line in marching formation, pilots in leather flight caps and gunners carrying their machine guns at shoulder arms, shouting out the new Air Corps anthem: *Off We Go into the Wild Blue Yonder!* Each time a unit departed for the war such ceremonies were repeated, with perhaps increasingly more emotion, especially after casualty figures became known.

The bombing program grew enormously. In March 1942 MacDill expanded with a huge bombing area at Avon Park General Bombing and Gunnery Range in the center of the state.[12] Acquiring first 107,059 acres of swamp and scrub, the military added another 111,165 acres the following year in neighboring Okeechobee County. The range consisted of approximately 352 square miles of territory and got its own Army Airfield in October 1942. By 1943 it was a fully integrated base, providing training in every aspect of aircraft bombardment. Avon Park expanded to become the largest bombing range in the South Atlantic United States. It included a 555-acre mock town on the shore of Lake Arbuckle. The range also offered a large floating target ship on Lake Kissimmee, and an eight-mile railroad target. A special town was erected there for the practice of incendiary bombing, and it was burned down repeatedly by the airmen in learning how to execute fire bombings. Bombardiers swore a special oath to guard the ingenious new Norden bombsight with their lives. Between 1942 and 1945 more bombs were dropped on Avon Park than on any enemy target.[13]

Frequently the bombing raids were joined by fighter planes flying escort. Fighter command's Orlando Army Air Forces School of Applied Tactics used eight thousand square miles of North Central Florida air space, from Tampa to Titusville and from Starke to Apalachicola (an area larger than New York State) for dogfights, and war games concluding with the fighter planes rendezvousing with bombers over Avon Park. Outside of Ocala, specialized aviation training was conducted at Dunnellon Army Airfield in the form of Troop Carrier squadrons training at dropping paratroopers, and towing glider planes loaded with troops, jeeps, and howitzers. Plywood glider planes were hammered together at a factory in DeLand.[14]

Army cargo planes towed wooden gliders full of soldiers across the Central Florida sky. When they neared the landing field the glider cable was unhooked from the aircraft. With no engines of their own, the gliders seemed to float effortlessly to earth. But the landings themselves were no more than controlled crashes. Mishaps were unforgiving. Bombs by the ton, parachutists, and gliders all descended purposefully on the Florida peninsula.

Florida also played an essential and largely unexamined role in the process of developing the Army Air Corps into an independent branch of service. Florida's empty hotel rooms contributed significantly to their selection to be the home of the new Officer Candidate School (OCS) of the Army Air

TABLE 8. B-24 Liberator Bomb Groups Trained in Florida

COMMAND	SQUADRONS	TRAINED IN FLORIDA	BASES/THEATERS/AWARDS
44th Bomb Group	66th, 67th, 68th, 404th	Jan 1941– Feb 1942	England. Distinguished Unit Commendation for the Battle of the Kiel Canal. Distinguished Unit Commendation for the Battle of Ploesti.
93rd Bomb Group	328th, 329th, 330th, 409th	15 May– 2 Aug 1942	England. Distinguished Unit Commendation for the North Africa Campaign. Distinguished Unit Commendation for the Battle of Ploesti.
98th Bomb Group	343rd, 344th, 345th, 415th	Feb–Jul 1942	Palestine, Egypt, Italy. Distinguished Unit Commendation for the North Africa Campaign. Distinguished Unit Commendation for the Battle of Ploesti.

Source: Compiled from Maurer, *Air Force Combat Units of World War II*, 70, 199–200, 202–3, 203–4, 222, 273, 274, 278, 281–82, 283, 81–82, 154, 156–58, 162–63, 166–67, 168–69, 338, 354–55, 101–2, 160–61, 168–69.

Corps. The Air Corps was striving to be autonomous, and in 1941 had won a measure of that autonomy with the new name, the "Army Air Forces" (AAF). The creation of an autonomous officer corps further institutionalized the differentiation from the Army. Officers in the AAF were previously graduates of the Army academy at West Point, or Army OCS. Ground fighting and riflery were their core curriculum. That was part of the problem. According to General Mitchell, appreciation of the air as a fighting environment "required an entirely different class of men from those which had heretofore constituted the officers in an army or a navy. In fact," he argued, "the physical requirements in the American Air Service are such that twenty-five percent of the officers accepted into the Regular Army between the ages of twenty and thirty cannot pass the physical examination."[15]

This was not simply a matter of the physical characteristics of greater visual acuity, hand-to-eye coordination, altitude tolerance, and response time that were required of aviators. Mitchell and his following believed that nonaviators simply could not exercise command of aviation forces effectively. "No

TABLE 9. B-17 Flying Fortress Bomb Groups Trained in Florida

COMMAND	SQUADRONS	TRAINED IN FLORIDA	BASES/THEATERS/AWARDS
29th Bomb Group	6th, 43rd, 52nd, 411th	May 1940–Jun 1942	Continental US, Guam. Distinguished Unit Commendation for the bombing of Japan.
88th Bomb Group	316th, 317th, 318th, 419th	Nov 1943–May 1944	Florida 3rd Army Air Force Trainer Group
91st Bomb Group	322nd, 324th, 401st	May–Jun 1942	England. Distinguished Unit Commendation for the bombing of Germany. Distinguished Unit Commendation (2nd) for the bombing of Germany.
92nd Bomb Group	325th, 326th, 327th, 407th	Mar–Jul 1942	England, France. Distinguished Unit Commendation for the bombing of Germany.
94th Bomb Group	328th, 329th, 330th, 409th	Jun–Jul 1942	England. Distinguished Unit Commendation for the North Africa Campaign. Distinguished Unit Commendation for the Battle of Ploesti.
97th Bomb Group	340th, 341st, 342nd, 414th	Feb–May 1942	England, Tunisia, Italy. Distinguished Unit Commendation for the bombing of Austria. Distinguished Unit Commendation for the Battle of Ploesti.
99th Bomb Group	346th, 347th, 348th, 416th	Jun–Jul 1942	Tunisia, Anzio, Normandy. Distinguished Unit Commendation for the invasion of Sicily. Distinguished Unit Commendation for the bombing of Austria.
100th Bomb Group	32nd, 352nd, 353rd, 419th	Jun 1942	England. Distinguished Unit Commendation for the bombing of Germany. Distinguished Unit Commendation for the Battle of Berlin.
463rd Bomb Group	772nd, 773rd, 774th, 775th	Nov 1943–Feb 1944	Italy. Distinguished Unit Commendation for the Battle of Ploesti. Distinguished Unit Commendation for the bombing of Germany.

COMMAND	SQUADRONS	TRAINED IN FLORIDA	BASES/THEATERS/AWARDS
483rd Bomb Group	815th, 816th, 817th, 840th	Nov 1943– Mar 1944	Italy. Distinguished Unit Commendation for the bombing of Germany. Distinguished Unit Commendation (2nd) for the bombing of Germany.

Source: Compiled from Maurer, *Air Force Combat Units of World War II*, 70, 199–200, 202–3, 203–4, 222, 273, 274, 278, 281–82, 283, 81–82, 154, 156–58, 162–63, 166–67, 168–9, 338, 354–55, 101–2, 160–61, 168–69.

one can know the air except one who works and travels in it, and a thorough air education can only be acquired by long study in this science and art."[16] Further, the general considered the greatest handicap to the development of military aeronautics in the United States was its leadership by non-aviators; they could not possibly know the problems of the field. Mitchell stated the cause of the problem succinctly: "This is because no corps of officers was especially trained, as a body, to specialize in aviation."[17]

If nothing proved more fundamental to this aeronautic philosophy than specialized education, Florida witnessed, then, its birth in the war years. With mobilization bringing into the Army Air Forces huge new levees and air fleets requiring officer leadership, and citing the wartime need to save time and money in construction (while bypassing consensus-building and permissions), Arnold seized on Miami Beach as a ready-made campus for an immediate Air Academy. The tourist town had seven thousand hotel rooms within a few miles' radius on the narrow island beside Biscayne Bay. Except for being empty of civilian guests, the hotels were fully operational. The hotels would serve as barracks, and with the concurrence of the city fathers and grateful hoteliers, the flyboys commandeered the town overnight for their own Officer Candidate School and related training. Leases were taken out on 188 hotels, 109 apartment houses, and 18 homes for senior officers.[18] Military Police (MPs) sealed off the causeways. Twenty-five percent of all AAF officers received their schooling on Miami Beach, about 125,000 officers.[19] An even larger number, 360,000 airmen, 20 percent of the enlisted Air Corps took basic training there.[20]

Noteworthy in addition to the ninety-day Officer Candidate School, the AAF established in the same town its specialized officer training school for direct appointment officers. Direct appointment officers were specialists in medicine and dentistry, chaplains, and former officers recalled to the service. The direct appointees were commissioned the day they joined. Frequently older than the officer candidates, the training of these professionals was less rigorous, and their numbers fewer. Still, the accession of these often-prominent members of the American elites further enhanced the standing of the AAF. Over thirteen thousand directly appointed officers went through the officer training school indoctrination. Its headquarters was the formerly exclusive Roney Plaza Hotel.[21]

For enlisted recruits two large basic training schools were set up: Number Four and Number Nine. These provided basic training for large numbers of airmen.[22] The enlisted men received indoctrination into the military, drill and ceremonies, and physical fitness. But there was a marked absence of the field training that was the hallmark of the Army Ground Forces. Instead, the course focused on classroom instruction in aviation matters, emphasizing Air Corps procedures and practices. A half-million personnel passed through these establishments.[23] When the basic training was completed, the future pilots and airmen went on to job training in their military operational specialty (MOS). There was yet another bonus to having Miami Beach for building up the Army Air Forces besides plentiful ready-made accommodations: it was close to advanced training at Air Corps bases all over Florida.

The Miami Beach curriculum was weighted toward aviation subjects: avionics, aerodynamics, the basics of flight, load mastering, aircraft maintenance, and the basics of waging war from the air. The golf courses of the resort town were converted into parade grounds, obstacle courses, and calisthenics arenas.[24] Swimming was taught in the ocean and the toney Venetian Pool. The Air Corps officer candidates were divided into fifty-man "flights." To address military health issues, the AAF took over the Biltmore Hotel in Coral Gables, giving it a new function as Army Air Forces Hospital Number One. The Nautilus Hotel on Miami Beach was also commandeered for the same purpose. The Biltmore's deluxe golf course was used for rest and recuperation (R&R) by military patients. The Breakers Hotel in Palm Beach and the Don Cesar Hotel in St. Petersburg were similarly converted into military hospitals.[25]

Besides the impact of the military on the city and the numbers of men training there, the exotic Florida location also proved especially attractive for patriotic publicity. The recruitment of movie star Clark Gable into the Officer Candidate School enhanced this association. The reason Gable gave for joining the service during World War II was the same reason held by the overwhelming number of Americans: He wanted to serve his country in time of war.[26] In December 1940 President Roosevelt had invited Gable and his wife, actress Carole Lombard, to the White House. The administration enlisted their help as spokespersons for the "Arsenal of Democracy" effort to aid to Britain. Gable and Lombard took the promotional work seriously. After Pearl Harbor the couple plunged into the war effort. Gable became chairman of the Screen Actors Division of the Hollywood Victory Committee organizing USO shows and entertainment to boost morale. Lombard sold war bonds. Sadly, on a war bonds tour, Lombard perished in a plane crash. Gable grieved in quiet and offered his services to the military.

General Arnold suggested the screen star could help the war effort by making a movie to promote the Air Corps. He offered the Academy Award winner a seat at the new Officer Candidate School in Florida. On August 12, 1942, Gable was sworn in. When he reported to Miami Beach, the media was waiting. Like the modern paparazzi, they peppered him with questions and requests for photographs. He responded by offering them a deal. He would pose for them to photograph as he shaved off his trademark mustache. In return, the reporters would then leave him alone to undergo his training.

A rich, famous, and overage officer candidate who had never graduated from high school, Gable was in the company of vigorous hand-picked young men with the highest motivation. The course went from morning until night six days a week, with physical fitness in between. To his credit the actor succeeded, graduating 700th in the first class of 2,600 officer candidates.[27] General Arnold came to Miami to officiate at the first graduation of his new officers filling the Miami Beach Golf Course. Newly minted Second Lieutenant Gable gave the graduation speech.[28]

The Officer Candidate School on Miami Beach also witnessed wartime social change. For the first time in history, African Americans were enrolled for commissions in the Army Air Forces. Each initial class of fifty cadets at the Officer Candidate School on Miami Beach contained at least one African American officer candidate.[29] Placing an African American soldier in the same unit with white soldiers offered momentous innovations.[30] First, it included World War II–era African Americans for the first time in combat units, from which they had been excluded before. Previously, they had been isolated in Army Services Command, usually as stevedores and laborers. Second, access to the Army Air Forces meant access to what was considered an elite branch of the military.[31]

Finally, completing the course awarded the African American a rank generally held in esteem by civil society, that of "an officer and a gentleman." Thus, if even in a small way, the military activity in Florida anticipated the push for establishing African American civil rights of the 1950s.

The trainees of the Air Corps OCS, OTS, and basic training schools were all quartered within the civilian community, as were significant numbers of Navy trainees across Biscayne Bay in the mainland city of Miami, and at sites in Broward County. Almost six hundred thousand military personnel lived and trained in the Miami, Miami Beach, Fort Lauderdale urban area, a region with a prewar population of less than half that number. As with the Jacksonville and Tampa Bay areas, these extraordinary numbers exemplified the nation's iconic wartime narrative of uniformed servicemen literally filling the space. Around the nation, 11 percent of the population were in uniform. In Florida the military presence amounted to more than 50 percent. Law and order was maintained by Army MPs and the Navy shore patrol who made the peninsula their own.

Florida might have guaranteed its place in the history of World War II and of the future Air Force solely by being a most important pioneer training ground for military airmen. Yet it had an equal or even more critical role as a supply base and staging area for the worldwide war effort. Created on July 7, 1942, to handle this effort was the Miami Intermediate Air Depot No. 6, a huge warehouse complex commanded by the Army Air Corps and run by thousands of civilians from the local community.[32] Most of the freight arrived by train. Both the railroads of Florida, the FEC, and the Seaboard Air Line, taken over and controlled by Army Transport Command, converged in Miami. There was a gigantic freight yard in Hialeah, adjacent to the Hialeah horse racing track. For most of the war, horse racing was banned, and the racetracks were commandeered by the military for supply dumps. The train line led from the freight yard and racetrack directly to the Air Depot No. 6 warehouses on the flight line of nearby Pan American Field and its contiguous Miami Army Airfield.[33] The civilian airlines of Pan American, Eastern, National, United, and Delta airlines were all concentrated there.[34] The federal government nationalized these civilian air carriers during the war but allowed them to operate on a charter basis for the military. Their cargo flights augmented the missions of Army Transport Command. Pan Am "Cannon Ball Express," cargo flights from Miami to Karachi, Pakistan, averaged 11,500 miles in three and a half days. Eastern Airlines flew 33,480,000 miles and carried 47,500,000 pounds of cargo and 130,000 passengers for Army Transport Command during the war.[35]

From the perspective of air-freight logistics, the tip of the Florida peninsula offered the logical embarkation point. Initially the air depot forwarded the materials needed to make the South Atlantic Route a dependable air bridge: the newly invented interlocking steel landing plates known as Marston Mat were laid down. Replacement aircraft engines and parts, aviation equipment, fuel, oil, controllers, and mechanics were all flown in.[36] The greatest airline of all time, the US Air Transport Command, sustained the effort. As the landing, refueling, and servicing points along the route were stabilized, so too were the military air embarkation points of Florida: Morrison Army Air Base in West Palm Beach and Miami Army Airfield. Morrison was the Transport Command point of command where aircraft crews received orders, inoculations, and briefings on overseas circumstances. Passengers, cargo, and mail departed from Miami.[37]

The Soviet Union was one sometimes overlooked destination of Florida's South Atlantic Route. The dangerous northern sea route known as the "Murmansk Run," into the Barents Sea and northern Russia, is well known. But there was also a southern sealift route delivering supplies to the Persian Gulf at Basra, Iraq, and from there by rail to Russia. It was supplemented by the airborne South Atlantic Route. Tehran was its terminal. One example illustrates the importance of this supply line. Between April and December 1942 the Air Transport Command used the Morrison-Miami aerial port to send 102 Lend-Lease B-25 bombers to Russia. The bombers were flown to Tehran, mostly by Pan Am contract pilots. From there Soviet pilots took the controls and flew them to Russia and the Eastern Front.[38] These warplanes augmented Russian forces just as the Battle of Stalingrad was being fought, the turning point of the war on the Eastern Front. There was no other way for the aircraft to have reached the war than from Florida.

Another great object of Florida's logistic war effort was support for China. American strategists recognized the necessity of keeping China in the war, thus tying down the large Japanese Kwantung Army. If China surrendered, those eight hundred thousand Imperial Japanese soldiers would be released to reinforce their Pacific Theater against the GIs.[39] The island-hopping campaign was already savagely opposed by the enemy at hand. Close to a million enemy reinforcements would make it that much harder.

It was essential that China be kept fighting. This meant, in turn, keeping the Chinese supplied. As the US forces fought their way across the Pacific, an additional strategic imperative emerged: Japan itself would ultimately have to be invaded and conquered. If the Japanese Army in China remained there long enough for the US fleet to get between them and their home islands, and thereby cut off their return home, the conquest of Japan itself would be much less daunting. It was a military necessity to keep China in the war.[40] Doing so was not easy.

In the summer of 1942 Florida's HALPRO raiders and other weaponry previously earmarked for China were diverted to beat back Rommel when he threatened the Suez Canal. Repercussions exploded. Generalissimo Chiang Kai-shek, the Chinese Nationalist leader, was furious. Via General Stilwell, Chiang issued Washington the "Three Demands" ultimatum.[41] He demanded three US divisions and five hundred aircraft at once, and five thousand tons of supplies a month. Otherwise, he threatened, China would make a separate peace with Japan. His first two demands were impossible ploys of negotiation meant to emphasize the third, the demand for massive monthly supplies. It made clear he would not continue to fight without major assistance. Strategically, the United States had to agree.[42] Thus China became the primary client of Florida's airlift for the rest of the war.

Airlift over the Himalayas was the only means of accomplishing the mission. Flying the Hump was an acquired skill taught thirty miles south of Miami at Homestead Army Airfield. As part of their contract to create the South Atlantic Route, Pan Am had hacked out an emergency landing strip on the edge of the Everglades at the southern tip of the peninsula. When the contract ran out, the landing strip was annexed by Air Transport Command and given the name of the nearby farming community.[43] In September 1942 Homestead Army Airfield formally opened. It assumed the geographically appropriate mission of maintaining the transport planes that flew the South

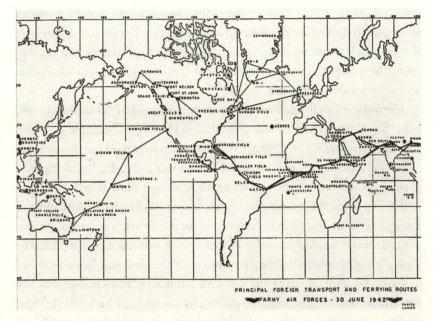

PRINCIPAL FOREIGN TRANSPORT AND FERRYING ROUTES
ARMY AIR FORCES - 30 JUNE 1942

The aerial warpath from Florida. The South Atlantic Route based in Florida was one of the three most important air routes of the war, and at thirty-six thousand miles roundtrip by far the longest. At the end of World War II, airlift had become so ingrained as a new military tool that the Air Force formally created in 1947 had three components: the bombers of SAC (Strategic Air Command), the fighter planes of TAC (Tactical Air Command), and the cargo planes of ATC (Air Transport Command). So experienced at beating air bridge challenges had the flyboys become that by 1948 the Berlin Airlift saw US Air Force cargo planes safely landing, unloading, and taking off again at a perfected rate of one-per-minute from Berlin's Tempelhof airport, one of the shorter runways of that era. Craven and Cate, *The Army Air Forces in World War II*. Vol. I, 329.

Atlantic Route.[44] These included the C-47 Skytrain, known as the Dakota, or simply christened the Gooney Bird. Another airlift plane even larger was the twin-engine C-46 Commando, sometimes known simply as "Dumbo," in reference to the Walt Disney cartoon elephant.[45] Appropriately, the acronym of the Air Transport Command, ATC, was sometimes said to stand for "Aid to China."

The FEC railroad ran south from Miami to Homestead and the air base flight line, allowing the place to store surplus air freight in transit. Homestead AAF first provided the periodic engine overhauls for the cargo planes of the Army Transport Command. As permanent facilities for the Miami Air Depot emerged and the concept of wartime airlift *throughput*, the rate of movement of supplies in and out of the system, became organized, Homestead Air Base devoted itself to training cargo pilots, navigators, loadmasters, and aircrewmen. The specialty of the 2nd Operational Training Unit was teaching pilots and aircrew how to "Fly the Hump."[46]

Until the Stilwell Road over the mountains and jungles of Burma (the other huge CBI project also supported from Florida) was completed late in the war, there was no other way to China except over the Himalayas. These tallest mountains on earth exceeded 23,600 feet in height, but flying over them was a military necessity. Every vehicle, every gallon of fuel, every gun and bullet to reach China in three years of war was flown in. The danger in flying over the desolate wind and snow-swept massif in the unarmed, unpressurized, heavily loaded propeller-driven aircraft was often compounded by Japanese fighter planes waiting to pounce on the slow and laden Dumbos and Gooney Birds. During the war four hundred planes crashed into the mountains, and sixteen hundred pilots and aircrewmen were killed. These numbers amounted to a plane crash every three days for three years. It was known grimly as the "Aluminum Trail." The death toll amounted to someone being killed flying it every day, day in and day out, for the three years the airlift operated. The mission took great aviation skill and good fortune.[47] The vast majority of the personnel who flew the Hump, almost seventeen thousand pilots, and fifteen hundred navigators, radiomen, loadmasters, and flight engineers, were trained at Homestead AAF in Florida.[48]

On March 3, 1943, the commander of the Army Air Forces himself came to South Florida for an extended stay. General "Hap" Arnold was a hard-driving workaholic who was creating and wielding the largest aviation force ever known. He lived and breathed aircraft production, aviation training, and aerial warfare.[49] His son was a cadet at West Point, and Arnold's sole pastime was an occasional round of golf. On February 28, at his quarters in Ft. Myer near the Pentagon, Arnold suffered a heart attack.[50] Three days later he was flown to Miami in a B-25 to recuperate.[51] He spent the next three weeks at Army Air Forces Hospital Number One, the former Biltmore Hotel, which had served as the temporary White House during the president's earlier visits.[52] Arnold had approved the hotel's conversion to a military hospital to support the medical needs of the thousands of airmen training in the area. Now he became its highest-ranking patient. The Air Corps chief was installed in the tower suite of the hotel, and his illness was kept top secret.[53] While recovering, Arnold puttered on the golf green, rode a PT crash boat around Biscayne Bay, and exercised command of his air forces.

Arnold's command was one of the largest military institutions in history. Over 2.4 million Americans served in the Air Corps. It flew over thirty-five thousand bombers alone. It was no accident he chose Army Air Forces Hospital No. 1 for his recovery. He knew Florida well. The Mighty Eighth Air Force, which bore the brunt of the air battle in the all-important European Theater, came largely from Florida. The critical China-Burma-India airlift originated there. From the window of the hotel/hospital tower, Arnold timed the steady stream of aircraft lifting off like clockwork from nearby Miami Army Airfield. He had worked for years building up Florida as a preeminent base for his air forces. The following year another heart attack brought him back to again exercise command from the same Florida hospital room window.[54]

Ailing or not, Arnold always pressed the offensive in war. Thus, he demanded the adoption of the B-29—the "Superfortress"—with a particular passion. The four-engine very heavy bomber, the largest aircraft of its day, could fly at forty thousand feet, beyond the range of anti-aircraft fire, had the first pressurized cabin, carried a payload of five thousand pounds of ordnance, and possessed a combat radius of sixteen hundred miles. A Billy Mitchell dream, the B-29 was intended to demonstrate once and for all that AAF bombing alone could bring an enemy to its knees. Much of the testing on the B-29 occurred in Florida. Beginning in autumn 1943 at Eglin Airfield Proving Ground, testing of the experimental XB-29 prototype model was done by the B-29 Accelerated Services Testing Group, whose commander and lead test pilot was Col. Paul Tibbets.[55]

For his service in the North African and European air campaigns, Tibbets had been promoted and nominated by General Doolittle as his best bomber pilot. Tibbets flew the XB-29 across Florida against captured enemy planes, including the Zero, Mitsubishi, and Messerschmitt, to perfect its combat worthiness. Its guns were sighted in over the Gulf. Test flights by "Tibbets' Troubleshooters" ranged as far as the Florida Keys.[56] In June 1944 the B-29 was deemed ready for war. Tibbets was directed to assemble fifteen of the Superfortresses and activate the 509th Composite Bomb Group for additional training for special missions.[57]

With the release of the B-29 for combat, the new bomber received orders for Operation Matterhorn. Matterhorn was the deployment to China-Burma-India Theater of five bomb groups composed entirely of the new B-29 for the express purpose of bombing Japan out of the war.[58] Arnold took personal command of the B-29s of the 20th Bomber Command, and its debut coincided with the initiation of two congressional bills to study a reorganization of the US military that would sanction autonomy for the AAF as a separate branch of service. In early 1945, elements of Operation Matterhorn collected on the recently captured island of Tinian in the Pacific to execute their bombing missions. They were joined by the 509th Composite Bomb Group.[59] Its specific mission was to drop the new kind of bomb secretly perfected by the Manhattan Project.

8

WOMEN, WORK, CAPTIVES, AND WOUNDED

Internal activity in Florida during the war was transformative. The civilian population was inundated by pan-military groups. Present were minority soldiers, female soldiers, enemy prisoners of war (POWs), and wounded soldiers. General Marshall's sweeping reorganization of 1942 created the Army Service Forces.[1] Large numbers of Women's Army Corps (WACs), and African American Army Service Forces trained in Florida.

Demographic geography was a factor in all these tumultuous visitations. Most Floridians were engaged in the war effort: A total of 15 percent were in uniform, and the rest of the males between eighteen and sixty-five years of age were all enrolled in the conscription pool. The labor force of the state was occupied with war work. Besides maintaining the ongoing military infrastructure of training and force projection, the primary industry was shipbuilding, and Florida's reserve of female workers joined this effort in large numbers.[2]

As Floridians moved to the cities for those patriotic and better-paying jobs, the farming sector was turned over to an unlikely group of new arrivals: German and Italian prisoners of war. They sometimes rejoiced at this fate. Yet another group of daily arrivals stamped *gravitas* on the entire Florida war effort: returning casualties. Because of its role as the embarkation point for one of the most important routes to the war, Florida was the point of return for thousands of wounded.

On the eve of the war there was no shipbuilding industry in Florida. There was the one earlier-noted contract with Kehler Shipbuilding of Tampa for a few vessels, but that was in default.[3] After Pearl Harbor, shipbuilding was underwritten by the US Maritime Commission, the War Shipping Administration, the Navy, and the Army. The entrepreneurial flair and the labor pool of enthusiastic Floridians created a production boom. At Jacksonville, Panama City, Tampa Bay, and Miami, Floridians and out-of-state workers converged to build ships.[4] Shipbuilding in Florida had its genesis in the two 1940 PT boat prototypes of the Miami Shipbuilding Company. From those came hundreds of PT boats built across the nation, including many in Miami and others by Huckins Yacht Co. of Jacksonville.[5] In early 1942 Merrill-Stevens Company of Jacksonville won the contract to build "Liberty ships." These used the exact same blueprints at shipyards around the nation, were virtually identical, and were built of prefabricated sections. Instead of time-consuming riveting, the ships were welded together.[6]

On September 27, 1941, President Roosevelt christened the first, the SS *Patrick Henry*, repeating the famous quote "Give me liberty or give me death!"[7] Thus inspiring the common name of the ship class. Liberty ships could carry 9,000 tons at 11 knots, and with 2,751 constructed, were the largest number of any class of ships ever built. They anticipated the modern container ship industry.[8]

The industry advanced another notch as the Merrill-Stevens Company set up the St. Johns River Shipbuilding Company near protective Naval Air Station Jacksonville.[9] With a subsidy of $17 million from the Maritime Commission, the ambitious shipyard could produce six Liberty ships at a time. On August 15, 1942, the keel of Florida's first Liberty ship, the SS *Ponce de Leon*, was laid. It would build eighty-two more.[10] The shipyard reached an efficiency of launching a boat into the water every forty days. In addition, the St. Johns Shipyard also built eleven Liberty ship tankers for transporting aviation fuel.[11] The government had ordered these in early 1945 in preparation for the invasion of Japan. Assuming the conquest of Japan would take at least two years of combat, the tankers were destined to keep the US warplanes flying in Japanese airspace. True to the production schedule, the ships were completed just before the invasion of Japan was scheduled to begin.

Other shipyards thrived in the area. Gibbs Gas Engine Company in downtown Jacksonville built fifty-three wooden Navy minesweepers, eighteen

Navy subchasers, and twenty-five tugboats. For the Army, Gibbs produced thirty-eight small boats and five barges and cranked out thirteen tugboats for the War Shipping Administration. Another company, the Arlington Shipbuilding and Engineering Corporation of Jacksonville, built tugboats for Lend-Lease to Britain. The Daytona Beach Boat Works built twenty Navy subchasers.[12]

Panama City experienced a larger burst of shipbuilding.[13] A $13 million award from the Maritime Commission got the J.A. Jones Construction Company started there from scratch. Although there was no prior shipbuilding experience in the area, the emergency was real, and the federal subsidies were enormous. Governor Holland dedicated the shipyard. Jones Construction christened the enterprise the Wainwright Shipyard in remembrance of General Jonathan Wainwright, the US commander in the Philippines who had been captured and was being held prisoner.[14] Workers flocked to the job. Almost overnight Bay County tripled to a sixty-thousand-person population.[15] The shipyard built dormitories, cafeterias, and clinics to accommodate the influx. Wainwright Shipyard laid its first Liberty ship keel on July 9, 1942; it was launched into the bay less than six months later, with Senator Claude Pepper officiating. Panama City built a hundred eight Liberty ships.[16] These included sixty-six standard Liberty ships, twenty-eight boxed aircraft Liberty ships (for shipping disassembled aircraft in crates). Eight tank transport Liberty ships were also built, the only eight such vessels for shipping tanks ever built.[17] In nearby Pensacola, the Warren Fish Boatyard built six Navy minesweepers and freighters.

This Florida industry took advantage of its assets: access to the sea and inland lakes, a willing and trainable population, and bountiful forests. Many of the vessels funded by the Emergency Shipbuilding Program were of simple wooden construction. In Central Florida, Lake Beresford outside Orlando typified this industry.[18] There the Beresford Shipyard used lumber from nearby Ocala and Lake George state forests to build fifty ammunition barges and thirty tugboats for the US Army.[19] The finished vessels were loaded aboard flatbed train cars and transported to the coast.

Similarly, cypress and mahogany hardwood from the Everglades and Key Largo were used by the Miami Shipbuilding Company to build more than a hundred PT boats of the rescue patrol craft (RPC) type on the Miami River.[20] The speedy RPC, lacking only torpedo tubes, was built for Army

Air Corps use in rescuing training pilots and crews who crashed at sea. They were called aviation rescue boats, or simply "crash boats." Many of the vessels were destined for Lend-Lease.[21] They went to Russia, to the Royal Navy, the RAF, and the British Dominions. Dooley Boatyard on the New River in Fort Lauderdale converted yachts for service with the Hooligan Navy and provided repairs for small craft at the Port Everglades Naval Facility.[22]

In Tampa, the Tampa Shipbuilding Company (TASCO) and McCloskey Shipyard became major shipbuilders. When the United States entered the war, TASCO had ten large (6,100 ton) half-built cargo ships. TASCO renamed them after volcanoes, finished them, and launched them into the war as Navy ammunition ships. Afterward, TASCO devoted its construction to Navy warships. These included twelve ammunition ships, twenty-four minesweepers, nine destroyer escorts, and three destroyer tenders. Many of its minesweepers went to Russia for the Lend-Lease program. Tampa's TASCO had no larger employer, and as a prime Navy contractor operated effectively as a War Department base. It was policed by the Navy shore patrol. The company also repaired battle-damaged warships and merchant marine ships.[23]

McCloskey Shipyard of Tampa built a unique type of Liberty ship. The owner, Matthew H. McCloskey Jr., was a construction contractor. He secured a $30 million contract to build ships of cement. No one ever produced such vessels. Because of the wartime shortage of steel, these ships were made of poured cement over rebar frameworks for the hull and superstructure. Internal bulkheads were of concrete. This construction took advantage of the nearby Florida Portland Cement Company, even as the mild weather helped the cement cure.

McCloskey named the first ship SS *Vitruvius*, after the first-century A.D. Roman military engineer and expert in concrete. The company produced a total of twenty-four such amazing Liberty ships. Two of them participated in the D-day invasion. The SS *Vitruvius* and SS *David O. Saylor* crossed the Atlantic to England prior to the invasion, sailing at three knots.[24] When the D-day invasion hit Normandy, the two cement ships were scuttled off Omaha Beach as part of a "gooseberry" artificial breakwater. They protected the "mulberry" pier of barges cobbled together to land men and materials for the invasion.[25]

Still another company, Tampa Marine and Bushnell Boatyards, built tugboats and barracks barges. The mostly wooden vessels were produced so quickly and uniformly that only the pennant and hull number distinguished them. The company laid keels for seventy-eight light tugboats destined for the Army. It also produced for the Navy nine unique three-story floating barracks for sailors' accommodations on foreign shores and at overseas outposts.[26]

The shipyards all demonstrated the institutionalized unity of private enterprise with the national government. In addition to the federal grants and subsidies to private corporations, otherwise described, the government shaped other aspects of the industry. The workers strove to win Efficiency Awards from the Navy and the Department of the Treasury.[27] Production involved military-like inspections and drives. The government and plant management promoted athletic tournaments and rivalries between the shipyards and local military teams. War bond rallies were a fixture at the yards, producing a steady source of war dollars. The authorities singled out large war bond purchasers for recognition and thanks. With young males in active military service, the labor force consisted primarily of older men and a great many women. Women workers centered in factories that produced both weapons and war materials. Newly salaried, they became an economic force in their own right. Florida shipbuilding welcomed them.

Practically every skill and job description were open to female workers. The government's Emergency Shipbuilding Program made a patriotic point of recruiting women. The emphasis on welding in the construction of the new ship types made that previously male-only job skill a female-dominated activity. "Joan of Arc-Welding" had an iconic presence in Jacksonville, Tampa, Miami, and Panama City.[28]

When Wainwright Shipyard opened in September 1942, women constituted 3.4 percent of the work force, most in clerical positions. By March 20, 1943, 10 percent of the workforce was female, performing every job in the shipways. Six months later that figure soared to 20 percent. Wainwright's 13,389-employee work force by December stood at 22 percent female.[29] The shipyard initially gave training for female clerical workers. Within a few months it launched the first welding class for women. The very next class in welding had two of the first female graduates as the instructors. Classes in ship fitting, plan reading, and electrical trades followed. These formerly male dominated trades paid higher wages than the clerical positions, and in addition offered affiliation with the labor unions, providing yet another entrée into previously all-male organizations.[30] Simultaneously, the Federal

Office of Education funded no-cost engineering courses at the University of Florida for the female shipyard workers.

Whether underemployed housewives, underworked farmhands, or members of Florida's significant numbers of unemployed—as demonstrated in the 1940 census, this war-inspired industrial frenzy found an extensive labor pool. Its extraordinary activity finds an easy measure in the statistics of Florida production:

- 148 Standard Liberty ships averaging 7,176 tons of steel apiece; 1,062,048 tons.
- 12 Aviation gas Liberty ships averaging 7,230 tons of steel; 86,760 tons.
- 28 Boxed aircraft Liberty ships averaging 7,176 tons of steel apiece; 200,928 tons.
- 6 Tanker Liberty ships averaging 7,230 tons of steel apiece; 43,380 tons.
- 8 Tank transport Liberty ships averaging 7,176 tons of steel apiece; 57,408 tons.[31]
- 24 Cement Liberty ships averaging 4,784 tons of steel; and 4,000 tons of cement.
- 12 Navy ammunition ships
- 17 Coastal freighters
- 70 Army barges and 9 Navy barracks barges
- 135 Army, Navy, and War Shipping Administration tugboats of wood construction
- 81 Navy minesweepers of wood construction
- 38 Navy subchasers of wood construction
- 9 Navy destroyer escorts
- 100 PT boats of wood construction[32]

This is a remarkable output for a state where there was minimal shipbuilding previously, and it reflects the wartime impact of Florida. Shipbuilding accounted for two-thirds of the industrial gains of wartime Florida.[33] The production of 226 Liberty ships was 10 percent of the national output. Over 1,565,340 tons of steel was used in their construction. The enthusiasm of the workforce can be measured by a single comparison: the first Florida Liberty ship in 1942, SS *Ponce de Leon*, took eight months to complete. By 1945 the Liberty ship SS *Thomas L. Haley* was built in two weeks.

As war work monopolized the citizenry of Florida, the agricultural base of the state suffered. Florida sought to remedy its farm worker shortage by using captured prisoners of war.[34] Over ten thousand German POWs were interned in the state.[35] The headquarters for the program was the Camp Blanding Provost Marshal General. The first POWs to arrive were captured sailors from the U-boats. They were housed at Camp Blanding in tents and barracks behind double fences topped with barbed wire and guard towers. After the invasion of North Africa, German soldiers of the *Afrika Korps* captured in Tunisia joined them.[36] Eventually Florida became home to twenty-five POW camps, including a second administrative center at Camp Gordon Johnston. In time, surrendering conscripts from regions conquered by the Nazis joined the camps. For some, being a POW in Florida was the most enjoyable part of their military service. They joked that the "PW" stenciled on their work shirts indicated they were "*Pensionierte Wehrmacht*" (retired from the German Army).[37]

Federal authorities put them to work farming tomatoes and green beans and harvesting sugarcane.[38] They brought in the citrus crops: the oranges, grapefruit, tangelos, pomelos, lemons, and limes.[39] They worked in the state forests cutting trees and milling logs for shipbuilding.[40] POWs incarcerated at bases worked in the mess hall kitchens, the laundries, and the officers' clubs. Others worked at base garages. POWs of the Kendall prisoner-of-war camp, now the site of Dadeland Mall in Miami, worked as orderlies at the US military hospital on Miami Beach.[41] POWs working at military bases earned ten cents daily in ration coupons good for cigarettes and toiletries. Those working on the farms and forests were paid eighty cents daily in the form of coupons, or government savings accounts. They performed the jobs Floridians had left for the patriotic and better-paying war work.[42]

Friction existed between diehard Nazis and those who were disenchanted with the Hitler regime.[43] It led to tension, fights, and strikes. US military police sometimes had to separate the factions.[44] There were occasional escape attempts, although only one POW in Florida was tragically successful in escaping from the camps. A young German soldier escaped from a working party in the sugarcane fields of Clewiston. He became lost and spent several hungry nights in the open while search parties closed in. Hungry, dehydrated, and disoriented, the man hanged himself with his belt.[45] The POW camps were all located at military bases, in state forests, and in farming areas. These unusual guest-workers went about Florida with a sometimes-surprising freedom of movement.

Compiled from Bellinger, this list presents the prisoner-of-war camps in Florida in 1944.

Camp Blanding (Army)
Homestead (Army Air Forces)
White Springs (Navy)
Banana River (Navy)
Kendall Miami (Army Air Forces)
Winter Haven (Army Air Forces)
Belle Glade (Army Air Forces)
Leesburg (Army Air Forces)
Camp Gordon Johnston (Army)
Bell Haven Miami (Army Air Forces)
MacDill Field (Army Air Forces)
Dale Mabry Field (Army Air Forces)
Clewiston (Army Air Forces)
Melbourne (Navy)
Eglin Field (Army Air Forces)
Dade City (Army Air Forces)
Orlando (Army Air Forces)
Telogia (Army)
Daytona Beach (Navy)
Page Field Fort Myers (Army Air Forces)
Marianna (Army Air Forces)
Drew Field (Army Air Forces)
Venice (Army Air Forces)
Whiting Field (Navy)
Green Cove Springs (Navy)

Military branch in parentheses indicates branch having jurisdiction over prisoners.

War mobilization affected the state's demography and social order in other ways. As Army Ground Forces left Florida to deploy overseas, their classroom seats were filled by Army Service Forces who followed.[46] Camp Blanding became an Army Service Forces Command, and Camp Gordon Johnston was redesignated a Service Forces Training Center. Specializing in functions of signals, supply, ordnance, medicine, chemicals, and transportation, the Army Service Forces absorbed most of the African American volunteers and draftees in the still-segregated army of World War II.[47] Assignment to combat arms was denied African American soldiers, except in two divisions comprised entirely of African American troops. Some of the work was highly technical; much of it was rigorous, grim, and arduous. In the wake of battle, it was the Army Service Forces who buried the dead, cleared away the ruins, and kept the trucks loaded and rolling.[48]

Nowhere was the dichotomy of US segregation more glaring than in the wartime armed forces. African American troops were expected to support whole-heartedly the war effort to destroy fascism yet abide by a system relegating them to an inferior position. With its large African American minority population, and its numerous African American soldiers in uniform, Florida witnessed early expressions of unrest against that system.

African Americans proved an important source of military manpower in the war. Of 9,838,725 persons drafted during the war, 1,056,841 were African Americans.[49] The Army contingent was largest: 885,945 African American draftees were 10.9 percent of the 8,108,531 conscripted. African American naval conscripts numbered 153,224; 10 percent of the total. The African American community offered 16,005 to the Marine Corps; 8.5 percent of its 188,709 conscripts. The Coast Guard's 1,667 African American conscripts were 10.9 percent of its total.[50] Constituting 11 percent of the total US population, the African American participation in the wartime armed forces stands at parity. Florida's minority contribution to the military was even greater. Over fifty thousand of its African American citizens joined the service: 20 percent of the Floridians in uniform were African American.[51]

These African American GIs, and their supportive families and communities, figured powerfully in Florida's demographics. With military bases across Florida, they were seldom sent far for training. Once in the barracks they were joined by African American soldiers from the north who were new to southern racism.[52] In such ways the war challenged Florida's mores of segregation. The wartime policy that encouraged soldiers to visit their hometowns whenever possible between training courses facilitated interaction between the African American GIs and their hometowns. Train rides of less than a day reaching most parts of Florida were plentiful, if governed by Jim Crow restrictions. Road trips by auto were rarer, but often soldiers on leave could simply walk home. Twenty-mile hikes were not considered hardships for the times. Florida's numerous African American GIs, often the pride of their community, were not insensible to the injustice of segregation in war, or of their place in the vanguard of its refutation. Racial tension was a fact of the war in Florida.[53]

Dale Mabry Army Airfield in Tallahassee was geographically only five miles from the state capitol building, which promulgated, administered, and enforced the separate and unequal segregation of the state. Geography numbered among several factors making it a hotbed for tensions. The population of Tallahassee was 40 percent African American, many living in the Frenchtown district.[54] Dale Mabry Airfield was visited often by the 332nd Fighter Group, the Tuskegee Airmen. This unit from Tuskegee Army Airfield in nearby Alabama was composed entirely of the first African American Army pilots and their crews. Members of this decorated unit were often at the Tallahassee airfield on training flights and were both a source of inspiration to the African American soldiers there and symbols of the struggle for equality, even as they challenged racial prejudices by their simple existence.[55]

Nearby Camp Gordon Johnston offered another source of frustration.[56] The camp continued to fit its GI nickname "Hell-By-The-Sea." Amenities were few, discomforts many.[57] Tallahassee was the only place for the soldiers to go on weekend passes. African American soldiers gravitated to Frenchtown. There were incidents of racial unrest in September 1942, and in August and October 1944.[58] On Easter Sunday in 1945, resentment spilled over when white Tallahassee police, reinforced by white MPs, reacting to boisterousness, began arresting African American soldiers. The scuffling, rock throwing, and confrontation escalated into a series of ugly riots.[59] It worsened that April. Hundreds of African American GIs gathered in Frenchtown for a going-away party, having been issued orders to depart for the upcoming invasion of Japan.[60] The soldiers unwound, fights broke out, stores were ransacked, and the Tallahassee police responded with tear gas. Dozens were arrested.[61]

MacDill Army Airfield in Tampa also figured in racial agitation. African

Americans constituted 25 percent of Tampa's population, and the African American community centered in a neighborhood known as The Scrub.[62] Again, African American GIs on leave gravitated to the local community. In July 1941, in June 1943, and in February 1944, the city police and African American airmen from MacDill faced off. The 1944 disturbance escalated into a riot when Tampa police and white MPs attempted to arrest an African American GI in The Scrub. A crowd estimated at four thousand gathered. Bottles were thrown from the crowd, and tear gas was released against them in return. Two dozen African American soldiers and civilians were arrested for riot.

The advent of women military personnel to both Florida and its armed forces was another transformative reckoning. History had no precedent for the mass enlistment of large numbers of female soldiers. The Coast Guard created the SPARS program (a nautical acronym of their motto *Semper Paratus*—Always Ready) composed of female coastguardsman.[63] Empty hotels in Palm Beach provided the barracks for the SPAR boot camp. From June 1943 until 1945, seven thousand SPARs trained in Palm Beach.[64]

Much larger by far, the Army Women's Army Corps (WAC) enlisted a hundred fifty thousand females during the war. The average WAC was between twenty-five and twenty-seven years of age, a high school graduate, unmarried, and with no dependents. One out of every five of the historic WACs, twenty-eight thousand women, trained at Daytona Beach in Florida.[65]

Three women led the campaign for women soldiers in Florida: US Representative Edith Nourse Rogers, First Lady Eleanor Roosevelt, and Florida educator Mary McLeod Bethune. As war approached, Eleanor Roosevelt suggested a "Women's Reserve" under the Office of Civilian Defense.[66] Congresswoman Rogers sponsored HR 4906 in May of 1941 to create a Women's Army Auxiliary Corps. The bill proposed a paramilitary civil service organization of twenty-five thousand women to assume clerical duties for male soldiers. The bill was sidetracked in the Bureau of the Budget, which failed to define a pay scale for women approximating the pay of soldiers doing the same duties. After Pearl Harbor, Rogers reintroduced the bill, increasing the proposal to recruit a hundred fifty thousand females. Language was inserted granting the women genuine military status.[67] The bill passed both Houses and the president signed into law on May 15, 1942, "An Act to Establish a Women's Army Auxiliary Corps (WAAC) for Service with the Army of the

US." The program was on the leading edge of both gender and racial issues. The legislation included enrollment of African American females in the program. Much of its activity would occur in Florida.

Bethune led the charge on two fronts. She strove for the inclusion of African Americans in the WAAC, just as she had earlier fought for their inclusion in the aviation Civilian Pilot Training program. The National Negro Council proposed Bethune to supervise African American recruitment into the WAAC.[68] She assisted the two African American recruiting officers for the WAAC in Florida, Dovey M. Johnson Roundtree and Ruth A. Lucas.[69] Almost sixty-five hundred African American females served in the WAAC and its successor WAC—a hundred forty-six of them as officers.[70] Throughout the war Bethune and the African American community worked for two victories of great seriousness: victory against the Nazis, and victory for equal rights.[71]

Bethune had only begun to fight. As a special assistant to the secretary of war, Bethune strove to help her home state. As the popular WAAC program grew to need a second training base, Bethune urged the Army to select Daytona Beach. Taking advantage of the empty hotel infrastructure, the Army concurred. Daytona Beach became WAAC Training Center No. 2. The Army leased the empty hotels, apartment houses, inns, and villas of the tourist town, activating the training center on October 1, 1942. The new recruits went for basic training to a tent city capable of housing six thousand recruits. After basic training they moved into hotels for skills training. Rogers meanwhile advanced legislation making the program officially a part of the Army. The "Auxiliary" nomenclature was dropped, redesignating it as the Women's Army Corps (WAC) on July 4, 1943. When the program began, females were eligible for just four military specialties. Within a year they were serving in a hundred fifty-five different Army jobs.[72] The Women's Army Corps in Daytona Beach drew considerable attention. Militarizing women aroused some opposition. A "whisper campaign" alleged impropriety and licentiousness.[73]

Because of the large numbers of WACs billeted amid Daytona Beach, both the allegations and the Army investigations focused on the civilian town:

> It was said that WAC trainees drank too much; that they picked up men in streets and bars; that they were registered with men in every hotel and auto court or had sexual relations under trees and bushes in

public parks; that the nearby military hospital filled to overflowing with maternity and venereal disease cases. Finally, it was seriously stated that WACs were touring in groups seizing and raping sailors and Coast Guardsmen.[74]

Investigations by the Army Service Command inspector general and Women's Army Corps headquarters rejected the complaints. Of the ten thousand women at the base in May 1943, only eighteen were pregnant, and sixteen of those women were married. The military police report for a typical Saturday night in Daytona Beach had only eleven discrepancies, all generally trivial in nature. There were two infractions of kissing and embracing in public, one WAC with no hat on, one without her identification card, and one enlisted WAC walking with a male officer. A bit more seriously, two were injured in an auto accident, two were found intoxicated, one AWOL returned, and one WAC was "retrieved from Halifax River in an intoxicated condition."[75] The information came to light that a few ex-WACs who had failed basic training and been discharged had kept their uniforms and remained in town wearing them. Their behavior prompted the worst charges. Venereal diseases in the WAC were practically zero, and pregnancy among unmarried WACs was one-fifth the rate of women in the civilian world. Twenty percent of the women of the Women's Army Corps received their training in Florida. They joined the Coast Guard SPARS and smaller numbers of Navy WAVES, serving at bases across the state.

The wounded were a final demographic group impacting on the state. Cargo planes returning from the battlefields landed every day at Florida airfields. Arriving in worn-out, and all too often shot-up, planes, the airlift ferried wounded soldiers to Florida hospitals. Those suffering "wounds not mortal" amounted to 670,846 personnel.[76] The US military suffered 1,082,245 killed and wounded during the war.[77] It is worth remembering this metric clarifying the seriousness of the war.

Florida's role as an aerial embarkation and debarkation port guaranteed that thousands of these wounded would return to the United States via Florida. Most came from the European and African-Mediterranean-Middle East theaters.[78] In 1943 casualties numbering 78,000 were evacuated to the US.[79] In 1944 that number increased by 300 percent.[80] Most went by hospital ship, but 121,000 of the worst injured were airlifted, many over the

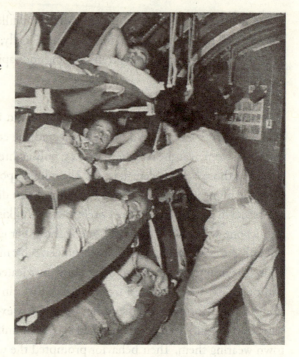

C-47 cargo plane converted for ambulance duty. The spartan experience of these first airborne medivacs ranged from inescapable monotony to ghastly mid-flight triage. Seventeen army nurses themselves gave their lives in airborne mishaps. Photo courtesy of Pictorial History of the Second World War: your Service Forces in Action. W.H. Wise and Co., Inc. New York. 1949. Vol. X, 263.

South Atlantic Route to Florida. Army transports and the civilian air carrier planes of Florida brought them home. Landing fields overseas were mostly co-located with the supply dumps and base hospitals behind the front. Once the planes from Florida landed and their outbound cargo of war materials was unloaded, whether bullets, bacon, or fresh soldiers, the aircraft were turned around to go back for more. The now-empty return flights often were loaded with the wounded being sent home, and they were usually the most seriously injured. Neurosurgery, maxillofacial surgery, plastic surgery cases, and the blinded had priority.[81]

The interior compartments of the cargo planes were reconfigured with racks for handling stretchers.[82] The wounded were manhandled aboard, signed over to the Army Transport Command, and joined by flight surgeons, nurses, and attendants. The accommodations were spartan.

The return flights in the unpressurized Dakotas and Dumbos were long, tedious, and often experiences of unmitigated suffering. The nonstop racket of the engines and shaking of the fuselage was punctuated by the occasional screams, prayers, or incoherent babble of the sufferers. Not all of them survived the flights. When the planes reached Florida, they usually landed at Miami Army Airfield, Morrison Army Air Base, or MacDill Airfield.

Each had a major military hospital on standby. In Miami, Army Air Forces Hospital No. 1, the former Biltmore Hotel, had been converted into a twelve-hundred-bed hospital treating the wounded. Morrison Air Base used the US Army's Ream General Hospital, formerly the Breakers Hotel of Palm Beach, with nineteen hundred beds. MacDill Field was linked to the Army Air Corps Station Hospital, formerly the Don Cesar Hotel of St. Petersburg.[83] Florida military hospitals also provided care for seriously injured members of the garrisons of the region requiring evacuation to the mainland.

From the Florida receiving hospitals the wounded were shipped by plane or often train to medical care around the nation; called the "Zone of the Interior."[84] In September 1944 the Zone of the Interior had 164,000 available general hospital beds, of which 153,000 were effective, which is to say, contained a wounded soldier. In addition, there were 53,000 effective convalescent hospital beds.[85] The emphasis at the convalescent hospitals was on returning the soldier to battle. On Miami Beach the Floridian, Pancoast, Gulf Stream, King Cole, Nautilus, and Tower hotels served as convalescent hospitals. In Daytona Beach, Welch Army Convalescent Center had 4,000 beds.[86]

WORLD WAR II MILITARY INSTALLATIONS OF FLORIDA

Northwest Florida Bases

Naval Air Station Pensacola
Bagdad Outlying Field, Naval Air Station Pensacola
Auburndale Outlying Field, Naval Air Station Pensacola
Bauer Outlying Field, Naval Auxiliary Aviation Facility Bronson Field
Bayou Outlying Field, Naval Auxiliary Air Station Corry Field
Bell Outlying Field, Naval Auxiliary Air Station Corry Field
Choctaw Outlying Field, Naval Air Station Whiting Field (adjacent Bagdad)
Chevalier Field, Naval Air Station Pensacola
Fountain Auxiliary Airfield, Naval Air Station Pensacola
Gonzalez Outlying Field, Naval Air Station Pensacola
Holm Airport (outside Pensacola)

Holley Outlying Field, Naval
　Air Station Whiting Field
King Outlying Field, Naval Air Station
　Pensacola
Milton Outlying Field, Naval Air
　Station Pensacola
Navarre Outlying Field, Naval Air
　Station Pensacola
Pace Outlying Field, Naval Auxiliary
　Air Station Ellyson Field
Pensacola Field #1
Pensacola Field #5 (near Gonzalez)
Pensacola Field #6 (near Gonzalez)
Pensacola Field #7
Pensacola Field #8 (near Muscogee)
Pensacola Field #9 (near Gonzalez)
Pensacola Municipal Outlying Field
Spencer Outlying Field, Naval
　Auxiliary Air Station Milton
Stump Outlying Field, Naval Auxiliary
　Air Station Corry Field
Naval Auxiliary Air Station Barin
Naval Auxiliary Air Station
　Bronson Field
Naval Auxiliary Air Station Corry Field
Naval Auxiliary Air Station
　Ellyson Field
Naval Auxiliary Air Station
　Saufley Field

Naval Air Station Whiting Field
Crestview Army Airfield
Eglin Army Airfield (near Valparaiso)
Eglin-Hurlburt Airdrome
　(Hurlburt Field)
Florosa Field (near Valparaiso)
Mossy Head Field (Eglin auxiliary #1)
Niceville Field (Eglin auxiliary #2)
Garniers Field (Eglin auxiliary #4)
Holt Field (Eglin auxiliary #6)
Mary Esther Field (Fort Walton Beach)
Tyndall Army Airfield (Panama City)
Marianna Army Airfield
Alliance Auxiliary Army Airfield
　(near Marianna)
Bascom Auxiliary Army Airfield
　(near Marianna)
Ellis Auxiliary Army Airfield
　(near Marianna)
Malone Auxiliary Army Airfield
　(near Marianna)
Apalachicola Army Airfield
Camp Gordon Johnston (Carrabelle)
Dale Mabry Army Airfield
　(Tallahassee)
Monticello Auxiliary Army Airfield
Quincy Auxiliary Army Airfield
Perry Army Airfield

Northeast Florida Bases

Naval Air Station Jacksonville
　· Jasper Outlying Field, Naval Air
　　Station Jacksonville
　· Branan Outlying Field, Naval Air
　　Station Jacksonville
　· Campville Outlying Field, Naval
　　Air Station Jacksonville
　· Cummer Outlying Field, Naval
　　Air Station Jacksonville

- Fernandina Outlying Field, Naval Air Station Jacksonville
- Fleming Island Outlying Field, Naval Air Station Jacksonville
- Francis Outlying Field, Naval Air Station Jacksonville
- Hart Outlying Field, Naval Air Station Jacksonville
- Herlong Outlying Field, Naval Air Station Jacksonville
- Madison Outlying Field, Naval Air Station Jacksonville
- Maxwell Outlying Field, Naval Air Station Jacksonville
- Middleburg Outlying Field, Naval Air Station Jacksonville
- Mile Branch Outlying Field, Naval Air Station Jacksonville
- Paxon Outlying Field, Naval Air Station Jacksonville
- Pomona Outlying Field, Naval Air Station Jacksonville
- Putnam Outlying Field, Naval Air Station Jacksonville
- St. Mary's Outlying Field, Naval Air Station Jacksonville
- Switzerland Outlying Field, Naval Air Station Jacksonville
- Trout Creek Outlying Field, Naval Air Station Jacksonville
- Kay Larkin Outlying Field, Naval Air Station Jacksonville (near Palatka)

Jacksonville Army Airfield
Jacksonville Army Airfield #2
Naval Auxiliary Air Station Cecil Field (near Jacksonville)
Naval Auxiliary Air Station Mayport (near Jacksonville)
Whitehouse Airport (near Jacksonville)
Fort Clinch #3 Army Post
St. Augustine Coast Guard Training Station
St. Augustine Outlying Field, Naval Air Station Jacksonville
Camp Blanding (near Starke)
Belmore Outlying Field, Naval Air Station Jacksonville
Carlisle Outlying Field, Naval Air Station Jacksonville (near Green Cove Springs)
Crystal Lake Army Air Base (Camp Blanding)
Naval Air Station Lake City
Lake Butler Outlying Field, Naval Air Station Lake City
Starke Army Airfield
Naval Auxiliary Air Station Green Cove Springs
Cross City Army Airfield
Horseshoe Point Auxiliary Army Airfield
Tennille Auxiliary Army Airfield
Alachua Army Airfield
Gainesville Municipal Airport
Keystone Heights Army Airfield
Montbrook Auxiliary Army Airfield (near Williston)
Stengel Field (Gainesville)
Bostwick Outlying Field, Naval Air Station Jacksonville
Palatka Air Operational Training Base

Naval Air Station Daytona Beach
- Bulow Outlying Field, Naval Air Station Daytona Beach
- Bunnell Outlying Field, Naval Air Station Daytona Beach
- New Smyrna Outlying Field, Naval Air Station Daytona Beach
- Tomoka Outlying Field, Naval Air Station Daytona Beach

Flagler Beach Coast Guard Patrol Station
Daytona Beach Women's Army Corps Training Center
Army Signal Corps School Daytona Beach
Ocala Auxiliary Army Airfield
Taylor Auxiliary Army Airfield (Ocala)
Cedar Keys Auxiliary Army Airfield
Crystal River Army Airfield
Dunnellon Army Airfield
Withlacoochee Auxiliary Army Airfield (Dunnellon)
Naval Air Station DeLand
Spruce Creek Outlying Field, Naval Air Station DeLand
Altoona Auxiliary Army Airfield
Bushnell Army Airfield
Leesburg Army Airfield

Minneola Auxiliary Army Airfield
Naval Air Station Banana River (Cape Kennedy)
Ryan Field (Apopka)
Naval Air Station Sanford
- Titusville Outlying Field, Naval Air Station Sanford
- Osceola Outlying Field, Naval Air Station Sanford

Cannon Mills Auxiliary Army Airfield (Orlando)
Gotha Army Airfield (Windermere)
Hoequist Auxiliary Army Airfield (Orlando)
Holopaw Field
Kissimmee Army Airfield
Orlando Army Air Base
Army Air Forces School of Applied Tactics, Orlando
Pinecastle Army Airfield (near Orlando)
Wallace Auxiliary Army Airfield (Orlando)
Winter Garden Army Airfield (near Orlando)
Brooksville Army Airfield
Zephyrhills Auxiliary Army Airfield
University of Florida Army ROTC and Navy ROTC (Gainesville)

Central Florida Bases

MacDill Field (Tampa)
Albert Whitted Airport (Coast Guard Air Station)
Drew Field (Tampa)
Dunedin Amphibian Tractor Detachment
Fort DeSoto (Mullet Key, Tampa Bay)
Hillsborough Army Airfield
Peter O. Knight Field

Pinellas Army Airfield (Clearwater)
St. Petersburg Coast Guard Station
St. Petersburg US Maritime Service Training Station
Wimauma Auxiliary Army Airfield (St. Petersburg)
Armor Auxiliary Army Airfield (near Bartow)
Bartow Army Airfield
Coronet Airport (near Bartow)
Drane Army Airfield (Lakeland)
Haldeman-Elder Field (Lakeland)
Hampton Auxiliary Army Airfield (Lakeland)
Lake Wales Army Airfield
Lakeland Army Airfield
Lakeland Municipal Airport
Lincoln Army Flying School
Leesburg Army Airfield
Leesburg Army Service Center
Plant City Auxiliary Army Airfield
Winter Haven Auxiliary Army Airfield
Naval Air Station Melbourne
· Malabar Outlying Field, Naval Air Station Melbourne
· Valkaria Outlying Field, Naval Air Station Melbourne
Naval Air Station Vero Beach
· Roseland Outlying Field, Naval Air Station Vero Beach
· Fort Pierce Outlying Field, Naval Air Station Vero Beach
Naval Auxiliary Air Station Witham (near Stuart)
· Stuart Outlying Field, Naval Auxiliary Air Station Witham
Naval Amphibious Training Base Fort Pierce
Passage Key Bombing Range
Avon Park Bombing Range
Avon Park Army Airfield
Conners Field (Okeechobee)
Hendricks Field (Sebring)
Okeechobee Auxiliary Army Airfield
Wauchula Auxiliary Army Airfield
Carlstrom Field (Arcadia)
Dorr Field (Arcadia)
Myrtle Beach Field (near Arcadia)
Wells Auxiliary Army Airfield (near Arcadia)

Southwest Florida Bases

Sarasota Army Airfield
Venice Army Airfield
Punta Gorda Army Airfield
Buckingham Army Airfield (in Fort Myers)
Fort Myers Airfield
La Belle Auxiliary Army Airfield
Page Field (North Fort Myers)
Bonita Springs Army Airfield
Naples Army Airfield
Immokalee Auxiliary Army Airfield
Belle Glade Auxiliary Army Airfield
Clewiston Army Airfield
Riddle Field (Clewiston)

Southeast Florida Bases

Camp Murphy Army Signal Corps (Hobe Sound)
Lake Worth Auxiliary Army Airfield
Lantana Auxiliary Army Airfield
Morrison Field Army Air Base (West Palm Beach)
Palm Beach Coast Guard Training Station
Boca Raton Army Airfield
ETTC Radio and Radar Technical Training School Boca Raton
Army Air Forces Distribution Center Boca Raton
Griffith AAF Field (Boca Raton)
Naval Air Station Fort Lauderdale
- North Pompano Outlying Field, Naval Air Station Fort Lauderdale
- Oakland Park Outlying Field, Naval Air Station Fort Lauderdale
- Pompano Outlying Field, Naval Air Station Fort Lauderdale

Naval Ball Gunner School, Hollywood
Naval Air Navigation School, Hollywood
Naval Ship Facility, Port Everglades
Port Everglades Coast Guard Patrol Base
NAAF North Pompano
NAAF West Prospect (Fort Lauderdale)
Naval Air Station Miami Mainside Field (Opa-locka)
Naval Air Station Miami Masters Field (Miami Gardens)
Naval Air Station Miami Municipal Field (Miami-Dade College North Campus)
- Davie Outlying Field, Naval Air Station Miami (Davie)
- Forman Outlying Field, Naval Air Station Miami (Dania)
- MacArthur Outlying Field, Naval Air Station Miami (Hollywood)
- North Perry Outlying Field, Naval Air Station Miami (Hollywood)
- South Perry Outlying Field (Miami-Dade College South Campus)

Miami 36 Street Airport
Miami Army Airfield
Miami Army Air Depot
Miami Beach Army Air Forces Officers Training School
Miami Beach Army Air Forces Basic Training Camp #2
Miami Beach Army Air Forces Basic Training Camp #9
Army Personnel Redistribution Center #7 (Miami Beach)
NAAF Dinner Key (Coconut Grove)
Coast Guard Station Dinner Key (Coconut Grove)
Navy Navigational School (Coconut Grove)
Naval Air Station Richmond LTA Navy Blimp Station (Richmond Heights)

- Banana River Outlying Field for Lighter Than Air (Navy Blimps)
- Meacham Outlying Field for Lighter Than Air (Navy Blimps)

Chapman Army Airfield (Pinecrest)
Homestead Army Airfield
Naval Base Key West
Naval Sound Training School Key West
Naval Submarine Base Key West
Naval Air Station Key West
Marathon Key Outlying Field (joint Army/Navy)
Fort Jefferson Coast Guard Seaplane Station
Naval Auxiliary Air Station Boca Chica
University of Miami Army ROTC, Navy V-5 and V-12 Officer Programs

Grand Hotels Converted into Military Hospitals

The Breakers of Palm Beach
The Nautilus of Miami Beach
The Biltmore of Coral Gables
The Don Cesar Resort of St. Petersburg
The Ponce de Leon Hotel of St. Augustine

Grand Hotels Converted for Training

The Boca Raton Club
The Beach Club of Miami Beach
The Surf Club of Miami Beach
The Hollywood Beach Resort
The McAllister Hotel of Miami
The Jacaranda Hotel in Avon Park
The Everglades Hotel of Miami
The Columbus Hotel of Miami

Racetracks Used as Supply Depots

Tampa Downs
Hialeah Racetrack
Tropical Park Racetrack
Gulfstream Park

In addition, many other venues, including bowling alleys, jai-alai frontons, dogtracks, fairgrounds, and innumerable smaller lodgings and establishments, were taken over by the military in Florida when it was a state at war.

Grades of naval establishments are thus: NAS is the acronym for Naval Air Station, the largest facilities. NAAS references Naval Auxiliary Air Station. NAF references Naval Air Facility. OLF is a naval acronym for Outlying Field. Grades of Army Air Corps establishments are so: the term "Field," as in MacDill Field, was applied to the largest installations. "Army Airfield" referred to medium installations. Army Auxiliary Airfield referred to the smaller establishments. In the cases of Orlando Army Air Base and Morrison Field Army Air Base, the station was officially designated an "Air Base." LTA is the naval abbreviation for Lighter Than Air.

Source: Compiled from Osborne, *World War II Sites in the United States*, 56–67, and *Florida World War II Heritage Trail.*

The importance of repairing the wounded and returning them to the battle was a grim reality of total war. Numbers mattered. Soldiers who had been wounded had experienced war in person. They had been bloodied. And, importantly, they had survived it. They had earned the red badge of courage. Their tried and proven worth required their return to the fighting.

They were no longer students, but graduates. As such, their military value as "effectives" was increased. Most were at least physically capable of fighting on. Hence, physical fitness and conditioning was emphasized to ensure the patients returned to active service. All hands were needed in the fight. As the war in Europe came to an end, the convalescent hospital program accelerated. It began providing reunions at the Florida convalescent centers for husbands and wives long separated by the war. The purpose was to strengthen morale among the troops and their families, indeed the entire nation. It was preparation for the hardest battle of the war that lay ahead. It was the battle that the US military, Florida, and the rest of the world braced for.

The invasion of Japan.[87]

9

A SUDDEN END TO WAR

Census and Remembrance

FDR's death in April 1945 and Germany's surrender in May did not slow Florida's militarization. Rather, it accelerated the military preparations for the huge undertaking of the conquest of Japan. The fruits of the Manhattan Project that ended the war so suddenly even had roots in Florida. The war came to an unexpected end, but Florida was changed forever from the war's influence. The 1950 Census clearly indicates how the war changed the backwater agrarian society the previous census had measured. If militarization developed the state, the state also contributed greatly to change within the military. Innovations tried first in Florida gave a new twist to postwar soldiering. This final chapter explores these three phenomena: Florida's role in the reduction of Japan, the changes the war brought to Florida, and changes Florida brought to the US military.

By 1945 war had become a way of life in the peninsula. The state was subordinated to the war effort. Florida hummed with wartime industry and practically total employment.[1] The peninsula was full of military installations and activity, guards, restricted areas, and surveillance. Something as ordinary as a civilian car traveling on a road was enough to draw attention. The bombing at Avon Park, Ocala National Forest, and Eglin Military Reservation went on with systematic regularity. Blimps armed with machine guns and bombs routinely patrolled the coastline, as did horsemen armed with rifles and dogs. Newspapers, radio, and travel were controlled. Gasoline, tires, shoe leather, and food were rationed, and the United States Postal Service brought what news there was.[2]

As Harry Truman stepped into the White House, the military shifted its focus to preparing for the second half of the war: the conquest of Japan. Codenamed Operation Downfall, the invasion was to begin in late 1945, and it was expected to take at least two years of fighting. The first landing to Kyushu, codenamed Olympic, was set for November 1, 1945. Operation Coronet, the follow-up invasion into Tokyo Bay on the main island of Honshu, was scheduled for March 1, 1946. The scale of the invasion may be seen in the number of troops assembled for it.

Troops numbering 395,000 went straight from Europe to the Pacific for the invasion. Another 408,200 soldiers were arriving in the Pacific after continental rest and recuperation in route. They were joined by 138,500 troops from the United States, making up a landing force of a million men. A force of 2.25 million soldiers was being positioned along the West Coast to serve as reinforcements and occupation force.[3] From a demographic standpoint, 5 percent of the 65 million US males counted in 1940 were to participate in conquering Japan.

The 1945 battles of Iwo Jima and Okinawa offered ghastly preludes.[4] Of the 30,000 US troops who stormed the island of Iwo Jima, 6,821 were killed in action, 23 percent of the force. Of 21,000 Japanese fighting on Iwo Jima, only 134 surrendered. The rest—over 99 percent—fought to the death.[5] At Okinawa, 65,631 US land and naval casualties were sustained.[6] Of these, 12,281, or 20 percent, were killed. Japanese losses were worse (of 100,000 Japanese defenders, only 7,000 lived to surrender). Ninety-three percent died fighting. Another 80,000 civilians lost their lives in the fighting.[7] Admiral Chester W. Nimitz warned:

> We must be prepared to take heavy casualties whenever we invade Japan. Our previous successes against ill-fed and poorly supplied units, cut down by our overpowering naval and air action, should not be used as sole basis of estimating the type of resistance we will meet in the Japanese homeland where the enemy lines of communication will be short and enemy supplies more adequate.[8]

Florida was the intermediate staging point for much of the preparation. The Army Air Forces established the "White Project" to transfer almost 6,000 warplanes from Europe to join the forces already in the Pacific. Almost 40 percent of that air fleet, 2,282 aircraft (primarily bombers) took the South Atlantic Route stateside, landing 25 planes a day for three months in Florida before going west to the Pacific. During the same May–August time the Army's "Green Project" airlifted 80,000 troops over the same route to Florida. It was the largest troop movement of the war by air. The government erected hundreds of temporary Quonset hut shelters at Miami Army Airfield to receive them. In a move anticipating the modern airline industry to come, Air Transport Command distributed preprinted survey cards to the soldiers, asking them to rate the service and efficiency of their flight.[9]

In addition to the Florida convalescent hospitals rehabilitating soldiers for fresh combat, the military set up "personnel redistribution centers" in the former hotels of Miami Beach, St. Petersburg, and Palm Beach, converting them from the training barracks they had already become. Air Corps personnel returning from the war in Europe were sent to these pleasant surroundings.[10] For between seven and thirty days, they received physical exams, dental work, psychological testing, rest, and recreation. After that they were shipped west. Those getting this "R&R" treatment (rest and recuperation) in Florida were personnel assigned to the invasion of Japan.[11]

Two one-plane US bombing missions, on August 6 and August 9, suddenly brought the war to its unexpected end. Not everyone was surprised. Col. Tibbets and some of his senior officers of the 509th Composite Squadron knew differently. Since arriving on the pacific island of Tinian to fly bombing attacks against Japan, the 509th continued practicing their special techniques for dropping the new and special bomb. Early on August 6, Tibbets took the yoke of his B-29 for a mission against the Japanese homeland armed with one single bomb, codenamed "Little Boy." The nose art painted on the aircraft fuselage bore the name *Enola Gay*, for Tibbets's mother, Enola Gay Tibbets.[12] Six of his twelve crewmembers had trained in Florida. At 0815 hours the *Enola Gay* appeared over Hiroshima and dropped the atomic bomb.[13]

When no immediate response came from the Japanese government, a second bombing mission was ordered for August 9. The Nagasaki mission also had Florida connections: The pilot, Captain Charles W. Sweeney, had served as an Eglin test pilot. The co-pilot 1LT Charles Donald Albury was a Miami High School graduate who had dropped out of the University of Miami to join the Army Air Corps.[14] Their B-29 was nicknamed *Bockscar*, a play on words for the gambling outcome when two rolled dice both present sixes: boxcars. The original plane commander was Captain Frederick C. Bock. The August 9 flight of *Bockscar* missed its first objective. After an hour of searching, the *Bockscar* appeared over Nagasaki at 1102 hours. It then released the weapon that was codenamed "Fat Man."

To his credit, President Truman followed up with a warning to the Japanese Empire that the United States would continue to drop such weapons on the home islands of Japan. One a week, every week, until *Dai Nippon* was reduced to ashes. This was the poker-play of a lifetime by the former artillery captain from the "Show Me" state. The United States had no other nuclear devices in its inventory at that time. The threat was a bluff.

The next day, Japan opened negotiations for surrender, their government asking only that terms would not "comprise any demand which prejudices the prerogatives of the emperor as sovereign ruler." August 15, Emperor Hirohito ordered the Japanese people to lay down their arms and surrender. The war had come to an end, just as suddenly as it had begun, and two years ahead of time.[15]

Euphoria gripped the victors. Celebrations erupted all over Florida, as they did across the rest of the United States. The wartime population and production centers of Jacksonville, Tampa Bay, and Miami were ecstatic, with none happier than the tens of thousands of soldiers in Florida who were on their way to join the invasion. On September 2, 1945, a Japanese delegation laid down their samurai swords and formally signed surrender documents aboard the battleship USS *Missouri* in Tokyo Bay.[16] General MacArthur delayed the ceremony until US General Jonathan Wainwright, captured and imprisoned in Japan since the fall of the Philippines, was located and brought aboard USS *Missouri*. The same honors were shown to the imprisoned British General Percival, who had surrendered Singapore. Gaunt and emaciated from years of privation in captivity, Wainwright and Percival stood to attention and solemnly witnessed the surrender.[17]

In Florida the governor issued a proclamation of victory. He declared a solemn commemoration for the twenty-four-hour period to follow. The proclamation urged that all liquor package stores, bars, tap rooms, juke joints, and other places dispensing alcoholic beverages were to remain closed during that period. Across the state Floridians went wild with celebrations. The ban on alcohol was ignored.

The war was over.

The impact the war had on Florida was one of its great legacies. Conversely, the effect Florida's role in the war had on the US military is the other. The Census of 1950, conducted in the spring of that year, provides metrics for measuring the impact of the war on Florida and its people. The census reported a phenomenal increase in population for Florida. Between 1940 and 1950 the population of the state had grown from 1,897,414 to 2,771,305, a 46 percent increase.[18] Florida's growth is especially significant within a national context—only California and Arizona exceeded Florida's increase. Florida's decade of growth more than tripled the average national increase of 15 percent.[19] The war marked a huge demographic watershed.

The census revealed another demographic shift: the rural state was urbanizing. The 1940 Census records a roughly 50/50 split between urban and country dwellers.[20] The 1950 statistics counted city dwellers at 65 percent of the population.[21] As revealing, people moved to larger urban centers, and thus the number of towns with populations under 1,000 shrank during the war, from 144 in 1940 to only 136 such hamlets in the 1950 Census.[22] The established urban areas grew apace. Metropolitan Miami in 1950 boasted nearly a half-million population. A new metropolitan center arose in Central Florida with Orlando.[23] Counting 52,367 within the city limits, and another 20,796 immediately adjacent, Orlando boasted a metropolitan population of 73,163. It was the first urban area in the interior of the state.[24]

Florida counties witnessed a pattern of growth. Clay County, near the metropolitan and military center of Jacksonville, witnessed the greatest expansion in Florida, with a 121 percent increase. Perhaps not surprisingly, Camp Blanding, the largest wartime base in Florida, was located there. In the Florida panhandle, Bay County and Okaloosa County experienced triple-digit growth. Bay County, host to the Wainwright Shipyard, doubled in population. Okaloosa County, home to Eglin Military Reservation, grew by 112 percent.[25] South Florida counties also registered very large gains in population. Broward County and Monroe County experienced increases of 110 percent and 112 percent, respectively.[26] Situated between them, Dade County registered the sixth largest growth increase with an 85 percent gain.

The smaller municipalities (less than 50,000) grew both in number and in size. The largest municipal increase in Florida was North Miami, a modest township in 1940 of 1,973 residents. The war decade brought explosive growth to 10,734 residents, a 444 percent increase. The neighboring municipality of Hialeah witnessed the second-largest increase in the state: its prewar population of 3,958 soared by 397 percent to 19,676, practically quadrupling.[27] The satellite municipalities of Coral Gables, Fort Lauderdale, and Hollywood doubled in size. The big metropolitan cities of Miami and Miami Beach experienced 45 percent and 65 percent population increases, respectively.[28] Military installations, including Naval Air Station Miami, the Miami Beach Army Air Forces Training Base, and the Navy Subchaser Training Center, major wartime installations, were in the immediate community. Miami Army Airfield, the critically important military aerial port of the South Atlantic Route, did not close along with the end of the war. In 1947 it was gifted to the civilian authorities, who simply renamed it Miami International Airport.

Municipalities in the Florida panhandle grew likewise. Pensacola expanded so much it was itself a metropolitan center in all but name, while Panama City's municipal population more than doubled in the war decade, from 11,610 persons in 1940 to 25,814 persons, an increase of 122 percent. In looking for cause and effect factors, the wartime shipyards of the city and nearby Tyndall Army Airfield were the only variables. The state capital of Tallahassee only grew by 67 percent, a relatively modest increase in comparison to the rest of Florida. But even that increase must be seen in contrast to the growth rate of 15 percent nationwide.

Key West represents an example of phenomenal growth that can only be attributed to the war. The island town always lacked a source of freshwater, except for rain collected in cisterns. The exponential growth of its wartime garrison demanded a better supply. Navy engineers drilled wells on the mainland in Florida City, installed pumps, and constructed a hundred-thirty-mile pipeline through the islands of the Florida Keys. The military pipeline brought potable water in plenty to the chain of islands for the first time in history. This ready supply of water enabled the Florida Keys to develop into a tourist haven.[29] Military improvements to public works such as this facilitated Florida's postwar growth.

Florida's singular preponderance of males to females during the war subsided quickly. The gender distribution of Florida in 1950 was 1,366,917 males to 1,404,388 females, a ratio of 49:51, conforming to national population norms.[30] The population of Florida aged slightly too. The median age had risen to 30.9 years in 1950, from the 1940 median of 28.9 years.[31] In 1950, 93

TABLE 10. Smaller Municipalities of Florida, 1950

MUNICIPALITY	POPULATION
Bradenton	13,604
Coral Gables	19,837
Fort Lauderdale	36,328
Fort Pierce	13,502
Hialeah	19,676
Key West	26,433
Lake Worth	11,777
Ocala	11,741
Pensacola	43,479
St. Augustine	13,555
West Palm Beach	43,162
Brownsville	20,269
Daytona Beach	30,187
Fort Myers	13,195
Gainesville	13,502
Hollywood	14,351
Lakeland	30,851
North Miami	10,734
Panama City	25,814
Sarasota	18,896
Warrington [a]	13,570

Note: Warrington was a "census-designated place," containing NAS Pensacola and base housing contiguous with the city of Pensacola. If Warrington were counted with Pensacola, it would make a fifth metropolitan area of over 50,000 in population in 1950.

Source: *US Census of Florida 1950*, Table 34, General Characteristics of the Population, For Metropolitan Areas, Urbanized Areas, and Urban Places of Ten Thousand or More: 1950, 10-56-58.

percent of the adult population of Florida, those persons 21 years of age or over, were native to the United States. Naturalized citizens were 5.2 percent. Aliens were just 1.3 percent.[32]

The census indicates the war brought on a marrying bee among Floridians. Between 1940 and 1950 the institution of matrimony grew noticeably. Of the marriageable population in Florida in 1940, 31 percent of the men were unmarried, as were 22 percent of the females.[33] By 1950 the percentage of unmarried men had dropped to 22.7 percent, while unmarried women decreased to 17 percent.[34] A boom of childbirth followed. In 1940 there were 151,968 children under five years old and 152,968 children between five to nine years; 16 percent of Floridians were between infancy and ten years of age.[35] In 1950 there were 290,745 persons under five years of age and 238,229 between the ages of five and nine years; in 1950 those between infancy and the age of ten amounted to 20 percent of all Floridians.[36]

In 1950, one in ten Floridians was born after the war. The numbers show a steady increase: 50,943 babies born in 1945, 113,806 babies born between 1946 and 1947, and 120,602 babies born between 1948 and 1949. In the spring of 1950, there were 56,337 babies under one year of age. In 1950, directly corresponding to the end of the war in 1945, there were 290,745 children five years or younger. The birth rate had doubled. Yet the 238,229 children born during the war and the postwar 290,745 children provided but one source of the population increase.

Returning GIs were another. Florida's own returning soldiers were augmented by another 594,917 adults. Many were former soldiers themselves. Kilroy liked what he saw in Florida during the war and began returning after the end of military service. Sergeant William E. Bills of Dallas, Texas, was typical in stating: "I've been to a lot of places since I got in the Army, and this is where I want to live."[37] Air-conditioning, a prewar rarity, made living in the Sunshine State idyllic year round. The wartime invention in Florida of DDT graced the citrus groves with bumper harvests.[38] Wide-open spaces, homestead exemptions, and GI-Bill mortgages were plentiful spurs to suburbanization. The young ex-GIs, empowered by the Veterans Readjustment Act of 1944, would change the landscape of Florida.

They were joined by another group coming to Florida, known generically as displaced persons. It should be remembered that President Truman did not declare the end of the unlimited national emergency until December 31, 1946. Chaotic wartime conditions prevailed in much of the world long after V-J Day. Europe and the Soviet Union were devastated. The British Empire had fallen apart. Its former domain of the subcontinent of India was tearing itself to pieces with religious and tribal and ethnic bloodshed. China polarized into civil war. Confused battles of liberation raged in the former Dutch East Indies, and French Indochina. Japan was a ruin, as was Germany, Italy, and most of Europe. The US Army of Occupation was all that was keeping those regions from anarchy. Amid the catastrophe wandered millions of homeless displaced persons. For many the only home they had ever known were the death camps.

Among them was the remnant of the Jewish community of Europe nearly annihilated in the war. Many sought refuge in the United States, and evinced a preference for settling in Florida. Certainly, the benign weather was a factor. Practically speaking, they also came because the transportation infrastructure raised into existence by the war made Florida relatively easy to get to. It may be also that war and extermination camp survivors preferred the safety offered by settling in what Florida in a very real sense had become: an impregnable military base surrounded by a moat on three sides.

The census shows stable postwar employment. The war boosted tourism to new heights in Florida. The Great Depression had devastated tourism, but the war restored it.[39] Florida had embraced the wartime visitors who flooded the peninsula: The soldiers, sailors, marines, and airmen were simply another type of tourist. As the war went on, Florida even courted northern war workers as well. By 1950 Florida had not only recovered its civilian tourist market but had increased it to five million visitors annually.[40] As tourism boomed, in concert with civilian aviation, so did employment in general, showing in 1950 a marked improvement over 1940 levels.

Florida's 1940 civilian labor force constituted 786,804 workers, male and female, of whom 677,833 were employed. The 1940 Census counted 103,471 unemployed, more than twice the 1950 number. Those unemployed were also a much larger percentage of the whole: 13.5 percent of the males, and 12.7 of the females. The 1950 civilian labor force numbered 1,057,479 workers, male and female. Of these, 47,864 persons were unemployed: 4.5 percent of the males, and 4.7 percent of the females. Those employed numbered 1,009,615 persons. In other words, between 1940 and 1950 Florida grew 331,782 paying jobs (1,009,615 less 677,833).[41]

The census reveals a new transition toward a government-oriented economy in Florida. In 1940 there were 5,500 persons holding paid noncivilian positions in the total labor force. Military positions counted in the labor force, but specifically not as part of the civilian labor force. In 1950 there were 89,166 such persons counted. A legacy of the war was that from 1940 to 1950 the number of paid military garrison positions grew by 83,666 jobs. National defense positions in Florida boomed by a stunning 1,600 percent.

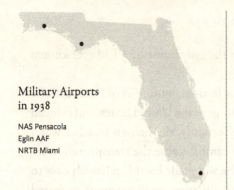

Military Airports in 1938

NAS Pensacola
Eglin AAF
NRTB Miami

Military Airports in 1945

Navy Airfields

NAS Banana River
NAAS Barin Field
NAAS Bronson Field
NAAS Cecil Field
NAAS Corry Field
NAS Daytona Beach
NAS DeLand
NAF Dinner Key
NAAS Ellyson Field
NAS Fort Lauderdale
NAAS Green Cove Springs
NAAS JAX Municipal #1

NAS Jacksonville
NAS Key West
NAS Lake City
NAAS Mayport
NAS Melbourne
NAS Miami
NAS Pensacola
NAS Richmond
NAS Sanford
NAAS Saufley Field
NAS Vero Beach
NAAS Whiting Field

Army Airfields

Alachua AAF
Apalachicola AAF
Avon Park AAF
Avon Park CPS
Bartow AAF
Boca Chica AAF
Boca Raton AAF
Brooksville AAF
Buckingham AAF
Carlstrom CPS
Clewiston BFT
Cross City AAF
Dale Mabry AAF
Dorr AAF
Drew AAF
Dunnellon AAF
Eglin AAF
Fort Myers AAF
Hendricks AAF
Hillsborough AAF

Homestead AAF
Jacksonville AAF
Keystone AAF
Kissimmee AAF
Lakeland AAF
Leesburg AAF
MacDill Field
Marianna AAF
Miami AAF
Montbrook AAF
Morrison Air Base AAF
Naples AAF
Ocala CPS
Perry AAF
Pinecastle AAF
Punta Gorda AAF
Tyndall AAF
Venice AAF
Zephyrhills AAF
Chapman CPS

Growth of Florida airports during the war. Compiled from Shettle, *United States Naval Air Stations of World War II*, and *Florida's Army Airfields of World War II*.

Notes: NRTB is the acronym for Navy Reserve Training Base. CPS is the acronym for Civilian Pilot School; this is a misnomer because all trainees were simultaneously enrolled in the army air corps reserve. BFT is the acronym for British Flight Training. Planes and facilities were provided by the US Army; instructors and students were Royal Air Force.

The federal military "occupation" of Florida during the war did not disappear at its end.[42]

Additionally, civil service government workers doubled, from 52,987 in 1940 to a 1950 count of 107,969 such workers.[43] Female participation in government work also doubled, from 19,053 workers to 38,860 workers. The related industry of public administration also grew from 21,942 persons to 51,959 persons, an increase of 250 percent. Public administration workers were over 25 percent female, triple the number in 1940. Conversely, the category of unpaid family workers in the home, a predominantly female category, had no increase in ten years, and shrank slightly from 14,740 persons in 1940 to 14,442 persons in 1950, despite the population boom.[44]

The war forged a permanent alliance between Florida and the aviation industry. Florida, a mainstay of the air war as an aviation academy and a launchpad for projecting aerial power, retained its aviation infrastructure. Tallahassee International Airport, Jacksonville International Airport, Orlando International Airport, Tampa International Airport, and Fort Lauderdale International Airport were all military airfields donated to the civilian community. Every airport in the state was either created in the war or enhanced enormously by it. These federal air bases, undamaged, pristine, and operating with military precision, were a tremendous endowment to Florida. A few airfields became school campuses or devolved into summer training camps for baseball teams, but most were within a few years turned over to the state and local civilian authorities.[45]

The new aerospace industry was another Florida beneficiary of the war. Its genesis was in the wartime Nazi V-1 and V-2 vengeance rockets captured and brought to Eglin Military Reservation for study. Nearby Apalachicola Gunnery School tinkered with the rockets and test fired them into the Gulf. Navy airships from Naval Air Station Richmond were positioned over the Gulf to observe their accuracy.[46] In July 1945 the blimps observed sixteen of the classified test firings.[47] The vengeance weapons worked. Yet there was a drawback in shooting them into the Gulf: a missile gone off course might hit Texas or Louisiana instead.

Meanwhile, Operation Paperclip was bringing émigré German scientists and engineers to settle into a government enclave at Huntsville, Alabama.[48] In 1947 Naval Air Station Banana River at Cape Canaveral was selected to become a guided missile experimentation station.[49] The World War II anti-submarine seaplane base had several advantages of location and place.

It was an isolated site easily secured. Its location fronting the Atlantic meant rockets could be fired great distances with little impact on the vast ocean. There were no friendly island nations likely to be affected. US outposts in the Bahama Islands were well situated downrange for observation and recovery. The Banana River Naval Air Station was taken over by the new Air Force and renamed Patrick Air Force Missile Test Center. Cape Canaveral would develop into NASA Cape Kennedy Space Center. Florida would be a major component of the US aerospace program for decades to come. It remains so to this day.[50] In 2021 Patrick Air Force Base was renamed Patrick Space Force Base.

If the war left a legacy of government interest and authority in Florida, it also fostered political domination of Florida by the victors as well. In the US Senate, Florida's wartime governor, Holland, moved up from Tallahassee to Washington in 1946 to assume the seat of dying Senator Andrews. Holland would serve in the Senate for the next twenty-five years. He was joined by George A. Smathers, marching home from thirty-nine months in the Marine Corps to take a seat in the US House and challenge Claude Pepper for the other Senate post. The New Deal was past, and FDR was gone; Pepper's postwar influence was diminished. The emergence of the Cold War and the new enemy of communism made his left-leaning suspect, and the GIs derisively dubbed him "Red Pepper." Smathers defeated him and ascended to serve eighteen years in the US Senate.

The Florida World War II cohort of veterans dominated the governorship of Florida after the war. Between 1949 and 1979, seven of the eight governors of Florida were former GIs.[51] This practically unbroken line of leadership with military experience was a powerful legacy to Florida directly linked to the war.

Gradually, Florida ceased to be a part of the "Old South," realigning itself instead as something of a fief of the federal government. The prewar political system in which the rural conservative representatives of North Florida exercised authority beyond their numbers would not long survive the war. Political change would begin with the Supreme Court–mandated reapportionment of the state, transferring power from rural and underpopulated North Florida to its urban centers, especially population-rich South Florida.[52] Florida would enter the New South, reemphasizing itself as a place to visit, while linking itself as a destination to its new powerhouse industrial engine of aviation.[53] The outlook of its people became more transient, urbane, and internationalist in character. Florida since the war has become a global center of travel and movement.

Florida's legacy to the US military was the other great impact of the war. The war prompted great changes within the standing military, which in the wake of World War II have remained. Between 1946 and 1952 President Truman made eleven working vacations to Naval Station Key West, amounting to a hundred seventy-five days. Although President Truman's affection for Key West was real enough, that alone does not account for the almost six months of his time in office spent there. Much of the time was devoted to creating the Department of Defense, establishing the Air Force, and military reorganization. Executive Order 9981, abolishing segregation in the armed forces, was planned and drafted by Truman with his Joint Chiefs of Staff at the Little White House.[54] His sojourns in Key West should be seen within context: that of the immediate postwar era. Florida was a bastion of the US military power and a proven center of its force projection around the world.

This was especially important with the abrupt emergence of the Cold War. Florida was an integral component of the US military ensemble. Key West during Truman's tenure was a military city. All the disciplines of warfare—warships, submarines, fighter planes, bombers, and all manner of land warfare—were represented by major installations there. Those inhabitants of the island who were not in the military were employed by it, or dependents of it. Key West and the rest of the state were at the highpoint of a robust military presence during the postwar reorganization of the US military.[55]

Florida contributions to the military reorganization may be seen most readily in its wartime role facilitating the emergence in 1947 of the Air Force as an independent branch of service. This momentous change did not begin when the war ended. Throughout the conflict it was a conscious pursuit by higher echelons of the US government, and by 1945 was the subject of active deliberation in Congress. If only informally, Florida provided much of the impetus for realizing General Mitchell's vision. In addition to providing the place and space where a large part of the Army Air Forces units formed up to fight World War II, the peninsula was moreover the boarding school for a large percentage of its personnel.

The establishment in Florida of the independent Officer Candidate School of the Air Corps was a critical element. A military service is led by its officer corps. Entering World War II, the Air Corps was led by Army Officers from

West Point. It emerged from the war led by its own Miami Beach officer corps. Miami Beach itself was reborn and flourished anew after the war, attracting even Army Air Corps Veteran Elliott Roosevelt (FDR's third son), who later served a stint there as mayor.[56]

When the Officer Candidate School moved out of its Miami Beach hotels near the end of the war, it did not reintegrate with the Army. Instead, the Air Corps Officer Candidate School moved into permanent quarters especially prepared for it at San Antonio, Texas, Aviation Cadet Center. By then, it was the Army Air Forces in name only. During the war approval for new bases and missions often involved interservice and governmental wrangling, not to mention the lead time of construction, and the consensus and agreements required first. If not for the island full of empty hotels Miami Beach provided, nestled within a state full of operating air bases, matters may have gone differently. Whether by serendipity or accident, the unique urban environment of Florida that allowed the first Army Air Forces OCS class to quickly convene within days after Arnold gave the order was nowhere else to be found.[57]

Moreover, Florida strengthened the hand of the AAF with another important card: air transport. The unplanned emergence of a third form of air power, airlift, owes as much to the South Atlantic Route that Florida pioneered as to the civilian DC-3 that flew it under coats of military green paint. By the end of the war this new military airlift capability was tried and proven. When the Air Corps first came to Florida it had two components: a strategic component of bomber aircraft and a tactical component of fighter planes. Florida provided the air space in which those two air combatant arms tested and perfected their techniques.

When the United States Air Force was created in the wake of the war, it had three components. Its two original combat arms developed into the Strategic Air Command (SAC) made up of bombing forces and the Tactical Air Command (TAC) composed of fighter aircraft. Yet the Air Force was born with a new and distinct third specialty that would morph from its Air Ferrying and Air Transport Command experience into Military Airlift Command (MAC). Much of the expertise came from flying Florida's long-drawn-out South Atlantic Route, hauling air cargo and passengers halfway around the world for years under profoundly arduous conditions, and overflying the tallest mountains on earth at the far end to deliver the goods.[58] Within a year of its birth the US Air Force would prove the importance of aviation transport with the Berlin Airlift of 1948.

Florida hosted much of the planning and implementation for the new Department of Defense at its Key West stronghold. The poker game between Truman and his generals and admirals at the isolated old Civil War Fort Jefferson in the Dry Tortugas predicated much of American life for the next century. The unwieldy troika of the War Department, State Department, and Navy Department was due for change, especially with the birth of the United States as global hegemon. The invention of the atomic bomb was reason enough to reorganize the US defense establishment. Florida was instrumental in training the pilots and crew of the *Enola Gay* and *Bockscar*, just as it trained tens of thousands of air force officers, and hundreds of thousands of enlisted personnel.[59] Florida facilitated the birth of the Air Force. Without an independent Air Force as a party to it, no Department of Defense would have been realistic.

One of the underlying concerns to be addressed by the new Department of Defense was the need for interservice cooperation in the increasingly complex mission of modern warfare. Florida's experience in the war was in some respects a model of joint service and the absence of rivalry. The twenty-four naval air stations and forty-seven Army airfields of Florida worked together within the peninsula's airspace to create air forces that were as capable of reducing powerful industrial states to submission as they were at controlling the 70 percent of the world that is water. Navy instructors from Pensacola helped train the Doolittle Raiders at Eglin.[60] Army pilots from MacDill helped fly the ASW patrols that drove back the U-boats. At the amphibious training centers of Camp Gordon Johnston and Fort Pierce, tens of thousands of soldiers and sailors trained together on all aspects of littoral warfare in relative harmony. During the several years of the military reorganization following World War II, Florida's experience was an example of joint service cooperation.

Topographically, the beaches of Florida were essential to winning the war. It has been said: "The Battle of Waterloo was won on the playing fields at Eton."[61] Words to that effect may apply to World War II and the Florida beaches. Florida was the US Army Amphibious Training Center of the war. JANET was in Florida.[62] The beaches of the state were crucial to developing the strategic doctrine and the tactical methods for prosecuting the war of seaborne invasions that the US waged. Its dozens of invasions from the sea were often executed against the least hospitable of coastlines on earth, and the most formidable of opponents. The disasters at Anzio and Tarawa, and the pyrrhic victories at Salerno and Iwo Jima, testify to the difficulties such combat presented. Florida was the elementary school where hundreds of thousands of GIs from shock troops to meteorologists were first exposed to the precise and dangerous art of amphibious warfare that ultimately brought victory. Again, whether by serendipity or accident, nowhere else in the continental US was there a state full of empty, benign beaches to practice on in privacy and acquire the essential playbook and experience to face the rocks and shoals, riptides, reefs, tides, and vagaries of the littoral environment, manned by the thoroughly dangerous enemies whom the GIs faced. It was perhaps apropos that the US command and control ship for many of its amphibious invasions, USS *Biscayne*, was named for that prominent Florida bay.[63]

In the broader sense of strategic geography, the many US seaborne invasions of the war may also be said to owe some of their success to the location of Florida in context to war production. The universal attack boat of the World War II landings, the Higgins boat, was mass produced in New Orleans, adjacent to Florida. Army Transport ships full of Higgins boats routinely plied the Florida realm heading either east or west to join the war. Furthermore, the majority of the larger amphibious landing vessels of the war such as the LSTs, sometimes called the "Prairie Navy," were built along the inland rivers of the US interior. Almost seven hundred LSTs of the cornfield fleet reached the open sea and the war via the principal ward of the Florida maritime marches: the Mississippi River.

Such vessels, specifically required for seaborne invasions, joined munitions and supplies of a more general nature that transited these sea lanes to the war only because of the protection afforded by having the Florida peninsula in US hands. One reason for pouring troops and infrastructure into the peninsula before the outbreak of the war that was never explicitly articulated at the time (certainly on purpose) was the fact that had the enemy gotten ground troops to French Guiana or Cuba, then Florida—with its inviting beaches—was the gateway to the US. The harder a target it was in those early war days, the better.

It is impossible to quantify how much the US victory in the war benefited from Florida's control of its sea lanes—a control it had to fight for desperately, as Admiral Mahan had foreseen. It is impossible even to quantify how much war material passed through the maritime realm of Florida (at least 10 percent of it was in Florida-built bottoms).[64] But a single example may serve to illustrate the importance of the Caribbean realm: The significant psychological victory of the Doolittle Raid in the otherwise-disastrous spring of 1942 occurred because the new aircraft carrier USS *Hornet* took on the Florida-trained B-25 bombers at NAS Alameda, California, and carried them deep into the Pacific Ocean to within range for the attack. But *Hornet* was built in Newport News, Virginia, and was on its first patrol. To reach its rendezvous with the Doolittle Raiders it first had to transit the Florida Straits and the Panama Canal. A single enemy torpedo hitting *Hornet* while in Florida waters, or even a lowly pipe bomb exploding at one of the Panama Canal locks, and the victorious Doolittle Raid would never have happened.[65]

To this day the Florida peninsula retains a centrality to the US military and to the defense establishment. Three of the ten unified combatant commands of the US Armed Forces are headquartered in Florida: Southern Command, Central Command, and Special Operations Command. The reasons for the military fondness are manifest. For example, the geographic appeal of Mayport Naval Station at the mouth of St. Johns River is a constant. US warships shoving off from Mayport can be out to sea in a matter of minutes, underway on any one of 180 degrees of headings. Likewise, friendly vessels seeking safe haven have 180 degrees of approach, while Mayport to this day retains the capability to easily close the mouth of the St. Johns River with submarine nets, denying that waterway to any foe. It is no accident that today Mayport is home to the 4th Fleet. At nearby Camp Blanding, seventy-three thousand acres of pristine pine barrens held by the Florida National Guard are exempt from Base Realignment and Closure (BRAC). The largest Coast Guard area of responsibility (AOR) in the world, Coast Guard 7th District (the old 7th Naval District), is based in Miami. Avon Park remains a bombing range. The longest runway in Florida remains at Homestead Air Force Reserve Base. The multitude of airports in Florida constitute a national strength, reaching as they do around the world. Florida is home to the third-largest population of veterans in the United States.

The factors of military geography, climate, and topography argued for

Florida as the mobilization site for turning out great numbers of trained soldiers, sailors, airmen, and merchant mariners. This arsenal produced over two million graduates: riflemen, cannoneers, pilots of all types, bombardiers, navigators, aircrews, mechanics, anti-submarine warfare experts, radar and sonar technicians, attack boat drivers, beach masters, commandos, frogmen, medics, and logisticians. Owing to its place in the Western Hemisphere it simultaneously stood watch over the Straits and the passages of the Caribbean. Had Florida lost the Battle of the Gulf Sea Frontier, had the Straits been closed, such strategic reverses could have decided the outcome of the war far differently. The combat air patrols flying daily over the realm from a dozen Florida bases and island outposts, joined by the Piper Cubs of the Civil Air Patrol, the splinter fleet keeping station at sea, and the coastwatchers ashore, all contributed to the war effort. US possession of the Florida peninsula was critical to its victory.

The GIs returned to Florida in large numbers after the war. But where those soldiers went in the between times, between their first visit to Florida and when they returned after the war, is seldom tracked. From Florida they went into the crucible of war. They went over the Aluminum Trail, and down the Burma Road, to Tunis and Cassino, Pointe du Hoc and Hiroshima. After such places their preference for Florida was understandable. The approximately 5,000 Floridians who did not return also deserves audit.[66] To the 4,674 service members KIA or missing between 1941 and 1945 may be added the many fatal training accidents, and the merchant mariners, pan-military, and civilian airline personnel who shared their fate. That number remains unknown.

By itself, 4,674 may seem a small number, but those losses suffered by the Floridians of the time represent as proportionately great a loss as that experienced by the entire US population in the Vietnam War.[67] The US population in 1970 stood at 205,052,174. The total war deaths from Vietnam were 58,282. That is .000284 percent of the 1970 population. The loss that Florida's 1940 population of 1,897,414 persons suffered of 4,674 deaths was much greater proportionately: .002463 percent. Moreover, the sacrifice of Floridians in World War II occurred in a much shorter time span of 1,363 days from December 7, 1941, to September 2, 1945.

The total number of US military personnel killed in Vietnam is 58,282, which includes nonhostile deaths of 10,786. The vast majority of the total,

Mail call for African American GIs building the Burma Road. With unshakable resolution these combat engineers of Florida fought against mountains, monsoons, malaria, jungles, and cobras. Enemy ambushes and aircraft bombings were regular features of the roadwork. Winding rigorously through the Burmese cordillera that was sometimes called the Stilwell Road or the Ledo Road, the soldiers themselves simply dubbed it the Long Snake. Its length of thirteen hundred miles was built at the average cost of the life of a soldier for each and every mile. Photo by Joe Davis, courtesy of the Col. Charles S. Davis Archive.

57,666 deaths, were between the years 1965 through 1972, a period of 2,920 days. This means the proportionately larger Florida losses of World War II, in contrast to Vietnam, were compressed to less than half the time and took place as subtraction from a peninsula population infinitely smaller than that of the United States as a whole.

The impact can only have been touching and sobering.

The people of Florida leaned into World War II wholeheartedly. They willingly submitted themselves to the *levée en masse*, offering up the flower of American youth. The leaders led by example with a common sense, practicality, and love of country that today may seem a puzzle. Behind the dreamy iconic memories of that war, and the glory days of that great generation; of big band music and newfound employment, uniforms and travel and excitement; a life-and-death struggle with the most profound ramifications was underway around the world. Civilized life hung in the balance, perhaps as never before. Hopefully, never again. Florida and its people rose to the occasion. The Floridians stood to the mark and helped deliver civilization.

This book speaks to that remembrance, and for our consideration of the importance of Florida's place and space in both war and peace. Lest we forget, Florida was central to the most harrowing, yet equally heroic, experience of recorded time, figuratively and literally. That is the message of *State of War: A History of World War II in Florida*.

NOTES

1. THE STICKS AND THE HICKS

1. See "World War II Military Installations of Florida" on page 133.
2. Mahan, *Mahan on Naval Warfare*, 16.
3. Reprinted from Mahan's "Strategic Features of Gulf and Caribbean." William E. Livezey, *Mahan on Sea Power* (University of Oklahoma Press, 1981), 130.
4. Mahan, *Mahan on Naval Warfare*, 27–30.
5. Mahan, 29.
6. Mahan, 65.
7. Although Mahan wrote when machinery was still fueled by coal, the replacement of coal by petroleum did not reduce the importance of the waters around Florida. The oil coming from Texas, Louisiana, Venezuela, and the Dutch West Indies refineries at Aruba and Curaçao made the waters of the region all the more strategic.
8. Morison, *The Two-Ocean War*, 117.
9. Mahan, *Mahan on Naval Warfare*, 31.
10. Corbett, *Some Principles of Maritime Strategy*, 361.
11. Matthew 24:28, King James Version.
12. Morison, *The Two-Ocean War*, 115.
13. Mahan, *Mahan on Naval Warfare*, 112.
14. Among the soldiers sent to strengthen the Philippines was Army 2d Lt. Alexander R. "Sandy" Nininger, of Fort Lauderdale. Nininger was posted to the Philippine Scouts.
15. See chapter 2.
16. Morison, *The Two-Ocean War*, 31–32.
17. Mahan, *Mahan on Naval Warfare*, 23.
18. Mormino, "World War II," 323.
19. Mitchell, *Our Air Force*, 12.
20. Mitchell, *Winged Defense*, 214.
21. Mitchell, *Skyways*, 63.
22. Mitchell, *Winged Defense*, 16–17.
23. Mets, *The Air Campaign*, 12.
24. Mitchell, *Winged Defense*, 5–6.
25. See chapter 3.
26. Craven and Cate, *The Army Air Forces in World War II*, 312.
27. Craven and Cate, 325.
28. Mitchell, *Our Air Force*, 200.

29. Mitchell, *Winged Defense*, 99.
30. Mets, *The Air Campaign*, 22.
31. *US Census of Florida 1940*, Table 4, Race, by Nativity and Sex, for the State, 14.
32. *US Census of Florida 1940*, Table 4, Race, by Nativity and Sex, for the State, 14.
33. Gannon, *Michael Gannon's History of Florida in Forty Minutes*, 48.
34. *US Census of Florida 1940*, Table 14, Foreign-Born White, by Country of Birth, by Sex, for the State, 32.
35. *US Census of Florida 1940*, Table 4, 14.
36. *US Census of Florida 1940*, Table 14, 32. Only 3,247 persons were of Spanish origin in 1940.
37. *US Census of Florida 1940*, Table 14, 32.
38. Jim Wiggins, *Florida and World War II*, 96.
39. Billinger, *Hitler's Soldiers in the Sunshine State*, xiv.
40. Mormino, "World War II," 326.
41. *US Census of Florida 1940*, Table 25, Indians, Chinese, and Japanese, by Sex, for Counties, and for Cities, 10,000 to 100,000, 75.
42. *US Census of Florida 1940*, Table 28, Race and Age, by Sex, with Rural Farm Population, for Minor Civil Divisions, by Counties, 106.
43. Mohl and Pozzeta, "From Migration to Multiculturalism," 395.
44. *US Census of Florida 1940*, Table 25, 75. Of the Yamato group, Tamotsu Kobayashi joined the US Army. He retired from the Reserves as a master sergeant and graduate of the University of Miami.
45. Ling, *Small Town, Big Secrets*, 25.
46. Rogers, "The Great Depression," 306.
47. *US Census of Florida 1940*, Table 20, Persons 14 Years Old and Over in the Labor Force, 43.
48. *US Census of Florida 1940*, Table 17, 36.
49. *US Census of Florida 1940*, Characteristics of the Population, Introduction, 6.
50. *US Census of Florida 1940*, Table 17, 36.
51. *US Census of Florida 1940*, Table 16, Persons 14 Years Old and Over, by Employment Status, Class of Worker, Race, and Sex, for the State, 34.
52. *US Census of Florida 1940*, Table 17, 36.
53. *US Census of Florida 1940*, Table 18—Employed Workers 14 Years Old and Over, by Major Occupation, Industry Group, 37.
54. Tebeau, *A History of Florida*, 418.
55. *US Census of Florida 1940*, Table 18, 37.
56. *US Census of Florida 1940*, Table 18, 37.
57. *US Census of Florida 1940*, Table 18, 37.
58. *US Census of Florida 1940*, Table 18, 37.
59. Lazarus, *Wings in the Sun*, 118, 143, 152, 171, 173.
60. MacDill AFB Library Base History Archive, *Miami Daily News*, Jan 13, 1941.
61. Lazarus, *Wings in the Sun*, 143.
62. *US Census of Florida 1940*, Table B-35—Age by Race and Sex, for the City of Miami: 1940, 141.

63. *US Census of Florida 1940,* Table 31—Composition of the Population for Cities of 10,000 to 100,000: 1940, 124.

64. *US Census of Florida 1940,* Table 28—Race and Age, by Sex, with Rural-Farm Population, for Minor Civil Divisions, by Counties, 91.

65. *US Census of Florida 1940,* Table C-35—Age, by Race and Sex for the City of Tampa: 1940, 150.

66. Mormino, "World War II," 326.

67. *US Census of Florida 1940,* Table A-35—Age, by Race and Sex for the City of Jacksonville, 132.

68. *US Census of Florida 1940,* Table 28, 94.

69. *US Census of Florida 1940,* Table 28, 91.

70. *US Census of Florida 1940,* Characteristics of the Population, Introduction, 3.

71. *US Census of Florida 1940,* Table 31, 124.

72. Leland and Oboroceanu, *American War and Military Operations Casualties,* Table I, 4.

73. The Navy was most partial to the distinction between Regular Navy and Navy Reserve. Nine out of ten in World War II were classed as Reserve component, despite serving on active duty for the duration of the war, often for five or six years.

74. Mormino, "World War II," 336.

75. Mormino, 335. From Florida's African American minority, fully 20 percent, one in five, all in the prime of life between eighteen and forty-five years of age, joined the US military during the war.

76. Morison, *The Two-Ocean War,* 131.

77. Mormino, "World War II," 338.

78. Colburn, "Florida Politics in the Twentieth Century," 356.

79. Rogers, "The Great Depression," 311.

80. Sherwood, *Roosevelt and Hopkins,* 93.

81. Colburn, "Florida Politics in the Twentieth Century," 357.

2. NAVAL AIR STATION FLORIDA

1. Mormino, "World War II," 324.

2. Matloff, *American Military History,* 410.

3. Sherwood, *Roosevelt and Hopkins,* 226.

4. Morison, *The Two-Ocean War,* 583.

5. Rogers, "The Great Depression," 308.

6. Cross, *Sailor in the White House,* 30. During the 1920s Roosevelt made two extended houseboat stays in the Florida Keys in the effort to find relief after being stricken with polio.

7. Morison, *The Two-Ocean War,* 583.

8. *Dai Nippon* translates as Greater Japan.

9. USS *Panay* was a river gunboat of the US Asiatic Fleet homeported at Manila Bay in the then-US commonwealth territory of the Philippine Islands. This fleet was destroyed in valiant, hopeless, and little-remembered sea battles against the IJN in the early months of 1942.

10. Perry, *The Panay Incident*.
11. Chang, *The Rape of Nanking*, 148.
12. Morison, *The Two-Ocean War*, 23.
13. PT boat prototypes No.1 and No.2 were built by Miami Shipbuilding Company. These cheap wooden vessels were powered by three Packard engines, carried three thousand gallons of fuel, and were capable of racing at forty-one knots for six hours. Hundreds were produced by American shipbuilders, among them Miami Shipbuilding and Huckins Yacht Company of Jacksonville.
14. Williamson, *Naval Air Station Jacksonville, 1940–2000*, 23.
15. Williamson, 24.
16. *Naval Station Mayport Base Guide*, 31–32.
17. Williamson, *Naval Air Station Jacksonville, 1940–2000*, 24.
18. McGovern, "Pensacola, Florida."
19. Mahan, *Mahan on Naval Warfare*, 29.
20. Roosevelt inspected NAS Pensacola August 8–9, 1938, after debarking from a tour of the Panama Canal Zone aboard USS *Houston* (CA 30). He took the salute of the new Pensacola aviation cadets at pass-in-review.
21. Cross, *Sailor in the White House*, 122.
22. Cross, 123.
23. Cross, 123.
24. Cross, 123.
25. Potter, *Bull Halsey*, 143.
26. H.R. 2880, 76th Congress. First Session.
27. Florida's third Medal of Honor recipient David McCampbell was among the instructors to pass through the base. Cmdr. McCampbell fought in the Pacific, and received the recognition on June 19, 1944, for thirty-four aircraft victories, a Navy record.
28. See table 2, Naval Training Stations in Florida During the War.
29. Arend, *Great Airports*, 88.
30. See "World War II Military Installations of Florida" on page 133.
31. Hoffman, *St. Petersburg Maritime Service Training Station*, 6.
32. Members of the US Maritime Service were awarded veteran status in 1988.
33. Koneazny, *Behind Friendly Lines*, 45.
34. Deese, *St. Petersburg, Florida*, 84.
35. Deese, 84.
36. Land, *The United States Merchant Marine at War*, 24.
37. See chapter 8.
38. Wynne and Barnes, "Still They Sail," 91.
39. Morison, *The Two-Ocean War*, 132.
40. Ogilvie and Miller, *Refuge Denied*, 24.
41. Ogilvie and Miller, 114.
42. While serving as the Army liaison to the CCC in the 1930s, Marshall became familiar with Florida while establishing CCC camps around the state. His enthusiastic support for the program brought him to the positive attention of the White House and the CCC creator, FDR.

43. Scarborough, "The Neutrality Patrol," 18–23.
44. Scarborough, 4.
45. Roth, "150 Years of Defense Activity at Key West," 48.
46. Cressman, *The Official Chronology of the US Navy in World War II*, 13–14.
47. Cressman, 14.
48. Gillis, *Fort Lauderdale, the Venice of America*, 52.
49. Burnett, *Florida's Past*, 188.
50. Cross, *Sailor in the White House*, 45. February 15–29, 1940, Roosevelt visited Pensacola again. He embarked in USS *Tuscaloosa* for a reinspection of the US Panama Canal Zone. Returning to Pensacola, Roosevelt addressed the crew. He warned them war in Europe could spread to the Americas, and the US military must prepare for war.
51. Morison, *The Two-Ocean War*, 30–31.
52. Library of Congress Veterans History Project. Oral History of Lt. Simon Bolivar Ruiz. Ruiz himself was severely wounded in the Vosges Mountains of France on Christmas Day, 1944.
53. Pepper with Gorey, *Pepper, Eyewitness to a Century*, 111.
54. "History of Conscription and the Selective Service System," 8.
55. "History of Conscription and the Selective Service System," 8.
56. *US Census of Florida 1940*, Table 8, Age, by Sex, for the State, 21.
57. Cross, *Sailor in the White House*, 135.
58. Sherwood, *Roosevelt and Hopkins*, 228.
59. Churchill, *Their Finest Hour*, 568.
60. En route FDR stopped his train at NAS Jacksonville for an inspection and briefing by the new base commander. To newspaper reporters present he declared himself "amazed" at the progress of the base.
61. Cross, *Sailor in the White House*, 137–38.
62. Sherwood, *Roosevelt and Hopkins*, 278.
63. Cressman, *The Official Chronology of the US Navy in World War II*. Those fifty-one seized German ships were transferred to the US Navy.
64. Vieques would serve as the main aerial and shipboard gunnery range for the Navy for the next sixty years.
65. Vaeth, *Blimps & U-boats*, 6–8.
66. "Miami Studied as Blimp Site," 1.
67. Van Treuren, *Airships vs. Submarines*, 206.
68. Shettle, *United States Naval Air Stations of World War II*, 233–34.

3. ARMY AIRFIELD FLORIDA

1. Matloff, *American Military History*, 430.
2. Lazarus, *Wings in the Sun*, 235. Joint Army-Navy boards met regularly to draw and redraw the map of Florida and the sectors of airspace over which each branch of service exercised cognizance for training activity.
3. Sandler, *Segregated Skies*, 9.
4. Sage-Gagne, *Pilots in the Sun*, 1–4.

5. Craft, *Embry-Riddle at War*.
6. Craft, 56–57.
7. Craft, 58.
8. Craft, 60.
9. Craft, 139.
10. Craft, 140.
11. Craft, 143.
12. Craft, 123.
13. Craft, 209.
14. Craft, 132.
15. Maurer, *Air Force Combat Units of World War II*, 9.
16. MacDill Base History Archive, MacDill Air Force Base Library. Tampa Tribune, October 24, 1939.
17. MacDill Base History Archive. Tampa Tribune, December 12, 1939.
18. Craven and Cate, *The Army Air Forces in World War II*, 5:128.
19. Matloff, *American Military History*, 428.
20. Maurer, *Air Force Combat Units of World War II*, 8.
21. Maurer, 81–82, 439, 459.
22. General Tinker gave his life at the Battle of Midway on June 7, 1942. The Osage warrior was killed in action while leading his bombers against the enemy fleet when his plane crashed at sea with all hands lost.
23. Williamson, *MacDill Air Force Base*, 44.
24. Maurer, *Air Force Combat Units of World War II*, 440.
25. Craven and Cate, *The Army Air Forces in World War II*, 1:309.
26. Shettle, *Florida's Army Airfields of World War II*, 10.
27. Gannon, *Florida: A Short History*, 104.
28. Florida posthumous fifth Medal of Honor recipient Thomas B. McGuire Jr. was among the pilots who trained there, and later taught there. Maj. McGuire was the second highest scoring US ace of the war, achieving thirty-eight victories in the Pacific before being killed in action over the Philippines on January 7, 1945.
29. Maurer, *Air Force Combat Units of World War II*, 440.
30. Maurer, 108–109.
31. See "World War II Military Installations of Florida" on page 133.
32. Hitler's decision to go east and invade his erstwhile ally the Soviet Union, rather than going west, may rank among the most fortuitous in US history.
33. Craven and Cate, *The Army Air Forces in World War II*, 1:315.
34. Craven and Cate, 1:316.
35. Craven and Cate, 1:318.
36. In the run-up to war, the occupations of Greenland by the US Army in April 1941 and of Iceland by the US Marines in July 1941 were in large part to secure airstrips to support the northern air route. In the aftermath of the war, President Truman offered to buy the strategic island of Greenland.
37. Craven and Cate, *The Army Air Forces in World War II*, 1:318.
38. Craven and Cate, 1:319.

39. See map of aviation routes in the South Atlantic on page 115.
40. Craven and Cate, *The Army Air Forces in World War II*, 1:320.
41. Craven and Cate, 1:320.
42. Craven and Cate, 1:326. The two aviators were Col. Caleb Haynes and Maj. Curtis LeMay. Major LeMay would go on to become chief of staff of the Air Force. Haynes was the grandson of Chang Bunker, one of the two conjoined Siamese twins, Eng and Chang, who settled in North Carolina after a show business career and sired large families. Caleb Haynes retired with the rank of major general. Another descendant of Chang Bunker is prominent Florida banking and political figure Adelaide "Alex" Sink. Sink was named the 2020 Citizen of the Year by the University of Florida Graham Center for Public Service.
43. Craft, *Embry-Riddle at War*, 69.
44. Craft, 69.
45. Craft, 71.
46. Glassman, "Keep 'em Flying."
47. Sage-Gagne, *Pilots in the Sun*, 30.
48. Sage-Gagne, 29.
49. As the war increased, hundreds of RAF and US pilot trainees were detailed to Cuba, where they were trained to fly by the Cuban Air Force.
50. Craft, *Embry-Riddle at War*, 71.
51. Freitus and Freitus, *Florida: The War Years, 1938–1945*.
52. General Blanding retired in 1940, but at the outbreak of war he was recalled by Governor Holland. Blanding served on active duty as the governor's aide-de-camp for the duration of the war.
53. Mormino, "World War II," 325.
54. *The Army Almanac*, 662.
55. Gannon, *Florida: A Short History*, 104.
56. Roosevelt, *Proclamation of Unlimited National Emergency*.
57. Roosevelt.
58. Roosevelt.
59. See "World War II Military Installations of Florida" on page 133.
60. Smith, *FDR*.
61. Morison, *The Two-Ocean War*, 67–68.

4. OFF WE GO!

1. Matloff, *American Military History*, 424–25.
2. Florida posthumous Medal of Honor recipient Alexander "Sandy" Nininger was killed in the fighting at Bataan on January 12, 1942. On February 5, 1942, the White House announced the award of the Medal of Honor to Nininger, the first Medal of Honor received in World War II. A monumental statue of Nininger stands today near the mouth of the New River in downtown Fort Lauderdale.
3. Brands, *Traitor to His Class*, 666.
4. Doolittle with Glines, *I Could Never Be So Lucky Again*, 231.
5. Doolittle with Glines, 243.

6. Lawson, *Thirty Seconds Over Tokyo*, 27.

7. Sims, *First Over Japan*, 16.

8. Lawson, *Thirty Seconds Over Tokyo*, 25.

9. Doolittle's navigator, Lt. James H. Macia, and six more of the Raider navigators received their training at the Pan American Airways school at the University of Miami. Box: Military Cooperation with Air Ferry Command. University of Miami archives. ASM0341 location 320-B-5–7.

10. Lawson, *Thirty Seconds Over Tokyo*, 29.

11. Salmaggi and Pallavisini, *2194 Days of War*, 234.

12. Morison, *The Two-Ocean War*, 139.

13. Brands, *Traitor to His Class*, 668. "Shangri-La" was a mythical land of mystery and enchantment in a popular fiction novel of the times, *Lost Horizon*. FDR's teasing joke about non-existent Shangri-La resonated with his radio audience, so much so that the navy commissioned one of its aircraft carriers coming off the 1944 assembly line the USS *Shangri-La*. Christened by General Doolittle's wife, Josephine, USS *Shangri-La* served in the later battles of Okinawa and the home islands.

14. Scott, *God Is My Co-Pilot*, 50.

15. Scott, 54.

16. Scott, 51.

17. Craven and Cate, *The Army Air Forces in World War II*, 7:404–5.

18. Scott, *God Is My Co-Pilot*, 65–67.

19. The Liberia Airport would remain under exclusive Pan American control for years after the war.

20. Craven and Cate, *The Army Air Forces in World War II*, 1:323–324.

21. Scott, *God Is My Co-Pilot*, 54.

22. Scott, 84.

23. General Stilwell was a native of Palatka, Florida.

24. Webster, *The Burma Road*, 39.

25. Scott, *God Is My Co-Pilot*, 105.

26. Craven and Cate, *The Army Air Forces in World War II*, 7:118. Unknown to Haynes, the fuel he transported over the Hump was for the Doolittle Raiders, expected to land in China after their mission of bombing Japan.

27. Craven and Cate, *The Army Air Forces in World War II*, 1:332.

28. Craven and Cate, 1:332.

29. Craven and Cate, 1:333.

30. At MacDill Field on February 10, 1942, training paused for a ceremony presenting the posthumous Medal of Honor of Sandy Nininger to his father, who had come to the base for the solemn occasion.

31. Craven and Cate, *The Army Air Forces in World War II*, 1:331.

32. Craven and Cate, 7:47.

33. Craven and Cate, 7:336.

34. Craven and Cate, 1:341.

35. Bomber Command simultaneously built another base across town: Buckingham Army Airfield.

36. Craven and Cate, *The Army Air Forces in World War II*, 1:342.

37. Maurer, *Air Force Combat Units of World War II*, 464–65. The American flyboys of the US Middle East Air Force staged out of RAF airfields at Ein Shemer, near Haifa, Ramat David, and Lod, adjacent Ben Gurion International Airport. Today these are major Israeli Air Force bases.

38. Craven and Cate, *The Army Air Forces in World War II*, 1:337.

39. Matloff, *American Military History*, 523.

40. Smith, *Camp Blanding*, 75–77.

41. Craven and Cate, *The Army Air Forces in World War II*, 1:60.

42. *Florida World War II Heritage Trail*, 10.

43. Jacqueline Cochran directed the WASP program, a consolidation of the Women's Flying Training Detachment (WFTD) and the Women's Auxiliary Flying Squadron (WAFS), which fielded women pilots flying in support of the Armed Forces. In 1977 its members were awarded veteran status by Congress.

44. Gaddis, *The Cold War*, 8.

45. Leland and Oboroceanu, *American War and Military Operations Casualties*, 2, table 1.

46. Leland and Oboroceanu, 2, table 1.

47. Leland and Oboroceanu, 2, table 1.

48. In 1987 the Maritime Service was awarded veteran status by act of Congress.

49. Leland and Oboroceanu, *American War and Military Operations Casualties*, 2, table 1.

50. There is no tabulation of those injured outside of combat theaters, except injuries resulting in death.

51. Brady, John T., "Mother Learns Long-Lost Son Died Great Hero for Country He Loved," *Boston Post*, February 7, 1942.

52. A few officers of the Philippine Scouts were Filipino graduates of West Point commissioned into the US Army.

53. The wording of the US military oath of allegiance to support and defend the Constitution of the United States has remained essentially the same since 1789.

54. Service Records of Dorothy Evelyn Blackwelder. Enlistment papers. NARA.

55. Blackwelder. *New York Times*, December 17, 1943. 1.

56. Service Records of Blackwelder. Death report. NARA.

57. Service Records of Blackwelder. Record of funeral. NARA.

58. Craven and Cate, *The Army Air Forces in World War II*, 7:49.

59. Craven and Cate, 7:46.

60. Craven and Cate, 1:319.

61. Cross, *Sailor in the White House*, 158–60.

62. The presidential train car *Ferdinand Magellan* is today a National Historic Landmark. It was always accompanied by the Army Signal Corps communications car *General Myer*, giving the president worldwide communications in real time whenever he was aboard.

63. Since Roosevelt could not swim, travel over water had to be of necessity by seaplane.

64. Spam was so much a staple of the soldiers' diet, they sometimes christened their field kitchens "Spamville." Resourceful GIs soon applied the handy lunch meat to such other military uses as lubricating their weapons and waterproofing their boots.

65. Despite being a world public figure, only a handful of photographs exist of Roosevelt

using a wheelchair, crutches, or braces. He was adamant to never be shown in any weakened physical condition.

66. Tibbets, *Return of the Enola Gay*, 71.
67. Maurer, *Air Force Combat Units of World War II*, 167.

5. ANCHORS AWEIGH

1. Gannon, *Operation Drumbeat*, 80–82.
2. Morison, *The Two-Ocean War*, 110.
3. Morison, 115.
4. Doenitz, *Memoirs: Ten Years and Twenty Days*.
5. See table 3.
6. Mahan, *Mahan on Naval Warfare*, 69.
7. Specifically, they are the Great Bahama Bank, the Little Bahama Bank, and the Cay Sal Bank.
8. The banks extend almost to Cuba, confining shipping along its north coast to the Old Bahama Channel.
9. Mahan, *Mahan on Naval Warfare*, 29–30.
10. Gannon, *Operation Drumbeat*, 347. Mexico was forced to declare war on Germany after its own ships were sunk.
11. With similar features and the farthest distance from the attackers, the western coast of the Gulf and the Bay of Campeche also saw fewer sinkings—six altogether. In the middle of the Gulf there were also only six lost, reflecting the difficulty of finding individual vessels on the open seas, specks on a sheet of deep water. Four outlying merchant ships were lost east of the Bahamas, sunk by U-boats coming and going from the battlefield by the Bahama channels.
12. Hoyt, *U-boats Offshore: When Hitler Struck America*, 18, 37, 132.
13. Scott, *God Is My Co-Pilot*, 54. One aspect of the battle seldom considered was the ecological damage caused by the sinking by torpedoes of thirty-five oil tankers, along with battle damage to several more, releasing their crude oil cargoes into the open seas. Aviators on patrol, as well as the civilians of the realm, routinely observed the coastline fouled with gooey tar-like oil slicks washed ashore. The devastation to marine life and habitat must have been catastrophic.
14. Morison, *The Two-Ocean War*, 115–17.
15. Morison, 109.
16. Morison, 116.
17. Morison, 136.
18. *The Miami Herald*, May 1942. The *Potrero del Llano* was steaming under the neutral flag of Mexico. Later it was learned that the U-564 misidentified it as the flag of Italy, and knowing no ships of that Axis power could be in these waters, torpedoed it as an enemy flying false colors.
19. Wiggins, *Florida and World War II*, 99–100.
20. Tebeau, *A History of Florida*, 420.
21. Tebeau, 420.
22. Wiggins, *Florida and World War II*, 99.

23. Statement by the White House concerning the sentences of eight Nazi saboteurs, issued August 8, 1942.
24. Noble, "The Beach Patrol and Corsair Fleet," 4.
25. Noble, 16.
26. Noble, 14.
27. Wright, *It Happened in Florida*, 56.
28. Three of these lookout towers remain today, in Stuart, Melbourne, and Ormond-by-the-Sea. The restored tower in Ormond Beach stands at 2160 Ocean Shore Blvd, Florida.
29. Lazarus, *Wings in the Sun*, 240.
30. Lazarus, 246–47.
31. Morison, *The Two-Ocean War*, 118.
32. Morison, 129.
33. As the defense of the Gulf Sea Frontier became stronger, the U-boats shifted their attacks south into the Caribbean and South America. Airship units patrolled the South Atlantic as far as Santa Cruz, Brazil. NAS Richmond, Florida, was their stateside headquarters for military supply, maintenance, and personnel concerns.
34. One doughty airship squadron deployed across the Atlantic and served first as antisubmarine patrol over the Straits of Gibraltar, then in support of the US invasions of Italy and France.
35. Mahan, *Mahan on Naval Warfare*, 131.
36. Mahan, 131.
37. Morison, *The Two-Ocean War*, 131.
38. Morison, 132.
39. Treadwell, *Splinter Fleet*, 19.
40. Treadwell, 116. Two serious complications during the battle were posed by Vichy-French Martinique. Martinique collaborated with German U-boats, providing them aid and comfort, fuel, and safe haven. Still graver was the military threat posed by the French Navy aircraft carrier and its escorts there. Had Vichy declared war the French squadron was quite capable to sortie forth and bomb and shell the Panama Canal, Tampa, Miami, Jacksonville, or even New York City. Knowing the US would ultimately invade France, and unwilling to antagonize the French military, the US maintained a studied neutrality toward Martinique until July 1943. At that time a US airborne invasion to neutralize the island was canceled at the last minute when the Vichy authorities on the island signaled their willingness to capitulate.
41. John F. Kennedy was an instructor of PT boat training there for six weeks while on temporary assignment awaiting back surgery for wounds received in the Solomon Islands. He was billeted at the toney Bath Club.
42. Noble, "The Beach Patrol and Corsair Fleet," 3.
43. Purdon, *Black Company*, 34.
44. Stafford, *Subchaser*, 8.
45. Rice, "The Submarine Chaser Training Center," 43.
46. Ogle, *Key West*, 199.
47. Wynn, *U-boat Operations of the Second World War*, 121.
48. Losses compiled from Wynn, *U-boat Operations of the Second World War*, 339–50; and *Florida World War II Heritage Trail*, 61–65.

49. Morison, *History of US Naval Operations in World War II*, 2:194.
50. Atwood, "An Incident at Sea," 57.

6. FLORIDA MILITARY ACADEMY COURSES

1. Smith, *Camp Blanding*, 56.
2. Taylor, *World War II in Fort Pierce*, 37.
3. US Army Ground Forces fielded ninety divisions during the war.
4. Matloff, *American Military History*, 461.
5. Matloff, 416.
6. Matloff, 426.
7. Matloff, 461.
8. Like the Roman two-legion camps of antiquity, Camp Blanding's hundred-seventy-thousand-acre size was large enough to accommodate two divisions at one time, allowing the soldiers to stage gigantic mock-battles against each other. One such contest pitted the Dixie Division of the Deep South against the 43rd National Guard Division of New England.
9. *The Army Almanac*, 687.
10. Mormino, "World War II," 324.
11. Leland and Oboroceanu, *American War and Military Operations Casualties*, 3–4.
12. Becker, "The Amphibious Training Center," 1.
13. Coles, "'Hell-By-The-Sea,'" 7.
14. Becker, "The Amphibious Training Center," 12.
15. Becker, 15.
16. Coles, "'Hell-By-The-Sea,'" 7.
17. Coles, 2.
18. Coles, 55.
19. Becker, "The Amphibious Training Center," 23.
20. Becker, 56.
21. Becker, 12.
22. Smith, *Amphibian*, 4.
23. Smith, 4.
24. Smith, 5.
25. Smith, 5.
26. Bradley and Blair, *A General's Life*, 112.
27. Bradley and Blair, 57.
28. Florida's second Medal of Honor recipient James Henry Mills fought in Italy. Pvt. Mills, US Army, received the medal for conspicuous gallantry and intrepidity at Cisterna di Littoria, Italy, on May 24, 1944. On Nov. 9, 1973, outside Gainesville, a terrible crime occurred when Mills and a friend stopped to help an apparently broken-down vehicle. It was a trap by three criminals. Mills and his friend were severely beaten, run over, and left for dead. Mills passed away on Veterans Day 1973. The hero is buried in Lakeland.
29. Becker, "The Amphibious Training Center," 58.
30. Becker, 58.

31. Becker, 59.
32. Becker, 60.
33. Becker, 8.
34. Becker, 59.
35. Becker, 60.
36. *The Army Almanac*, 653.
37. Babcock, *War Stories*, 29.
38. *The Army Almanac*, 653.
39. Matloff, *American Military History*, 541.
40. Koneazny, *Behind Friendly Lines*, 42.
41. Koneazny, 56.
42. Koneazny, 60.
43. Koneazny, 60.
44. Koneazny, 63–66.
45. Taylor, *World War II in Fort Pierce*, 8.
46. Taylor, 8.
47. Rottman, *US Special Warfare Units in the Pacific Theater, 1941–1945*, 38.
48. Taylor, *World War II in Fort Pierce*, 37.
49. Taylor, 46.
50. Pushies, *Weapons of the Navy SEALS*, 12.
51. Pushies, 12.
52. Pushies, 12.
53. Pushies, 12.
54. Rottman, *US Special Warfare Units in the Pacific Theater, 1941–1945*, 38.
55. Taylor, *World War II in Fort Pierce*, 46.
56. Blackwell, "Report on Navy Combat Demolition Units in Operation Neptune," 1.
57. Blackwell, 3.
58. Blackwell, 4.
59. The popular war movie *Saving Private Ryan* depicted a small group of soldiers engaged in the D-day invasion. The captain in charge (played by Tom Hanks) and his team are accurately depicted by their uniform patches as members of the 2nd Rangers. Their soldier-interpreter companion wears the 29th Division insignia.
60. *The Army Almanac*, 652, 653, 661.
61. Taylor, "The Frogmen of Florida," 91.
62. Taylor, 289–90.
63. Taylor, 294.
64. These warfare units evolved into the Navy SEAL (Sea, Air, Land) teams of today.
65. Taylor, *World War II in Fort Pierce*, 64.
66. General Eisenhower once enumerated the four tools with which the GIs won their war. In his expert opinion these were the Willys Jeep, the Norden bombsight, the M1 Garand rifle, and the Higgins boat.
67. Wynne and Moorhead, *Florida in World War II*, 213.
68. A few of these storied vehicles are in use today around the world as amphibious tour buses.

69. Wynne and Moorhead, *Florida in World War II*, 214.
70. Taylor, *World War II in Fort Pierce*, 82–83.
71. Taylor, 127.
72. Callwell, *Military Operations and Maritime Preponderance*, 360.

7. BOMBS AWAY AND OVER THE HUMP

1. Arnold, "Report of the Commanding General of the Army Air Forces to the Secretary of War," 303.
2. Maurer, *Air Force Combat Units of World War II*, 439.
3. Maurer, 70.
4. Wynne and Moorhead, *Florida in World War II*, 82.
5. MacDill Base History Archive, MacDill Air Force Base Library.
6. MacDill Base History Archive, MacDill Air Force Base Library.
7. Doolittle with Glines, *I Could Never Be So Lucky Again*, 254.
8. Doolittle with Glines, 255.
9. Maurer, *Air Force Combat Units of World War II*, 200.
10. Smith, *The Mighty Eighth in the Second World War*, 288–91.
11. Army Command and General Staff College (ACGSC), MLHIC Series.
12. Wiggins, *Florida and World War II*, 42.
13. Wiggins, 42.
14. Lazarus, *Wings in the Sun*, 231.
15. Mitchell, *Our Air Force*, 112.
16. Mitchell, 110.
17. Mitchell, 111.
18. Denfield, "Camp Miami," 72.
19. Tebeau, *A History of Florida*, 417.
20. The War Department appreciated the savings in time and money in the arrangement and duplicated such arrangements at St. Petersburg, Clearwater, Daytona Beach, and Palm Beach, taking over entire blocks of hotels there to serve as troop accommodations.
21. Denfield, "Camp Miami," 78.
22. Florida's fourth Medal of Honor (posthumous) recipient Robert Edward Femoyer trained at Miami Beach. Femoyer served as a navigator with the Eighth Air Force. On November 2, 1944, on a bombing mission over Germany, 2d Lt. Femoyer was mortally wounded when his B-17 sustained heavy battle damage. He remained at his battle station and was instrumental in navigating the successful return of the damaged aircraft, dying minutes after it landed.
23. Tebeau, *A History of Florida*, 417.
24. Denfield, "Camp Miami," 76.
25. LaRoue and Uguccioni, "World War II and Beyond," 14.
26. Denfield, "Camp Miami," 77.
27. Upon being commissioned in the Air Corps Gable went to Flexible Gunnery School at Tyndall Army Airfield in North Florida. Posted overseas as an aerial gunner, he served in several combat missions over Germany. His bomber came under fire from flak and enemy

fighters, suffering battle damage and crewmembers killed and wounded. Flak shards just missed Gable's head.

28. Denfield, "Camp Miami," 77.

29. Sandler, *Segregated Skies*, 32–33.

30. Sandler, 77–78.

31. The US military was not integrated during the war. The Army fielded two segregated infantry divisions composed entirely of Black soldiers, the 92nd Division in Italy and 93rd Division in New Guinea. The rest of the Black troops in the Army were assigned to Army Service Forces, or segregated Air Corps units.

32. Craven and Cate, *The Army Air Forces in World War II*, 7:59.

33. Craven and Cate, 7:49. The two airfields were separated only by the railroad tracks and swale.

34. The Defense Reorganization Act of 1947–48 awarded veteran status and GI Bill eligibility to all personnel of those civilian airlines who had worked with Army Transport Command during the war.

35. Tebeau, *A History of Florida*, 420–22.

36. Tebeau, 421.

37. Craven and Cate, *The Army Air Forces in World War II*, 7:47.

38. Craven and Cate, 7:331.

39. Sherry, *China Defensive*, 26.

40. Matloff, *American Military History*, 464.

41. Spector, *Eagle Against the Sun*, 338.

42. Spector, 339.

43. Craven and Cate, *The Army Air Forces in World War II*, 7:42.

44. *Florida World War II Heritage Trail*, 45.

45. Craven and Cate, *The Army Air Forces in World War II*, 7:43.

46. Craven and Cate, 7:44.

47. Craven and Cate, 7:115. Over 1,659 US pilots and crewmen were accounted for as killed or remain missing, lost while flying the Hump.

48. *Florida World War II Heritage Trail*, 45. The China-Burma-India Theater Air Transport Command was the first noncombat unit ever awarded the Presidential Unit Citation, at the personal direction of President Roosevelt in 1944.

49. Craven and Cate, *The Army Air Forces in World War II*, 2:266.

50. Coffey, *Hap*, 304.

51. Coffey, 305.

52. Coffey, 306.

53. Coffey, 307.

54. Coffey, 308.

55. Caron and Meares, *Fire of a Thousand Suns*, 99.

56. Caron and Meares, 115.

57. Tibbets, *Return of the Enola Gay*, 153. Two of the test pilots were female WASPs: Dora Dougherty and Didi Moorman.

58. Craven and Cate, *The Army Air Forces in World War II*, 6:54–55.

59. Craven and Cate, 5:518.

8. WOMEN, WORK, CAPTIVES, AND WOUNDED

1. Matloff, *American Military History*, 430.
2. Wynne and Moorhead, *Florida in World War II*, 51.
3. Wynne and Barnes, "Still They Sail," 92.
4. Wynne and Moorhead, *Florida in World War II*, 49.
5. Wynne and Moorhead, 50.
6. Pelt, "The Liberty Ship," 120.
7. Morison, *The Two-Ocean War*, 133.
8. Pelt, "The Liberty Ship," 120. With wartime shipbuilding advances, the Liberty ships were augmented by a newer Victory ship class that was larger, faster, and better armed. Built primarily on the West Coast, over 500 Victory ships went to sea, some remaining in service through the Vietnam War. Today, the SS *American Victory* serves as a floating museum at the Port of Tampa Bay.
9. Wynne and Moorhead, *Florida in World War II*, 49.
10. Sawyer and Mitchell, *The Liberty Ships*, 142–148.
11. Tim Colton. http://www.ShipBuildingHistory.com. Accessed Nov. 10, 2021.
12. Wynne and Moorhead, *Florida in World War II*, 49–50.
13. Mormino, "World War II," 328.
14. Pelt, "Wainwright Shipyard," 4–5.
15. Cvitovich, *Images of America*, 103.
16. Mitchell and Sawyer, *The Liberty Ships*, 83–86.
17. Pelt, "The Liberty Ship," 122.
18. Wynne and Moorhead, *Florida in World War II*, 51.
19. Colton. http://www.ShipBuildingHistory.com. Accessed Nov. 10, 2021.
20. Wiggins, *Florida and World War II*, 116.
21. Wynne and Moorhead, *Florida in World War II*, 50.
22. Wynne and Moorhead, 49.
23. Mormino, *Hillsborough County Goes to War*, 52.
24. Mormino, 53–54.
25. Morison, *The Two-Ocean War*, 407.
26. Mormino, *Hillsborough County Goes to War*, 54.
27. Wynne, "Still They Sail," 94.
28. Mormino, "World War II," 338.
29. Pelt, "The Liberty Ship," 133.
30. Pelt, "The Liberty Ship," 137.
31. Compiled from Sawyer and Mitchell, *The Liberty Ships*, 83–86, 142–48, 184–85.
32. Compiled from Sawyer and Michell, Wynne and Moorhead, Mormino, and Colton.
33. Mormino, "World War II," 329.
34. Billinger, "With the Wehrmacht in Florida." A total of 435,788 captured enemy soldiers, mostly German, were interned in CONUS during the war.
35. Billinger, *Hitler's Soldiers*, 8.
36. Billinger, 10.
37. Billinger, xv.

38. Tebeau, *A History of Florida*, 418.
39. Mormino, "World War II," 326.
40. Billinger, *Hitler's Soldiers*, 32.
41. Billinger, 33. The ultramodern Dadeland Shopping Center in Miami stands on the site of this prisoner-of-war camp.
42. Wiggins, *Florida and World War II*, 103.
43. Billinger, *Hitler's Soldiers*, 71.
44. Billinger, 77–80.
45. Billinger, "The Other Side Now."
46. Billinger.
47. Matloff, *American Military History*, 462.
48. Matloff, 464.
49. *Selective Service and Victory*, 187–88.
50. *Selective Service and Victory*, 188.
51. Gannon, *Operation Drumbeat*, 335.
52. Mormino, "GI Joe Meets Jim Crow," 26.
53. Mormino, "World War II," 336.
54. Mormino, 336.
55. Mormino, 335.
56. Becker, "The Amphibious Training Center," 58.
57. Evans, "The Origins of Tallahassee's Racial Disturbance Plan," 351.
58. Mormino, "GI Joe Meets Jim Crow," 26.
59. Mormino, 27.
60. Mormino, 29.
61. Mormino, 30.
62. *US Census of Florida 1940*, Table C-35, Age, by Race and Sex, for the City of Tampa, 150.
63. Tilley, "A History of Women in the Coast Guard," 3.
64. Tilley, 3.
65. Treadwell, *The Women's Army Corps*, 55.
66. Treadwell, 16.
67. Morden, *The Women's Army Corps, 1945–1978*.
68. Bethune, *Mary McLeod Bethune*, 173.
69. Putney, *When the Nation Was in Need*, 32.
70. Putney, viii.
71. Brands, *Traitor to His Class*, 516.
72. Treadwell, *The Women's Army Corps*, 192.
73. Treadwell, 193.
74. Treadwell, 210.
75. Treadwell, 209.
76. Congressional Research Service. Table 1. 4.
77. There is no tabulation of those injured outside of combat theaters, except where the result was in death.
78. Wiltse, *US Army in World War II*, 141.
79. *Army Service Forces Statistical Review*, 69.

80. *Army Service Forces Statistical Review*, 250.
81. Wiltse, *US Army in World War II*, 50.
82. Wiltse, 139.
83. LaRoue and Uguccioni, *The Biltmore Hotel*, 88.
84. Smith, *The Medical Department: Hospitalization and Evacuation, Zone of Interior*, 341.
85. Military hospital beds containing a patient were termed "effective."
86. Wiltse, *US Army in World War II*, 189.
87. In anticipation of this invasion the War Department had placed an order for another seven hundred thousand Purple Heart medals, the serious military decoration for those killed or wounded in battle.

9. A SUDDEN END TO WAR

1. Mormino, "World War II," 328.
2. Newspapers early in the war confined reporting to articles and photo essays of human interest and local color about soldier life, bases springing up, sports and war bond contests, USO dances, and morale boosting, such as:
Miami Daily News, June 7, 1942, "Navy Speeds Blimp Base." George Goodwin.
Miami Herald, April 11, 1943, "Metamorphosis of Miami." Sigrid Arne.
Miami Daily News, Sept. 24, 1944, "Homestead Air Base: West Point of the ATC." Milt Solen.
Censorship and the reality of combat close to home influenced what coverage there was. Radio was dominated by military control. Television did not exist. As the war was winding down was there more factual reporting, such as:
Miami Daily News, May 8, 1945, "Torpedoed Ships Sank on Our Doorstep." Art Robinson.
Miami Daily News, June 3, 1945, "Blimps Made War History." Jess Houseman.
Miami Herald, December 30, 1945, "Nazi Attack Hit Florida Travel." Thomas W. Hagen.
3. Matloff, *American Military History*, 526.
4. Doughty and Gruber, *American Military History*, 570.
5. Among the Americans killed on Iwo Jima was Platoon Sgt. Ernest Ivy Thomas Jr. of Tampa. Thomas went by the nickname "Boots" and was among the Marines who raised the initial US flag over Mount Suribachi. (A larger, more widely publicized second flag-raising was later the same day.) Boots Thomas was killed in action eight days later.
6. Florida's sixth World War II Medal of Honor recipient Pvt. Robert M. McTureous Jr., USMC, was among the fallen at Okinawa, June 7, 1945. McTureous was posthumously awarded the medal "for conspicuous gallantry and intrepidity at the risk of his life above and beyond the call of duty" during the battle there.
7. Doughty and Gruber, *American Military History*, 570.
8. Spector, *Eagle Against the Sun*, 544.
9. Craven and Cate, *The Army Air Forces in World War II*, 7:215.
10. Craven and Cate, 7:217.
11. Craven and Cate, 7:558.
12. The apartment house in Miami where Tibbets grew up still stands in the neighborhood there.

13. Matloff, *American Military History*, 526.

14. *The Miami Herald*, June 4, 2009, 1. Albury returned to Florida and flew for many years for Eastern Airlines in relative anonymity.

15. The ceremony was delayed by Gen. MacArthur until the arrival of US Gen. Wainwright and British Gen. Percival, who had recently been freed from POW camps. They stood among the victorious witnesses at the surrender on USS *Missouri*.

16. There is some confusion over which date is V-J Day. One may consider any of three dates as V-J Day. August 14, 1945, was the day the Japanese government signaled to the US its intent to surrender. August 15, 1945, was when news of this was announced to the world. President Truman declared September 2, 1945, the date of the surrender aboard the USS *Missouri*, as V-J Day.

17. General Wainwright's wife, Adele, spent much of the war in a secluded home on Miami Beach.

18. *US Census of Florida 1950*, Table 1, Population of Florida, Urban and Rural: 18 to 1850, 10–16.

19. Tebeau, *A History of Florida*, 417.

20. It should be understood this does not mean actually residing within municipal boundaries. The 1940 Census counted urban residence as within a few hours travel proximity to the urban core.

21. *US Census of Florida 1950*, Table 2, Population in Groups of Places According to Size: 1950, 10–16.

22. *US Census of Florida 1950*, Table 3, Population in Groups of Places According to Size: 1900 to 1950, 10–17.

23. *US Census of Florida 1950*, Table 9, Population of Urbanized Areas: 1950, 10–16.

24. *US Census of Florida 1950*, Table 9, Population of Urbanized Areas: 1950, 10–16.

25. *US Census of Florida 1950*, Table 5, Area and Population of Counties, Urban and Rural: 19 to 1950, 10–19.

26. *US Census of Florida 1950*, Table 5, Area and Population of Counties, Urban and Rural: 19 to 1950, 10–19.

27. *US Census of Florida 1950*, Table 4, Population of Urban Places of 10,000 or More from Earliest Census to 1950, 10–18.

28. *US Census of Florida 1950*, Table 4, Population of Urban Places of 10,000 or More from Earliest Census to 1950, 10–18.

29. Ogle, *Key West*, 198–99.

30. *US Census of Florida 1950*, Table 13, Color by Sex, for the State, Urban and Rural, 19 to 1950, 10–31.

31. *US Census of Florida 1950*, Table 16, Age by Color and Sex for the State: 1880 to 1950, 10–35.

32. *US Census of Florida 1950*, Table 17, Citizenship and Nativity of the Population 21 Years of Age and Over, for the State, 10–37.

33. *US Census of Florida 1950*, Table 21, Marital Status by Color, for the State, Urban and Rural, 1950, and for the State, 1940, 10–38.

34. *US Census of Florida 1950*, Table 21, Marital Status by Color, for the State, Urban and Rural, 1950, and for the State, 1940, 10–38.

35. *US Census of Florida 1950*, Table 15, Age by Color and Sex, for the State, Urban and Rural: 1950 and 1940, 10–34.

36. *US Census of Florida 1950*, Table 15, Age by Color and Sex, for the State, Urban and Rural: 1950 and 1940, 10–32.

37. "Sergeant Rates Miami No. 1 Town," *Miami Herald*, June 7, 1945.

38. Tebeau, *A History of Florida*, 419.

39. Tebeau, 414.

40. Mohl and Mormino, "The Big Change in the Sunshine State," 437.

41. *US Census of Florida 1950*, Table 26, Labor Force, 1950 and 1940, and Gainful Workers, by Color and Sex, for the State, 10–41.

42. *US Census of Florida 1950*, Table 27, Employment Status by Color and Sex, for the State: 1950 and 1950, 10–41.

43. *US Census of Florida 1950*, Table 29, Class of Worker and Major Occupation Group of Employed Persons, by Sex, for the State: 1950 and 1940, 10–44.

44. *US Census of Florida 1950*, Table 29, Class of Worker and Major Occupation Group of Employed Persons, by Sex, for the State: 1950 and 1940, 10–44.

45. Some functioned as dual civilian/military airports throughout the Cold War.

46. Fleet Airship Wing Two War Diary. 16–24 March, 23–24 May 1945.

47. Navy Airship Squadron ZP-21 War Diary. July 1945.

48. Lipartito and Butler, *A History of the Kennedy Space Center*, 34.

49. Lipartito and Butler, 47.

50. Lipartito and Butler, 37.

51. Mormino, "World War II," 340. Only State Senator Charley Eugene Johns, named acting governor when McCarty died in office, was not a veteran. At that time the state had no lieutenant governorship and Senate President Johns filled the position unelected per Florida's constitution for fifteen months. Running for the office in 1955, he was defeated by Navy veteran LeRoy Collins, who won handily by 66,125 votes.

52. Tebeau, *A History of Florida*, 440.

53. The Greater Miami area acquired the nickname "The Sixth Borough," in reference to its specific connection with the northern metropolis of New York.

54. MacGregor, *Integration of the Armed Forces*, 291.

55. GIs returning stateside on terminal leave at the end of their enlistment continued to be sent to the Miami Beach "R&R" centers throughout 1946.

56. The four sons of President Roosevelt all served in the US military during World War II. Col. Franklin Roosevelt, USMC, was nearly killed during a raid on Makin Island, an obscure atoll in the Pacific.

57. Arnold, "Report of the Commanding General of the Army Air Forces," 220.

58. In 1947 British war leader Winston Churchill predicted the Cold War with the observation that "an Iron Curtain is descending over Europe."

59. The only crewman aboard both atomic missions, Radar Countermeasures Officer, 1st Lt. Jacob Beser, was trained at Boca Raton Army Radar School.

60. Morison, *The Two-Ocean War*, 139.

61. Attributed to Wellington.

62. See chapter 6.

63. The Hawaiian Islands replicate many of the same tactical advantages. But practicing to invade Europe from Hawaii required monumental logistics across twenty-five hundred miles of the ocean, rather than the easy access afforded by the rail system linking Florida with the rest of the East Coast. Above all, training in Hawaii confounded a grand strategy of Europe First.

64. An application of the "hidden hand of the marketplace" driving the military-industrial complex in this situation of total war may be the fact that every ship sunk off Florida equated to the laying of a new keel.

65. Loaded troop ships never transited Florida's risky sea passages, but always launched from the East Coast and West Coast ports of embarkation straight onto the comparative safety of the open seas.

66. *Florida World War II Heritage Trail*, 3.

67. NARA. Vietnam War US Military Fatal Casualty Statistics.

BIBLIOGRAPHY

PRIMARY SOURCES

Becker, Col. Marshall O. "The Amphibious Training Center: Study Number 22." In *Army Ground Forces*. US Army, 1946.

Blackwell, LTJG H. L., Jr., USNR. "Report on Navy Combat Demolition Units in Operation 'Neptune.'" Department of the Navy. July 5, 1944.

Selective Service and Victory: The 4th Report of the Director of Selective Service. US Government Printing Office, 1948.

Seventeenth Census of the United States. Volume II. Characteristics of the Population. Part 10: Florida.

Sixteenth Census of the United States. Volume II. Characteristics of the Population. Part 2: Florida-Iowa.

General Doolittle's Report, April 18, 1942. War Department, Washington, June 5, 1942.

Halsey-Doolittle Raid, April 1942, War Department, Headquarters of the Army Air Forces, Washington, July 9, 1942.

War Diary: Fleet Airship Wing Two. 16–24 March, 23–24 May 1945. NARA.

War Diary: Gulf Sea Frontier. September 1945. NARA.

War Diary: Navy Airship Squadron ZP-21. July 1945. NARA.

SECONDARY SOURCES

Allen, Thomas B., and Norman Polmar. *Code-Name Downfall: The Secret Plan to Invade Japan—And Why Truman Dropped the Bomb*. Simon & Schuster, 1995.

Arend, Geoffrey. *Great Airports: Miami; A Picture History*. Air Cargo News, 1986.

Army Service Forces Statistical Review: December 1941–August 1945. War Department, US Government Printing Office, 1946.

Arnold, H. H. "Report of the Commanding General of the Army Air Forces to the Secretary of War." In *The War Reports of General George C. Marshall, General H. H. Arnold, Fleet Admiral Ernest J. King*. Lippincott, 1947.

Atwood, Anthony D. "An Incident at Sea: The Historic Combat between U.S. Navy Blimp K-74 and U-Boat 134." Thesis, Florida International University, 2003.

Babcock, Robert O. *War Stories: Utah Beach to Pleiku*. St. John's Press, 2001.

Bellafaire, Col. Judith A. *The Women's Army Corps: A Commemoration of World War II Service*. Center of Military History, US Army. US Government Printing Office, 1995.

Bethune, Mary McLeod. *Mary McLeod Bethune: Building a Better World, Essays and Selected*

Documents, edited by Audrey Thomas McCluskey and Elaine M. Smith. Indiana University Press, 1999.

Billinger, Robert, Jr. *Hitler's Soldiers in the Sunshine State: German POWs in Florida*. University Press of Florida, 2000.

Billinger, Robert, Jr. "The Other Side Now: What Blanding Prisoners of War Told the Wehrmacht." *Florida Historical Quarterly* 73, no. 1 (1994).

Billinger, Robert, Jr. "With the Wehrmacht in Florida: The German POW Facility at Camp Blanding, 1942–1946." *Florida Historical Quarterly* 58, no. 2 (1979).

Bradley, Omar N., and Clay Blair, *A General's Life*. Simon & Shuster, 1983.

Brands, H. W. *Traitor to His Class: The Privileged Life and Radical Presidency of Franklin Delano Roosevelt*. Doubleday, 2008.

Burnett, Gene M. *Florida's Past: People and Events That Shaped the State*. Vol. 2. Pineapple Press, 1997.

Callwell, C. E. *Military Operations and Maritime Preponderance: Their Relations and Interdependence*. William Blackwood and Sons, 1905.

Caron, George R., and Charlotte E. Meares, *Fire of a Thousand Suns: The George R. "Bob" Caron Story, Tail Gunner of the Enola Gay*. Web Publishing Company, 1995.

Chang, Iris. *The Rape of Nanking: The Forgotten Holocaust of World War II*. Putnam, 1997.

Churchill, Winston. *Their Finest Hour*. Houghton Mifflin, 1949.

Coffey, Thomas M. *Hap: The Story of the US Air Force and the Man Who Built It, General Henry H. "Hap" Arnold*. Viking Press, 1982.

Colburn, David R. "Florida Politics in the Twentieth Century." In *The New History of Florida*, edited by Michael Gannon. University Press of Florida, 2012.

Coles, David J. "'Hell-By-The-Sea': Florida's Camp Gordon Johnston in World War II." *Florida Historical Quarterly* 73, no. 1 (1994).

Corbett, Julian S. *Some Principles of Maritime Strategy*. Longmans, Green & Co., 1911.

Craft, Stephen G. *Embry-Riddle at War: Aviation Training During World War II*. University Press of Florida, 2009.

Craven, W. F., and J. L. Cate. *The Army Air Forces in World War II*. 7 vols. Office of Air Force History, 1948–1952.

Cressman, Robert J. *The Official Chronology of the US Navy in World War II*. Naval Institute Press, 1999.

Cross, Robert F. *Sailor in the White House: The Seafaring Life of FDR*. Naval Institute Press, 2003.

Cvitkovich, Eileen. *Images of America: Bay County*. Arcadia Publishing, 2000.

Deese, A. Wynelle. *St. Petersburg, Florida: A Visual History*. The History Press, 2006.

Denfeld, D. Colt. "Camp Miami: The Palm Playground Turns Serious During World War II." *Journal of America's Military Past* 33, no. 2 (2007).

Department of the Army. *The Army Almanac: A Book of Facts Concerning the United States Army*. The Military Service Publishing Company, 1959.

Doenitz, Karl. *Memoirs: Ten Years and Twenty Days*. Da Capo Press, 1959.

Doolittle, General James H. "Jimmy," with Carroll V. Glines. *I Could Never Be So Lucky Again*. Bantam, 1991.

Doughty, Robert A., and Ira D. Gruber. *American Military History and the Evolution of Warfare in the Western World.* D.C. Heath and Company, 1996.

Evans, Jon. "The Origins of Tallahassee's Racial Disturbance Plan: Segregation, Racial Tensions, and Violence During World War II." *Florida Historical Quarterly* 79, no. 3, (2001).

Florida World War II Heritage Trail. Florida Department of State, Division of Historical Resources, 2004.

Freitus, Joseph, and Anne Freitus. *Florida: The War Years, 1938–1945.* Wind Canyon, 1998.

Gaddis, John Lewis. *The Cold War : A New History.* Penguin Books, 2005.

Gannon, Michael. *Florida: A Short History.* University Press of Florida, 1993.

Gannon, Michael. *Michael Gannon's History of Florida in Forty Minutes.* University Press of Florida, 2007.

Gannon, Michael. *Operation Drumbeat: The Dramatic True Story of Germany's First U-boat Attacks Along the American Coast in World War II.* Harper & Row, 1990.

Gillis, Susan. *Fort Lauderdale: The Venice of America.* Arcadia Publishing, 2004.

Glassman, Steve. "Keep 'em Flying: Riddle's Wild Blue Yonder." *South Florida History Magazine,* Summer 1989.

Selective Service System, "History of Conscription and the Selective Service System." US Government Printing Office, 2003.

Hoffman, Michelle L. *St. Petersburg Maritime Service Training Station.* Arcadia Publishing, 2006.

Homan, Lynn M., and Thomas Reilly. *Wings over Florida.* Arcadia Publishing, 1999.

Hoyt, Edwin P. *U-boats Offshore: When Hitler Struck America.* Scarborough, 1978.

Kleinberg, Howard. *The Stingaree Century: A 100-Year History of Miami High School.* Centennial Press, 2003.

Koneazny, John J. *Behind Friendly Lines: Tales from World War II.* General Store Publishing House, 2001.

Land, Emory S. *The United States Merchant Marine at War: Report of the War Shipping Administrator to the President.* War Shipping Administration, 1946.

Largent, Will. *RAF Wings over Florida: Memories of World War II British Air Cadets.* Purdue University Press, 2000.

LaRoue, Samuel D., Jr., and Ellen J. Uguccioni. *The Biltmore Hotel: An Enduring Legacy,* Centennial Press, 2002.

LaRoue, Samuel D., and Ellen Uguccioni, "World War II and Beyond: A Hotel Transformed." *South Florida History* 30, no. 2 (2002).

Lawson, Ted W. *Thirty Seconds over Tokyo.* Blue Ribbon Books, 1944.

Lazarus, William C. *Wings in the Sun: The Annals of Aviation in Florida.* Tyn Cobb's Florida Press, 1951.

"The Ledo Road." *Life Magazine,* August 14, 1944.

Leland, Anne, and Mari-Jana Oboroceanu. *American War and Military Operations Casualties: Lists and Statistics.* Library of Congress, Congressional Research Service, 2010.

Ling, Sally J. *Small Town, Big Secrets: Inside the Boca Raton Army Air Field During World War II.* The History Press, 2005.

Lipartito, Kenneth, and Orville R. Butler. *A History of the Kennedy Space Center.* University Press of Florida, 2007.

MacGregor, Morris J. Jr. *Integration of the Armed Forces, 1940–1965*. Center of Military History, US Army, US Government Printing Office, 1985.

Mahan, Alfred Thayer. *Mahan on Naval Warfare: Selections from the Writings of Rear Admiral Alfred T. Mahan*. Little, Brown and Company, 1941.

Matloff, Maurice, ed. *American Military History*. Office of the Chief of Military History, US Army, US Government Printing Office, 1968.

Maurer, Maurer, ed. *Air Force Combat Units of World War II*. Department of the Air Force, Office of Air Force History, 1983.

McGovern, James R. "Pensacola, Florida: A Military City in the New South." *Florida Historical Quarterly* 59, no. 1 (1980).

Meilinger, Col. Phillip S., ed. *The Paths of Heaven: The Evolution of Airpower Theory*. Air University Press, 1997.

Mets, David R. *The Air Campaign: John Warden and the Classical Airpower Theorists*. Air University Press, 1999.

"Miami Studied as Blimp Site." *Homestead Leader*, International News Service, Dec. 4, 1939.

Mitchell, William "Billy." *Our Air Force: The Keystone of National Defense*. E.P. Dutton & Co., 1921.

Mitchell, William "Billy." *Skyways: A Book on Modern Aeronautics*. J.B. Lippincott Company, 1930.

Mitchell, William "Billy." *Winged Defense*. G.P. Putnam's Sons, 1925.

Mohl, Raymond A., and Gary Mormino. "The Big Change in the Sunshine State: A Social History of Modern Florida." In *The New History of Florida*, edited by Michael Gannon. University Press of Florida, 1996.

Mohl, Raymond A., and George E. Pozzetta. "From Migration to Multiculturalism: A History of Florida Immigration." In *The New History of Florida*, edited by Michael Gannon. University Press of Florida, 1996.

Morden, Bettie J. *The Women's Army Corps, 1945–1978*. Vol. 2. Center of Military History, US Army. US Government Printing Office, 1988.

Morison, Samuel Eliot. *History of US Naval Operations in World War II*. Vol. 2. Little, Brown, 1954.

Morison, Samuel Eliot. *The Two-Ocean War: A Short History of the United States Navy in the Second World War*. Little, Brown and Company, 1963.

Mormino, Gary R. "GI Joe Meets Jim Crow: Racial Violence and Reform in World War II Florida." *Florida Historical Quarterly* 73, no. 1 (1994): 23–42.

Mormino, Gary R. *Hillsborough County Goes to War: The Home Front, 1940–1950*. Tampa Bay History Center, 2001.

Mormino, Gary R. "World War II." In *The New History of Florida*, edited by Michael Gannon. University Press of Florida, 1996.

Muir, Helen. *The Biltmore: Beacon for Miami*. Pickering Press, 1987.

Naval Station Mayport Base Guide. US Naval Station, 2008.

Noble, Dennis L. "The Beach Patrol and Corsair Fleet." In *The U.S. Coast Guard in World War II*, Coast Guard Historian's Office, 1992.

Ogilvie, Sarah A., and Scott Miller. *Refuge Denied: The St. Louis Passengers and the Holocaust*. University of Wisconsin Press, 2006.

Ogle, Maureen. *Key West: History of an Island of Dreams.* University Press of Florida, 2003.
Osborne, Richard E. *World War II Sites in the United States: A Tour Guide and Directory.* Riebel-Roque Publishing, 1996.
Patterson, Gordon. "Hurston Goes to War: The Army Signal Corps in Saint Augustine." *Florida Historical Quarterly* 74, no. 2 (1995).
Pelt, Peggy Dorton. "The Liberty Ship: Unique Cargo Ship of World War II." *Selected Annual Proceedings of the Florida Conference of Historians.* Vol. 2, 1994.
Pelt, Peggy Dorton. "Wainwright Shipyard: The Impact of a World War II War Industry on Panama City, Florida." PhD diss., Florida State University, 1994.
Pepper, Claude Denson, with Hays Gorey. *Pepper: Eyewitness to a Century.* Harcourt Brace Jovanovich, 1987.
Perry, Hamilton Darby. *The Panay Incident: Prelude to Pearl Harbor.* Macmillan, 1969.
Potter, E. B. *Bull Halsey.* Naval Institute Press, 1985.
Purdon, Eric. *Black Company: The Story of Subchaser 1264.* Naval Institute Press, 2000.
Pushies, Fred J. *Weapons of the Navy SEALs.* MBI Publishing, 2004.
Putney, Col. Martha S. *When the Nation Was in Need: Blacks in the Women's Army Corps During World War II.* Scarecrow Press, Inc., 1992.
de Quesada, Alejandro M. *World War II in Tampa Bay.* Arcadia Publishing, 1997.
Rice, Charles W. "The Submarine Chaser Training Center: Downtown Miami's International Graduate School of Anti-Submarine Warfare during World War II." *Tequesta* 70 (2010).
Rogers, William W., "The Great Depression." In *The New History of Florida,* edited by Michael Gannon. University Press of Florida, 1996.
Roosevelt, Franklin D. *Proclamation of Unlimited National Emergency.* May 27, 1941.
Roth, Clayton D., Jr. "150 Years of Defense Activity at Key West." *Tequesta* 30 (1970).
Rottman, Gordon L. *US Special Warfare Units in the Pacific Theater, 1941–1945: Scouts, Raiders, Rangers, and Reconnaissance Units.* Osprey, 2005.
Sage-Gagne, Waneta. *Pilots in the Sun: Primary Pilot Training Schools in Lakeland and Avon Park, Florida, 1940–1945.* Friends of the Library, 1990.
Salmaggi, Cesare, and Alfredo Pallavisini. *2194 Days of War: An Illustrated Chronology of the Second World War.* Gallery Books, 1977.
Sandler, Stanley. *Segregated Skies: All-Black Combat Squadrons of World War II.* Smithsonian Institute Press, 1992.
Sawyer, L. A., and W. H. Mitchell. *The Liberty Ships: The History of the 'Emergency' Type Cargo Ship Constructed in the United States During World War II.* Redwood Press, 1970.
Scarborough, William E. "The Neutrality Patrol: To Keep Us Out of World War II?" *Naval Aviation News,* April 1990.
Scott, Col. Robert L. *God Is My Co-Pilot.* Charles Scribner's Sons, 1943.
Sherry, Mark D. *China Defensive: The U.S. Army Campaigns of World War II.* US Army Center of Military History, Pub. 72–38, US Government Printing Office, 2003.
Sherwood, Robert E. *Roosevelt and Hopkins: An Intimate History.* Harper Publishers, 1949.
Shettle, M. L., Jr. *Florida's Army Airfields of World War II.* Schaertel Publishing, 2009.
Shettle, M. L., Jr. *United States Naval Air Stations of World War II.* Vol. 1, *Eastern States.* Schaertel Publishing, 1995.

Sims, Jack A. *First over Japan: An Autobiography of a Doolittle-Tokyo Raider.* Southpointe Press, 2002.
Smith, Col. Clarence McKittrick. *The Medical Department: Hospitalization and Evacuation, Zone of Interior.* Office of the Chief of Military History, Department of the Army, 1956.
Smith, Graham. *The Mighty Eighth in the Second World War.* Countryside Books, 2001.
Smith, Jean Edward. *FDR.* Random House, 2007.
Smith, Oliver. *Amphibian: Camp Gordon Johnston Association Newsletter.* Winter 2008.
Smith, W. Stanford. *Camp Blanding: Florida Star in Peace and War.* Triangle, 1998.
Spector, Ronald H. *Eagle Against the Sun: The American War with Japan.* Macmillan, 1985.
Stafford, Edward Peary. *Subchaser.* Naval Institute Press, 1988.
Stilwell, Joseph W. *The Stilwell Papers.* Sloane Hadden, 1948.
Tanner, Stacy Lynn. "From Pearl Harbor to Peace: The Gendered Shipyard Experience in Tampa." Master's thesis, Florida State University, 2005.
Taylor, Robert A. *World War II in Fort Pierce.* Arcadia Publishing, 1999.
Taylor, Robert A. "The Frogmen in Florida: US Navy Combat Demolition Training in Fort Pierce, 1943–1946." *Florida Historical Quarterly* 75, no. 3 (1997).
Tebeau, Charlton W. *A History of Florida.* University of Miami Press, 1971.
Tibbets, Paul W. *Flight of the Enola Gay.* Buckeye, 1989.
Tibbets, Paul W. *The Reminiscences of Brigadier Gen. Paul Tibbets, Jr.* Aviation Project, Oral History Research Office, microfiche, Columbia University, 1961.
Tibbets, Paul W. *Return of the Enola Gay.* Midcoast Marketing, 1998.
Tibbets, Paul W., with Clair Stebbins and Harry Franken. *The Tibbets Story.* Scarborough House, 1978.
Tilley, John A. "A History of Women in the Coast Guard." *Commandant's Bulletin,* Office of the Coast Guard Historian, 1996.
Treadwell, Col. Mattie E. *The Women's Army Corps.* Vol. 1. Center of Military History, US Army, US Government Printing Office, 1954.
Treadwell, Theodore R. *Splinter Fleet: Wooden Subchasers of World War II.* Naval Institute Press, 2000.
Vaeth, J. Gordon. *Blimps & U-boats: US Navy Airships in the Battle of the Atlantic.* Naval Institute Press, 1992.
Van Treuren, Richard G. *Airships vs. Submarines.* Atlantis, 2009.
Weatherford, Doris. *American Women During World War II: An Encyclopedia.* Routledge, 2010.
Webster, Donovan. *The Burma Road: The Epic Story of the China-Burma-India Theater in World War II.* Farrar, Straus and Giroux, 2003.
Wiggins, Jim. *Florida and World War II: A Personal Recollection.* Heritage Books, 2008.
Williamson, Ronald M. *Naval Air Station Jacksonville, 1940–2000.* Turner Publishing Company, 2001.
Williamson, Steven A. *MacDill Air Force Base.* Arcadia Publishing, 2011.
Wiltse, Charles M. *US Army in World War II.* Vol. 2, *The Medical Department.* Office of the Chief of Military History, Department of the Army, 1965.

Wright, E. Lynne. *It Happened in Florida: Remarkable Events That Shaped History.* Morris Book Publishing, 2010.

Wynn, Kenneth. *U-boat Operations of the Second World War.* Naval Institute Press, 1997.

Wynne, Lewis N., and Carolyn J. Barnes. "Still They Sail: Shipbuilding in Tampa During World War II." In *Florida at War*, edited by Lewis N. Wynne. St. Leo College Press, 1993.

Wynne, Nick, and Richard Moorhead. *Florida in World War II: Floating Fortress.* History Press, 2010.

INDEX

Page numbers in *italics* refer to illustrations.

1st Infantry Division/Big Red One, 89, 99
2nd Battalion of Army Rangers, 98–99
2nd Engineer Amphibian Brigade, 92
2nd Operational Training Unit, 116
2nd Ranger Battalion, 99, 173n59
3rd Army Air Force Trainer Group, 108
4th Fleet, 157
4th Infantry Division/Ivy Division, 95–96, 99
5th Air Force, 56
6th Cavalry (mechanized) Regiment, 90
6th Naval Beach Battalion, 99
7th Amphibious Scouts/Special Service Unit #1, 98
7th Naval Beach Battalion, 99
8th Air Force/Eighth Bomber Command, 103, 117, 174n22
10th Air Force, 57
20th Bomber Command, 118
21st Bomb Group, 104
28th Infantry Division/Keystone Division, 95
29th Bomb Group, 41, 108
29th Division, 173n59
29th Infantry Division/Blue and Gray Division, 89, 99
30th Infantry Division/Old Hickory, 89
31st Infantry Division/Dixie Rifles, 47, 48, 89, 172n8
36th Infantry Division/Texas Division, 89
38th Infantry Division/Cyclone Division, 92, 95
43rd Infantry Division/Winged Victory, 89, 172n8
45th Engineering General Services Regiment, 59
63rd Infantry Division/Blood and Fire, 89
66th Infantry Division/Black Panthers, 89

79th Infantry Division/The Cross of Lorraine, 89
88th Bomb Group, 108
91st Bomb Group, 108
92nd Bomb Group, 108
92nd Division, 174n31
93rd Division, 174n31
94th Bomb Group, 108
97th Bomb Group, 68, 108
99th Bomb Group, 108
100th Bomb Group, 108
124th Infantry Regiment of Florida, 47, 48
156th Regiment of Military Police, 90
265th Florida Coastal Artillery Regiment, 48
320th Bomb Group, 104
322nd Bomb Group, 104
322nd Fighter Group/Tuskegee Airmen, 128
323rd Bomb Group, 104
344th Bomb Group, 104
386th Bomb Group, 104
387th Bomb Group, 104
391st Bomb Group, 104
394th Bomb Group, 104
397th Bomb Group, 104
463rd Bomb Group, 108
483rd Bomb Group, 109
508th Parachute Regiment/Red Devils, 90
509th Composite Group, 117, 118, 143

Abucay, Bataan, Philippine Islands, 62
Accra, Gold Coast, 53, *54*, *56*, 66
Act to Establish a Women's Army Auxiliary Corps (WAAC) for Service with the Army of the US, An, 129–30
Aerospace industry, 151–52

Africa: and air routes, 8, 43, 53, *54, 56;* Casablanca conference participants in, 67; maps of, *54, 56, 115;* Pan American Airways and, 14; Project X aircraft in, 57

Africa-Middle East Wing Command, 65

African Americans: and Burma Road construction, 59, *159;* and Civilian Pilot Training program, 130; and civil rights, 112, 130; and combat units, 112, 127; in Deep South, 10; as draftees, 127; enlistment by, 127, 163n75; in Florida, 10, 11, 163n75; and Great Depression, 11; populations of, 10; as proportion of US population, 127; and racial unrest, 128; segregated divisions of, 174n31; and US Army Air Corps/US Army Air Forces, 111–12, 174n31; and US Army Service Forces, 112, 119, 127, 174n31; and Women's Army Auxiliary Corps, 130

African-Mediterranean-Middle East Theater of Operations, 101, 131

Afrika Korps, 58, 125

Agriculture: Axis prisoners of war and, 119, 125; and DDT, 148; fruit and vegetable cultivation, 11, 12, 125, 148; in pre–World War II Florida, 12; sugarcane cultivation, 12

Aircraft: A-20 light bombers, *vi;* air carrier planes, 132; and anti-submarine actions, 85; anti-submarine seaplanes, 151; B-18s, 29, 81; B-24 bombers, 45, 52, 53, 55, 58, 102, 103; B-25 bombers, 51, 66, 113, 116, 157; B-26 bombers, 66, 102, 103, 104; B-29 bombers ("Superfortresses"), 117–18, 143–44; barrage balloons, 94; bombers, 28, 38, 41, 49, 50–51, 52, *115,* 117, 143, 153, 154; C-46 Commandos ("Dumbos"), 115, 116, 132; C-47 cargo planes, 52, *132;* C-47 Skytrains ("Dakotas" or "Gooney Birds"), 115, 116, 132; C-54 cargo planes, 67; cargo planes, 38, 106, *115,* 131; clippers, 21, 67; Clipper Ship seaplanes, 44; Dakota transport planes, 8; DC-3s, 154; dive bombers, 22; fighter planes, 22, *23,* 38, 41, 42, 49, 106, *115,* 116, 153, 154; four-engine planes, 43; gasoline for, 52; glider planes, 106; heavy bombers, 39, 55; landing plates for, 113; materials for, 4, *73;* Messerschmitts, 117; Mitsubishis, 117; Norden bombsight for, 106; P-39 Airacobras, 41; P-40 Warhawks, 41; P-51 Mustangs, 41; Piper Cubs, 158; range of, 52; scout planes, 22; seaplane bombers, 24, 28; seaplanes, 24, 31, 33; shipment of parts for, 121; single-engine fighter planes, 66; torpedo bombers, 22; transport planes, 114, 132; Troop Carriers, 106; warplanes, 31, 120, 142; XB-29 prototype bomber, 117; Zeros, 117. *See also* Airships/blimps/zeppelins; B-17 bombers

Air crews: African American, 128; aviation maintenance officers, 38; bombardiers, 38, 68, 102, 103; cargo pilots, 116; controllers, 58, 113; engineers, 58; ground crews, 103; guards, 59; gunners, 102, 103, *105;* loadmasters, 116; maintenance personnel, 103; mechanics, 59, 102, 113; navigators, 38, 53, 55, 68, 102, 116, 168n9, 174n22; pilots, 38, 53, 55, 68, 102, 103, 116, 128, 166n28; radiomen, 55, 102, 103; technicians, 59; training of, 55–56

Airport Development Program (ADP), 44

Airships/blimps/zeppelins: bases for, 33–35, 77–79, 171n33; characteristics of, 33, *78;* crews for, 33, 77, *78;* engines for, 33, 77; equipment and weapons on, 33, 77, *78;* places assigned to, 77, *78,* 79, 141, 171n33, 171n34; post–World War II, 151; production of, 22, 33, 77; shooting down of, *30;* surveillance by, 33, 77–*78,* 141, 171n33; types of, 33, 77; and *U-176* sinking, 85; US Army and, 41; US Navy and, 33, 35, 77–79, 139, 151

Airship Wing Two, 79

Akron, Ohio, 77

Alabama, 10, 41, 47, 128

Alachua Army Airfield, 135, *150*

Alameda, CA, 51, 157

Alaska, 5

Albert Whitted Airport, 136

Albury, Charles Donald, 143, 178n14

Al-Can Highway, 5

Alcoa Puritan (ship), 82

Aleutian Islands, 5

Algeria, 42, *54, 56,* 66, 89

Alliance Auxiliary Army Airfield, 134

Altoona Auxiliary Army Airfield, 136

Aluminum Trail, *57,* 158

Amapala (ship), 83

Amazone (ship), 82

Amazon region, 56, 57

American Historical Association, 2

Amphibious warfare: in European Theater, 156;

in Pacific Theater, 98, 156; training for, 87–88, 91–96, 97, 98–100, 101, 155, 158; unit for, 98; US Army and, 87, 91, 97, 155; US Navy and, 97
Anacostia, Washington, DC, 76
Andrew Jackson (ship), 84
Andrews, Charles O., 18, 152
Andros Island, Bahamas, 71, *73*
Antigua, *3*, 6
Antilles, 2
Anti-submarine warfare (ASW): aircraft for, 77–79, 81, 85; characteristics of, 74; civilians and, 74, 76–77, 79, 86; communications for, 77, *78*, 81; equipment and weapons for, 72–73, 77, *78*, 80, 81, 85; Florida Civil Defense Agency and, 76; Florida Defense Force and, 76–77; listening stations for, 81; Royal Navy and, 74, 85; strategies for, 74, 76, 81; training for, 74, 77, 158; US Army and, 77, 155; US Coast Guard and, 76; US Navy and, 73–74, 77–81; vessels for, 74, 79–80, 81, 85
Antwerp, Belgium, 28
Anzio, Italy, 89, 108, 156
Apalachicola, FL, 106
Apalachicola Army Airfield, 134, *150*
Apalachicola Bay, 92, 96
Apalachicola Gunnery School, 151
Apalachicola National Forest, 13
Apopka, FL, 136
Aquila Force: and 10th Air Force, 57; aircraft for, 52; contribution of, to aerial transportation system, 59; destination of, 52; experiences of, 53–54; and HALPRO expedition, 58; as hasty operation, 52, 55; orders for, 52; and Project X, 55, 56; and South Atlantic Route, 52; US State Department and, 52
Arabia, 52
Arabian Sea, *56*, *57*
Arauca (ship), 28–29, 32
Arcadia, FL, 46, 137
Arcadia Chamber of Commerce, 37
Ardennes, 89, 95
Argentina, 42
Arizona, 145
Arkansas (state), 41
Arkansas River, 4
Arlington Shipbuilding and Engineering Corporation, 121

Armor Auxiliary Army Airfield, 137
Army Air Corps Station Hospital, 133
Army Air Forces Distribution Center Boca Raton, 138
Army Air Forces Hospital No. 1, 133
Army Air School of Applied Tactics, 136
Army-Navy Amphibious Command, 97
Army Personnel Redistribution Center #7, 138
Army Service Command Inspector General, 131
Army Signal Corps School Daytona Beach, 136
Army Student Training Corps, 18
Arnold, Harold Harley "Hap": and B-29s of 20th Bomber Command, 118; characteristics of, 116; and civilian flight schools, 37; and Clark Gable, 111; in Florida, 116–17; and Franklin D. Roosevelt, 40; health of, 116–17; on importance of bombardment, 102; and Joint Chiefs of Staff, 40; and MacDill Field/Southeast Air Base, 39; and Miami Beach, 109; and military hospitals, 116; rank of, 40; and Royal Air Force pilot training, 45–46; and strategic bombardment, 40; as US Army Air Corps/Army Air Forces commander, 8, 37, 116; and US Army Air Corps/Army Air Forces officer candidate school, 154; and US Army Air Forces training site, 109
Aruba, 161n7
Ascension Island, *54*, *56*, 66, 67
Asia: and air routes, 8, 14, 43–44, 52; Douglas MacArthur in, 62; Japanese aggression in, 19; map of, *115*; World War II in, 5
Assam, India, 54, *57*
Assam Airfields, *57*
ASW. *See* anti-submarine warfare (ASW)
Atenas (ship), 83
Atkinson Airfield, 52, 53, *54*
Atlantic Airways Ltd., 53
Atlantic Narrows: and Allied air routes, 43; blimp passage over, *78*; extent of, 53; location of, 53; as potential route for Axis forces, 42, *44*, 48; travel to Casablanca conference over, 67
Atlantic Ocean: and air routes, 8, *54*, *56*, *56*; and anti-submarine warfare (ASW), 77; currents of, 2; and Florida, 72; maps of, *3*, *44*, *54*, *56*; shipping in, *3*; U-boat battles in, 74; US defenses along, 23, 25; as US frontier, 5
Atlantic Sector, 23

Atlas Mountains, 67
Atomic bombs, 68, 155
Auburndale Outlying Field, Naval Air Station Pensacola, 133
Australia, 56, *115*
Austria and Austrians, 10, 108
Avon Park, FL, 37, 139, 141
Avon Park Army Airfield, 137
Avon Park Bombing Range, 137, 157
Avon Park CPS, *150*
Avon Park General Bombing and Gunnery Range, 106
Azores Islands, 8, 48, *56*

B-17 bombers ("Flying Fortresses"): Aquila Force and, 52; and bombing of Germany, 174n22; dependability of, 40; Eighth Bomber Command/8th Air Force and, 103, 174n22; fleets of, 102; as four-engine aircraft, 8, 40; fuel capacity of, 52; importance of, 40; introduction of, 8; at MacDill Field dedication, 41; numbers of, 40; Paul Tibbets and, 68; photo of, *105;* Project X and, 55, 56; range of, 40, 52, 53; training on, 108–9; weapons on, 40. *See also* Aircraft
B-29 Accelerated Services Testing Group, 117. *See also* Aircraft: B-29 bombers
Bagdad Outlying Field, Naval Air Station Pensacola, 133
Bahamas Banks, 71, 170n7, 170n8
Bahamas Islands: as British territory, 6; characteristics of, 71; and Florida Straits, 70; maps of, *3, 73;* U-boat attacks near, *73,* 170n11; US defenses in, 6, 152
Bahamians, 10
Baja California (ship), 84
Ball Gunner School, 26
Baltimore, MD, 64
Banana River, 22, 24, 34. *See also* Naval Air Station Banana River
Banana River Outlying Field for Lighter Than Air, 139
Banana River prisoner of war camp, 126
Barents Sea, 113
Bartow Army Airfield, 41, 137, *150*
Bascom Auxiliary Army Airfield, 134
Base Re-Alignment Committee (BRAC), 157
Basra, Iraq, 45, 113

Bastogne, Belgium, 104
Bataan peninsula, Philippine Islands, 50, 55, 62–63, 167n2. *See also* Philippine Islands
Bathurst, Gambia, 53, *56*
Battle of Britain, 29
Battle of Siegfried Line, 104
Battle of the Bulge, 90, 104
Bauer Outlying Field, Naval Auxiliary Aviation Facility Bronson Field, 133
Bauxite, 4, *73,* 74
Bayboro Harbor, 27
Bay County, FL, 121, 145
Bay of Campeche, 170n11
Bayou Outlying Field, Naval Air Station Corry Field, 133
Beach Club Hotel, 139
Bearn (ship), 31
Belém, Brazil, 52, 53, *54,* 67
Belgium, 28, 29, 104
Belle Glade Auxiliary Army Airfield, 137
Belle Glade prisoner of war camp, 126
Bell Haven Miami prisoner of war camp, 126
Bell Outlying Field, Naval Auxiliary Air Station Corry Field, 133
Belmore Outlying Field, Naval Air Station Jacksonville, 135
Ben Gurian International Airport, 168n37
Benjamin Brewster (ship), 84
Benson (ship), 32
Beresford Shipyard, 121
Berlin, Germany, 108, *115,* 155
Bermuda, *3,* 6, 23, *54*
Beser, Jacob, 180n59
Bethune, Mary McLeod, 37, 129, 130
Billinger, Robert D., Jr., 126
Bills, William E., 148
Biltmore Hotel, 24, 110, 116, 133, 139
Bimini, Bahamas, 81
Biscayne (ship), 156
Biscayne Bay: flying school on, 38; Miami and, 15, 112; Miami Beach on, 109; presidential flight over, 67; PT boats in, 117; seaplane station on, 26; US-Cuban ceremony on, 85
Blackwelder, Benjamin, 64
Blackwelder, Dorothy Evelyn, 63–65
Blackwelder, Earl, 64
Blackwelder, Everitte, 64
Blackwelder, Harvey, 64

Blackwelder, Percy Mae, 64
Blanding, Albert H., 47, 167n52
Blimps. *See* Airships/blimps/zeppelins
Boca Chica Army Airfield, *150*
Boca Raton, FL, 49, 82, 138, *139*
Boca Raton Army Airfield, 11, 138, *150*
Boca Raton Army Radar School, 180n59
Boca Raton Club, 139
Bock, Frederick C., 144
Bockscar (airplane), 143–44, 155
Bonita Spring Army Airfield, 137
Boston, MA, 14
Bostwick Outlying Field, Naval Air Station Jacksonville, 135
Bradenton, FL, 41, 147
Bradley, Omar, 93
Branan Outlying Field, Naval Air Station Jacksonville, 134
Brazil: and air routes, 43, 45, 53, *54;* airships in, 35, *78,* 171n33; and Aquila Force flyover, 52; and Atlantic Narrows, 42, 53; aviation training in, 39; bauxite from, 4; and distance to Ascension Island, 66; and distance to Atkinson Airfield, 52; and distance to Cape Verde Islands, 48; Franklin D. Roosevelt in, 67; map of, *54;* Nazi influence in, 45; offshore islands of, 45; Pan American Airways in, 45; and potential Axis threat, 43; and relations with United States, 43, 45; US Air Transport Command in, 65; US facilities in, 6, 45, 52, *78;* US Navy leaders and, 33
Breakers Hotel, 110, 133
British Flying Training Schools (BFTS), 46, *150*
British Guiana, 4, 6, *44,* 45, 52, *54*
British Malaya, 50
British Navy, 29, 33, 74, 99
Brooklyn, NY, 25
Brooksville Army Airfield, 41, 136, *150*
Broward County, FL, 26, 112, 145
Brownsville, FL, 147
Buckingham Army Airfield, 137, *150,* 168n35
Bulow Outlying Field, Naval Air Station Daytona Beach, 136
Bunker, Chang, 167n42
Bunker, Eng, 167n42
Bunnell Outlying Field, Naval Air Station Daytona Beach, 136
Bureau of the Budget, 129

Burger, Ernst P., 75, 76
Burma, 54, *57,* 59, 116
Burma Road/Stilwell Road/Ledo Road, 59, 116, 158, *159*
Bush, George Herbert Walker, 26
Bushnell Army Airfield, 41, 136

Cacalilao (ship), 83
Cairo, Egypt, 53, *56,* 58, 65
Callwell, C. E., 101
Calgarolite (ship), 83
California, 51, 145
Caloosahatchee River, 92
Camp Blanding: as Army Service Forces Command, 127; Axis prisoners of war at, 125, 126; characteristics of, 98; Crystal Lake Army Air Base at, 135; establishment and construction of, 47, 92; location of, 87, 135, 145; number of soldiers trained at, 91; returning soldiers at, 91; size of, 47, 145, 157, 172n8; training at, 47, 48, 59, 87, 89, 90, 91, 172n8; units at, 47, 48, 59, 89, 90, 172n8; as US Army headquarters in Florida, 91
Camp Blanding Provost Marshal General, 125
Camp Carrabelle Army Amphibious Training Center. *See* Camp Gordon Johnston
Campeche Banks, 70
Camp Foster, 20, 24, 47
Camp Gordon Johnston: African American soldiers at, 127, 128; Axis prisoners of war at, 125, 126; characteristics of, 91, 92, 93, 94, 96, 98, 128; establishment and construction of, 92; location of, 87, 91, 134; mission statement of, 93; naval equipment at, 92–93, 96; Omar Bradley on, 93; opening of, 91; size of, 92; as staging port, 96; training at, 87, 91–96, 97, 127, 155; units at, 95, 96
Camp Murphy Army Signal Corps, 138
Campville Outlying Field, Naval Air Station Jacksonville, 134
Canada and Canadians, 4, 10, 22, 29, 46, *54*
Canadian Coastal Zone, *23*
Cannon Mills Auxiliary Army Airfield, 136
Cape Canaveral, FL, 24, 69–70, 82, 151
Cape Cod, MA, 91, 92
Cape Ferrol, 85
Cape Florida, 71
Cape Kennedy, 136

Cape Kennedy Space Center, 152
Cape Verde Island, 48, *54*
Caribbean basin and Caribbean Sea: and air routes, 8, 43, *54*, 67; Alfred Mahan on, *3*, 5, 24; and anti-submarine warfare, 77, *78*, 79, 80, 171n33; Axis and, 31, *44;* British territories in, 6, 29, *30*, 31; currents in, 2; Franklin D. Roosevelt and, 20, 25, *30*, 31, 67; maps of, *3*, *44;* military importance of, 5, 24, 26; and shipping routes, *3*, 40; U-boat battles in, 69, 74, 171n33; and US defenses, 6, 22, 29, *30*, 31, 33, 35, 40, 54, 65, 158; US Navy war games in, 24
Caribbean Defense Command, *23*, *44*
Caribbean Sea Command, 29
Caribbean Sea Frontier, *23*
Caribbean Wing Command, 65
Carlisle Outlying Field, Naval Air Station Jacksonville, 135
Carlstrom Field, 38, 137, *150*
Carlstrom Riddle Aeronautical Institute, 38
Carolina Sector, *23*
Carrabelle, FL, 134. *See also* Camp Gordon Johnston
Carrabelle River, 95
Carrabulle (ship), 83
Casablanca, Morocco, *56*, 65, 67
Castilla (ship), 84
Casualties: in childbirth, 64; female, 60, 63–64, *132;* killed, vi, 21, 49, 60, 61, 63, 70, *73*, 74, 89, 95, 99, 103, 116, 131, *132*, 142, 158–59, 166n22, 166n28, 167n2, 169n50, 174n22, 174n27, 175n47, 177n77, 178n5, 178n6; numbers of, 142, 169n50, 177n77; rehabilitation and return to duty of, 133, 140, 142; wounded, 21, 60, 61, 89, 95, 99, 103, 119, 131–33, 140, 142, 165n52, 171n41, 174n27, 177n77
Cay Sal Bank, 170n7
CBI. *See* China-Burma-India (CBI) Theater of Operations
Cecil Field, 25
Cedar Keys Auxiliary Army Airfield, 136
Central America, *3*, 42–43
Central Command, 157
Central Defense Command, *23*, *44*
Central Europe, 89, 95
Central Florida, 136–37, 145
Chapman, Victor E., 38
Chapman Army Airfield, 139

Chapman CPS, *150*
Chapman Field, 38
Charleston, SC, 14
Charts (term), 71
Chesapeake Bay, 97
Chesapeake Bay Sector, *23*
Chesapeake region, 14
Chevalier Field, Naval Air Station Pensacola, 133
Chiang Kai-shek, 21, 114
Chicago, IL, *vi*
Chief of Naval Operations, 40
China: airlifts to, 54–55, 114–15, 116; Aquila Force and, 52; Chiang Kai-shek and, 114; Doolittle Raiders and, 51, 52, 168n26; and Japan, 21, 50, 58, 98, 114, 116; map of, *57;* post–World War II civil war in, 148; and Stilwell Road, 59; strategic importance of, 114; and US defenses, 52, 58, 88, 98
China-Burma-India (CBI) Theater of Operations: and airlifts, 59, 102, 117; Air Transport Command in, 175n48; and bombing of Japan, 118; and preparations to invade Japan, 98; and Stilwell Road, 59, 116
Choctawhatchee National Forest, 20, 41
Choctaw Outlying Field, Naval Air Station Whiting Field, 133
Churchill, Winston, 29, 31, 39, 67, 180n48
Cincinnati, OH, 75
Cisterna di Littoria, Italy, 172n28
Cities Service Empire (ship), 70, 82
City Service Toledo (ship), 84
Civil Air Patrol (CAP), 17, 77, 158
Civil Air Patrol Squadron Three, 77
Civil Defense Wardens, 17
Civilian Conservation Corps (CCC), 27, 164n42
Civilian Pilot Training (CPT) Program, 37, 46, 130
Clare (ship), 83
Clay County, FL, 145
Clearwater, FL, 15, 136, 174n20
Clewiston, FL, 39, 46, 125, 137
Clewiston Army Airfield, 137
Clewiston British Flying Training School, *150*
Clewiston Flight School, 46
Clewiston prisoner of war camp, 126
Coastal Picket Patrol, 79
Coast Guard Station Dinner Key, 138
Coast Watchers, 76–77
Cochran, Jacqueline, 14, 169n43

Coconut Grove, FL, 26, 67, 138
Colabee (ship), 82
Cold War, 152, 153, 180n45, 180n48
Collins, LeRoy, 180n51
Colorado, 4
Columbus (ship), 28
Columbus Hotel, 139
Comayagua (ship), 83
Connors Field, 137
Conscription, 30–31, 48–49
Continental United States (CONUS), 5
Convalescent hospital program, 140
Coral Gables, FL, 110, 139, 146, 147
Corbett, Julian Stafford, 5
Corn Island, FL, 76
Coronet Airport, 137
Corpus Christie, TX, 73
Corregidor Island, 50, 56. *See also* Philippine Islands
Corsair Fleet, 79
Coventry, England, 7
Cozumel, Mexico, 73
Crestview Army Airfield, 134
Cross City Army Airfield, 41, 135, *150*
Crystal Lake Army Air Base, 135
Crystal River Army Airfield, 136
Cuba: anti-submarine blimps in, 78, 79; and Axis threat, 156; maps of, *3, 23, 44, 73;* and Old Bahama Channel, 71, 170n8; pilot training in, 167n49; and SS *St. Louis,* 28; U-boat battles near, 73, 81, 82, 83, 84, 85, 86; US airstrips in, 45; war games near, 24
Cuban Navy, 85
Cubans, 39
Cummer Outlying Field, Naval Air Station Jacksonville, 134
Curaçao, *3,* 161n7
Curtiss, Glenn, 14
Czechoslovakia and Czechs, 10

Dade City prisoner of war camp, 126
Dade County, FL, 15, 145
Dadeland Shopping Center, 125, 176n41
Dahlgren (ship), 30
Dakar, Senegal, 48, 53, *54, 56*
Dakar Bulge, 53
Dale Mabry Airport, 41
Dale Mabry Army Airfield, 126, 128, 134, *150*
Dale Mabry Boulevard, 41

Dallas, TX, 148
Dania, FL, 138
Dasch, George John, 75, 76
David McKeklvey (ship), 83
David O Saylor (ship), 122
Davie Outlying Field, Naval Air Station Miami, 138
Davis, Bert, 95–96
Daytona Beach, FL: as coastal location, 15; convalescent hotel in, 133; Greenwood Cemetery in, 65; military housing in, 15, 130, 174n20; military training in, 39, 129, 136; naval air station at, 25, 34, 135, *150;* population of, 16, 147; as smaller municipality, 15, 16; WAVES in, 64; Women's Army Corps in, 129, 130–31, 136
Daytona Beach Boatworks, 121
Daytona Beach prisoner of war camp, 126
Daytona Beach Women's Army Corps Training Center, 136
D-day: aircraft in, 78, 104; casualties during, 99; events of, 99; medals and awards for participants in, 104; movie depiction of, 173n59; paratroopers in, 90; United States and, 89, 95, 96, 99; watercraft in, 122
Death Camps, 149
"Deep in the Heart of Texas," 67
Defense Reorganization Act of 1947–48, 175n35
DeLand, FL, 25, 34, 106, 136, *150*
Delisle (ship), 82
Delray Beach, FL, 82
Delta Airlines, 14, 113
Democratic Party, 17
Dinner Key, FL, 26, 34, 67, 138, *150*
Displaced persons, 148–49
Dog Island, 91
Dominican Republic, *44,* 45
Domino (ship), 84
Donald Duck Navy, 80
Don Cesar Hotel/Resort, 110, 133, 139
Dooley Boatyard, 122
Doolittle, Jimmy, 51, 103, 117
Doolittle Raid and Raiders, 50, 51–52, 155, 157, 168n9, 168n26
Dorman Outlying Field, Naval Air Station Miami, 138
Dorr Army Airfield, 38, 137, *150*
Dougherty, Dora, 175n57
Douhet, Giulio, 7

Draft/conscription, 30–31, 48–49
Drane Army Airfield, 137
Dresden, Germany, 7
Drew Army Airfield, *150*
Drew Field Municipal Airport/Drew Field, 41, 126, 136
Dry Tortugas, FL, 82, 83, 84, 155
Dunedin, FL, 100
Dunedin Amphibian Tractor Detachment, 136
Dunnellon Army Airfield, 41, 106, 136, *150*
Dutch East Indies, 50, 148
Dutch Guiana, 4
Dutch West Indies, 161n7
Duval County, FL, 15

Earhart, Amelia, 14
East Coast Embarkation Centers, 101
Eastern Airlines, 14, 38, 59, 113, 178n14
Eastern Defense Command, *23, 44*
Eastern Front, 113
Eastern Sea Frontier, *23*
Eastern Sun (ship), 83
Eastport, FL, 22
Eclipse (ship), 82
Edward Luckenbach (ship), 84
Eglin Army Airfield/Eglin Military Reservation: activities at, 141; auxiliary fields of, 134; Axis prisoners of war at, 126; characteristics of, 51; Doolittle Raiders at, 51, 155; as gift to US Army, 20; location of, 20, 51, 134, 145; map of, *150;* and Nazi V-1 and V-2 Vengeance Rockets, 151; proving ground at, 117; size of, 41
Eglin-Hurlburt Airdrome (Hurlburt Field), 134
Egypt, 43, 45, 52, *56*
Ein Shemer airfield, 168n37
Eisenhower, Dwight D., 173n66
El Alamein, Egypt, 58
El Fasher, Sudan, 53
El Geneina, Sudan, 53
Elizabeth (ship), 83
Ellis Auxiliary Army Airfield, 134
El Obeid, Sudan, 53
Embry, Talton Higbee, 37
Embry-Riddle schools, 37–39
Emergency Shipbuilding Program, 121, 123. *See also* Shipbuilding
Emile Bertin (ship), 31

Empire Buffalo (ship), 82
England. *See* Great Britain
English Channel, 2, 70
Enola Gay (airplane), 68, 143, 155
E.P. Theriault (ship), 83
Escola Tecnica de Aviacao (Technical Aviation School), 39
Esparta (ship), 82
ETTC Radio and Radar Technical Training School Boca Raton, 138
Europe: and air routes, 8, 43; and Allied supply convoys, 90; German aggression in, 19; Holocaust survivors in, 149; map of, *115;* post–World War II, 148; transfer of planes from, 143; US military police in, 90; World War II in, 5
Europeans, 10
European Theater of Operations, 94, 101, 103, 104, 117, 131
Everglades, 26, 77, 100, 114, 121
Everglades Hotel, 139

Faja de Oro (ship), 83
Father of Waters, 72
FEC Railroad, 112, 115
Federal (ship), 82
Federal Office of Education, 123–24
Femoyer, Robert Edward, 174n22
Ferdinand Magellan (train car), 66, 169n62
Ferebee, Thomas, 68
Fernandina, FL, 22
Fernandina Beach, FL, 82
Fernandina Outlying Field, Naval Air Station Jacksonville, 134
Fernando Noronha islands, Brazil, 45
Flagler Beach Coast Guard patrol station, 136
Fleming Island, FL, 24
Fleming Island Outlying Field, Naval Air Station Jacksonville, 134
Flexible Gunnery School, 174n27
Florida: aerospace industry in, 151; African American troops from, 127–28; African American population of, 127; agriculture in, 119, 125, 148; and airlifts, 55, 114, 117, 154; airports in, 6, 157; and air routes, 43–44, 65–66, 113, 154; air shows in, 36; and anti-submarine warfare, 76–77, 79, 141; and Atlantic Ocean, 72; aviation in, 6, 14, 16; Axis prisoners of war in, 10,

119, 125–26; Axis spies in, 10–11; Axis threat to, *44*, 48; B-29 testing in, 117; and bombing of Japan, 50, 51; bombing squadron activation ceremonies in, 103–5; Caribbean Wing of Air Transport Command in, 65; changing character of residents of, 152–53; Civil Air Patrol in, 77; civilian aviation training in, 37–39; Civilian Conservation Corps in, 164n42; contributions of, to World War II, 159–60; Democratic Party in, 17–18; demography in, 9–11, 12, 146–47, 162n36; ecological damage in, 86, 170n13; economic activities in, 12–14, 15; Eighth Air Force in, 117; as embarkation point, 119; employment and unemployment in, 11–12, 124, 141, 149–51; and end of World War II, 144; expanded military presence in, 19, 22; female military personnel in, 119; Frank Knox in, 32; Franklin D. Roosevelt and, 20, 24, 31, 32, 66–67, 116; geography and climate of, 1, 16, 37, 149, 157; George C. Marshall in, 164n42; governors of, 14, 18, 41, 46, 152, 167n52, 180n51; Great Depression in, 11–12, 13; and Gulf Stream current, 71; Hap Arnold in, 116–17; Holocaust survivors in, 149; increased numbers of marriages and birthrates in, 147–48; labor force in, 11–12, 149; land mass of, 9; and Manhattan Project, 141; maps of, *3, 23, 44, 73, 150;* as maritime state, 1–2; media control in, 74–75, 141; military aviation in, 19, 22; military draft/conscription in, 31, 48–49, 119; military enlistment in, 10; military facilities in, 1, 2, 6, 11, 34, 49, 133–39, *150*, 155; military housing in, 13; military importance of, 1–6, 8, 43, 153–58, 161n7, 180n63; military personnel in, 35, 112; minority soldiers in, 119; and Mississippi River, *3*; National Guardsmen from, 47; natural resources in, 15; and Neutrality Patrol, 28; New Deal in, 17; news of Pearl Harbor attack in, 49; Overseas Highway in, 24; and Panama Canal, 2, *3,* 4, 5; as part of New South, 152; as part of US Southeastern District, 41; population of, 9–11, 14–15, 17, 35, 101, 145, 146, 179n20; post–World War II, 149, 151, 152, 157, 180n45; and post–World War II reorganization of US defenses, 153; and preparations to invade Japan, 141, 142–43, 144; presidential elections in, 17–18, 20; racial segregation in, 127–28; railroads in, 13–14, 15, 101, 112, 180n63; rationing in, 141–42; residents of, killed or missing in action, 158–59; returning soldiers in, 140, 148; rural nature of, 14, 15; and sea lanes, 15; shipbuilding in, 27–28, 80, 97, 119, 120–23, 124, 157, 180n64; social order in, 127–28; and SS *St. Louis,* 28; as staging area, 112; and Stilwell Road construction, 116; as supply base, 112; threats to, 31; tourism in, 74, 149; transportation in, 15, 162n36; transportation of planes to, 59–60; travel controls in, 141; travel infrastructure in, 162n36; troops from, 119; U-boats along, 69–70, *73,* 74, 82–86; underwater topography of west coast of, 72; urbanization in, 145; and US air power, 36–37; US Army Air Corps in, 8, 36; US Army Ground Forces in, 87–88; US Army in, 37; and US defenses, 36; US Navy in, 37; US Navy leaders in, 32–33; veterans in, 157, 180n51; wartime industrial gains in, 124; wealth in, 14; Women's Army Auxiliary Corps in, 130; before World War II, 19, *23,* 28; wounded soldiers in, 119, 131–33, 140

Florida, military training in: African Americans and, 59, 119, 130; for airlifts, 102, 114, 116; amphibious, 87–88, 91, 101, 158; anti-submarine, 158; of Army rangers, 96; aviation, 6, 19, 22, 25–26, 35, 37–39, 41–42, 49, 102, 104, 106, 107, 108–9, 114, 116, 158; basic, 47, 87, 138; bombing, 6, 26, 38, 39, 41, 102–3, 104, 106, 108–9, 158; centers of, 15; civilians and, 17, 35, 37–39, 46, 49; of commandos, 158; Doolittle Raiders and, 51; of enlisted personnel, 155; of *Enola Gay* and *Bockscar* atomic bombing crews, 155; fatalities during, 158; fighter plane, 39, 41, 42, 106; of infantry, 47, 88, 89, 95, 101; inter-service, 155; of logisticians, 158; of mechanics, 102, 158; medical, 158; National Guard and, 29–30, 47, 89; of navigators, 38, 102, 158; number of graduates of, 158; number of persons involved in, 35; of officers, 27, 97, 106–7, 138, 154, 155; of paratroopers, 106; and racial integration, 27; on radar, 49, 158, 180n59; on radio signaling, 49, 102; Royal Air Force and, 39, 45–46, 49; on sonar, *30,* 49, 158; for South Atlantic Route and Flying the Hump, 114, 116; SPARS and, 131; state's suitability for, 1–2, 6, 16, 22, 155–56; US Army Air Corps/Army Air Forces and, 36, 37, 38–39, 41–42, 46, 104, 107, 108–9; US Army and, 47, 87, 89, 95, 96, 165n2;

US Army Reserve and, 37, 49; US Coast Guard and, 27; US Marine Corps and, 19; US Maritime Service and, 26–27; US Navy and, 19, 22, 25, 26, 35, 38–39, 49, 165n2; WACs and, 119, 131; WAVES and, 131; on weaponry, 6, 102, 158; women and, 119, 131
Florida-Brazil coastal corridor, 43
Florida Civil Defense Agency, 76
Florida Defense Force, 47, 49, 76–77
Florida Gator, The (airplane), vi
Florida Gulf Coast, 91
Florida Keys, 117, 163n6. *See also* Key Biscayne, FL; Key Largo, FL; Key West, FL
Florida National Guard, 18, 20, 24, 46–47, 48, 157
Floridan Hotel, 133
Florida panhandle, 146
Florida Portland Cement Company, 122
Florida Power and Light Company, 47
Florida Sector, *23*
Florida State University System, 35
Florida Straits: anti-submarine warfare in, 77–79, 81, 85; characteristics of, 70; defenses for, 24, 33, 35, 158; depth of, 71; German ships in, 28–29; and Gulf Stream current, 2; military importance of, 25; and shipping, 71; and transport of Doolittle Raid aircraft, 157; U-boat battles in, 69, 71, 74–75, 83, 85, 86, 170n18
Florosa Field, 134
Flying the Hump, 55, *57*, 114, 116, 168n26, 175n47. *See also* South Atlantic Route
Fort Clinch #3 Army Post, 135
Fort Desaix, 31
Fort DeSoto, 136
Fort Jefferson, 155
Fort Jefferson, FL, 76
Fort Jefferson Coast Guard Seaplane Station, 139
Fort Lamy, 53
Fort Lauderdale, FL: Alexander R. "Sandy" Nininger in, 61; Franklin D. Roosevelt in, 32; Germans in, 29; harbor at, 1; Hepburn Board in, 22; naval air station at, 26, 34, 138, *150*; number of military personnel in, 112; population of, 15, 112, 146, 147; as populous area of Florida, 74; shipbuilding in, 122; statue of Alexander R. "Sandy" Nininger in, 167n2; U-boat battles near, 74, 82; US soldiers from, 161n14
Fort Lauderdale International Airport, 151

Fort Meade, MD, 66
Fort Myers, FL: as coastal location, 15; Doolittle Raiders at, 51; Gulf of Mexico at, 92; HALPRO expedition at, 58; military installations at, 41, 58, 126, 137, *150*; population of, 16, 147; as smaller municipality, 15, 16
Fort Myers Army Airfield, 58, 137, *150*
Fort Pierce, FL, 71, 82, 147
Fort Pierce Naval Amphibious Training Base: Army Rangers trained at, 96, 98–99; Attack Boat School at, 100; characteristics of, 98; details of training at, 87, 97, 98–101; landing craft at, 100–101; location of, 98, 137; number of service members trained at, 87, 101, 155; opening of, 98; US Army Ground Forces at, 87
Fort Pierce Outlying Field, Naval Air Station Vero Beach, 137
Fort Walton Beach, FL, 134
Fountain Auxiliary Airfield, Naval Air Station Pensacola, 133
Four Base Plan, 39
France: declaration of war on Germany by, 28; German occupation of, 29; maps of, *56*; surrender of, *44*; territories of, 42; treasury of, 31; US ambulance driver in, 99; US bomb groups in, 104, 108; US invasion of, 94, 171n34, 171n40; US troops in, 89, 165n52
Francis Outlying Field, Naval Air Station Jacksonville, 135
Freetown, Sierra Leone, 53
French Alps, 30
French Equatorial Africa, 53, *56*
French Guiana, 43, 156
French Indochina, *57*, 148
French Navy, 31, 171n40
French North Africa, 48
French Riviera, 30
French West Africa, 42, *44*, *54*, *56*
Fritz Hotel, 38
Ft. Myer, VA, 116

Gable, Clark, 111, 174n27
Gaddis, John Lewis, 60
Gainesville, FL, 15, 16, 41, 135, 136, 147
Gainesville Municipal Airport, 135
Galapagos Islands, 33
Galveston, TX, *3*

INDEX

Gambia, 45, 53, *54*
Gambia River, 67
Garniers Field (Eglin auxiliary #4), 134
General Meyer (train car), 169n62
George Calvert (ship), 83
Georges Island, 91
Georgia, 10, 41
German Navy, 69–70
Germans, 10, 90, 119, 125–26, 151
Germany: and 1939 invasion of Poland, 28; and 1940 bombing of Great Britain, 29; and 1940 invasion of France, Holland, and Belgium, 29; after World War II, 148; and Allied forces, 88; as Axis power, 10; bombing of, 104, 108, 109, 174n22, 174n27; declaration of war against United States by, 69; declarations of war against, 28, 170n10; rise of Nazis in, 19; seizure of ships of, 32, 165n63; surrender of, 141
Gertrude (ship), 84
Gettysburg, PA, 64
Ghana, 66
Gibbs Gas Engine Company, 120
GI Bill, 175n35
Gold Coast, 53, *54*, *56*
Gonzalez Outlying Field, Naval Air Station Pensacola, 133, 134
Goodyear, 14, 33, 77, 98
Gotha Army Airfield, 136
Grand Bahama, 71
Great Bahama Bank, 170n7
Great Britain: and air routes, 43; declaration of war against Germany by, 28; and Egypt, 43; and English Channel, 2; and Pan American Airways, 45; post–World War II, 148; territories and colonies of, 6, *30*, 43, 50, 53, 58, 66, 148; as US ally, 88; and US assistance, 6, 31, 32, 43, 45–46, 111, 121, 122; and US defenses, 6, 29, 43, 45, 104; US forces in, 108; wartime struggles of, 29, 33, 42, *44*, 69
Great Depression, 11–12, 13, 74
Greater Miami, FL, 15, 180n53
Great Lakes, 4
Great War/World War I, *3*, 7, 18, 27, 38
Green Cove Springs, FL, 22–24, 25, 34, 135, *150*
Green Cove Springs prisoner of war camp, 126
Green Island (ship), 82
Greenland, 6, 166n36

Greenville Flying Academy, 37
Greenwood Cemetery, 65
Grenada Passage, 2
Griffith Army Air Forces Field, 138
Guadalupe, 43
Guam, 50, 108
Guantanamo, Cuba, 6, *23*, 73
Gulfamerica (ship), 82
Gulf Coast, 72
Gulf of Mexico: and anti-submarine warfare, 79; and bomber testing, 117; Franklin D. Roosevelt in, 20; German merchant ships in, 28; maps of, *3*, *44*, *73*; maritime routes in, *3*; Mechanized Landing Craft flotilla in, 92; and military training, 51, 95, 102; as part of US frontier, 3; rockets fired into, 151; shipping in, 4; U-boat battles in, 69, *73*, 82, 83, 84, 85, 86, 170n11; and US defenses, 37, 40, 87; and US Southeastern District, 41; waters of, 2
Gulfoil (ship), 83
Gulfpenn (ship), 83
Gulfprince (ship), 83
Gulf Sea Frontier: anti-submarine measures in, 77, 81, 171n33; headquarters of, 74, 80; map of, *23*; military importance of, 158; U-boat battles in, 69, *73*, 82–85, 86
Gulf State (ship), 86
Gulf Stream, 2, 71
Gulfstream Hotel, 133
Gulfstream Park, 139
Guyana. *See* British Guiana; French Guiana; Portuguese Guiana

Hagan (ship), 81, 84
Haifa, Israel, 168n37
Haiti, *3*, *44*, 45
Halderman-Elder Field, 137
Halifax River, 131
Halo (ship), 82, 83
HALPRO expedition, 52, 57–58, 59, 114
Halsey (ship), 82
Halsey, William F. "Bull," Jr., 22
Halverson, Harry E., 58
Hamburg, Germany, 28
Hampton Auxiliary Army Airfield, 137
Hampton Roads (ship), 83
Hanks, Tom, 173n59

Harbeson City, FL, 95
Hart Outlying Field, Naval Air Station Jacksonville, 135
Hastings Field, 53, *54*, *56*
Haupt, Herbert, 75
Havana, Cuba: and Florida Straits, 71; maps of, *3*, *73*; and search for *U-157*, 81; and SS *St. Louis*, 28; U-boat battles near, *73*, 84, 86
Hawaiian Islands, 5, 180n63
Haynes, Caleb, 53, 54, 167n42, 168n26
Hector (ship), 83
Hendricks Army Airfield, 137, *150*
Hepburn, Arthur J., 22, 24
Hepburn Board, 22–24
Heredia (ship), 83
Herlong Outlying Field, Naval Air Station Jacksonville, 135
Hermis (ship), 84
Hialeah, FL, 68, 112, 146, 147
Hialeah Racetrack, 112, 139
Higgins, Andrew, 100
Hillsborough Army Airfield, 41, 136, *150*
Hillsborough County Commission, 39
Himalaya Mountains, 55, *57*, 114–15, 116
Hirohito, Emperor, 144
Hiroshima, Japan, 7, 143, 158
Hispanics, 162n36
Hitler, Adolf, 32, *44*, 50, 166n32
Hobe Sound, FL, 49, 81, 82, 138
Hoequist Auxiliary Army Airfield, 136
Holland, 29, 43, 104
Holland, Spessard B.: and Albert H. Blanding, 167n52; and creation of Florida Defense Force, 47; as Democrat, 18; as governor of Florida, 14, 18, 41, 46, 47, 121, 152, 167n52; and military aviation, 14, 18, 41, 46; and shipbuilding, 121; as US senator, 152; as veteran, 18
Holley Outlying Field, Naval Air Station Whiting Field, 133
Hollywood, FL, 26, 138, 146, 147
Hollywood Beach Hotel/Resort, 26, 139
Hollywood Victory Committee, 111
Holm Airport, 133
Holocaust, 28
Holopaw Field, 136
Holt Field (Eglin auxiliary #6), 134
Homestead Air Force Reserve Base, 157
Homestead Army Airfield, *54*, 114–15, 116, 139, *150*

Homestead Ledger, 33
Homestead prisoner of war camp, 126
Homing pigeons, 77
Honshu, Japan, 142
Hooligan Navy, 79, 122
Hornet (ship), 51, 157
Horseshoe Point Auxiliary Army Airfield, 135
Houma, LA, 79
Houston (ship), 24, 164n20
Howell, George, 27
HR 4906, 129
Huckins Yacht Company, 120, 164n13
Hump Route, 55, *57*, 114, 116, 168n26, 175n47. See also South Atlantic Route
Hungary and Hungarians, 10
Hunter College, 64
Huntsville, AL, 151
Hurlburt Field, 134
Hyde Park, 66

Iceland, 80, 166n36
Illinois River, 4
Immokalee Army Airfield, 41
Immokalee Auxiliary Army Airfield, 137
India: and air routes, 43, 53, *57*; Aquila Force and, 52, 54; as British territory, 43; post–World War II, 148; Project X aircraft in, 57; and Stilwell Road, 59
Indian River, 92, 98, 100
Infantry, 29–30, 47, 88–90, 93–94, 95, 101
Intercity Peninsula, Tampa Bay, 39, 41
Iran, 43, 53, *56*
Isle of Pines, Cuba, *73*, 79
Israeli Air Force, 168n37
Italians, 10, 119
Italy: African American troops in, 174n31; as Axis power, 10; blimps in, *78*; post–World War II, 148; US forces in, 94, 108, 109, 171n34, 172n28
Iwo Jima, Japan, 142, 156, 178n5

Jacaranda Hotel, 139
Jacksonville, FL: and 1938 aviation war games, 39; and end of World War II, 144; female welders in, 123; harbor at, 1; Hepburn Board in, 22–24; maps of, *23*, *73*; and military facilities, 20, 22–24, 34, 135, *150*; military personnel in, 112; and military training, 15, 20, 35; Nazi saboteurs in, *73*, 75; and Pensacola, FL, 24; population

of, 15; and railroads, 13; as seaport, 14; and shipbuilding, 15, 120, 121, 123, 164n13; threats to, 171n40; U-boat battles near, *73, 82*; and US military presence in Florida, 36
Jacksonville Army Airfield, 135, *150*
Jacksonville Beach, FL, 75
Jacksonville Chamber of Commerce, 24, 47
Jacksonville International Airport, 151
Jacksonville Municipal Airport, 25
Jacksonville Naval Air Training Operating Base, 24–25, 164n27
J.A. Jones Construction Company/Wainwright Shipyard, 121
Jamaica, *3, 6, 44, 73, 78, 79*
Jamaicans, 10
J.A. Moffett Jr. (ship), 84
Japan: Allied preparations to invade, 98, 114, 120, 128, 141, 142–43, 177n87; atomic bombing of, 68, 143–44; and Burma, 54; and China, 21, 114, 116; December 1941 attacks by, 49, 50; Imperial forces of, 42, 51, 62–63, 114; Kwantung Army of, 114; post–World War II, 148; and pressures on Allied forces, 88; rise of aggression in, 19; surrender of, 144, 178n16; traditional bombing of, 52, 58, 108, 118, 168n26
Japanese, 11, 142
Jasper Outlying Field, Naval Air Station Jacksonville, 134
Java Arrow (ship), 82
Jeanne D'Arc (ship), 31
Jews, 149
Johns, Charles Eugene, 180n51
Johnson, Dovey M. Roundtree, 130
Johnston, Gordon, 91
Joint Army/Navy Experimental Testing (JANET) Board, 98, 155
Joint Chiefs of Staff (JCS), 40, 67, 153
Joseph Conrad (ship), 27
Joseph M. Cudahy (ship), 82

Kano, Nigeria, 53
Karachi, Pakistan, 53, 56, *57,* 113
Kauffman, Draper L., 99–100
Kauffman, James L., 80
Kay Larkin Outlying Field, Naval Air Station Jacksonville, 135
Keating, Frank Augustus, 92
Keegan, John, 60

Kehler Shipbuilding, 120
Kendall Miami prisoner of war camp, 125, 126, 176n41
Kennedy, John F., 171n41
Kerling, Edward John, 75
Key Biscayne, FL, 81
Key Largo, FL, *30,* 74, 121
Keystone Army Airfield, 135, *150*
Key West, FL: blimps at, *78;* as coastal location, 15; and Florida Straits, 71; Franklin D. Roosevelt in, 24; and fresh water, 146; growth of, 146; Gulf Sea Frontier headquarters at, 74, 80; harbor at, 1; Harry S. Truman in, 153, 155; Hepburn Board in, 22; maps of, *3;* military facilities at, 19, 24, 28, 34, 35, 49, 79, 139, *150;* mine field at, 81; and Overseas Highway, 24; population of, 16, 147; post–World War II, 153; and search for *U-157*, 81; as smaller municipality, 15, 16; and tourism, 146; U-boat battles near, 84, 85; and US military presence in Florida, 36; USS *Dahlgren* in, *30;* before World War II, 19
Key West Naval Station, 28
Khartoum, Sudan, 53, *56*
Kilroy, 17
King, Ernest J., 22, 32, 40, 74
King Cole Hotel, 133
King Outlying Field, Naval Air Station Pensacola, 133
Kingston, Jamaica, *3*
Kiowa tribe, *105*
Kissimmee Army Airfield, 41, 136, *150*
Knox, Frank, 32, 33
Knoxville City (ship), 83
Kobayashi, Tamotsu, 162n44
Kobe, Japan, 51
Korsholm (ship), 82
Kyushu, Japan, 142

La Belle Auxiliary Army Airfield, 137
Laertes (ship), 82
Lake Arbuckle, 106
Lake Beresford, 121
Lake Butler Outlying Field, Naval Air Station Lake City, 135
Lake City, FL, 25, 34
Lake George State Forest, 121
Lakehurst, NJ, 35
Lake Kissimmee, 106

204 INDEX

Lakeland, FL, 147
Lakeland Army Airfield, 41, 46, 137, *150*
Lakeland Municipal Airport, 37, 137
Lake Okeechobee, 92
Lake Pontchartrain, 97
Lake Wales Army Airfield, 137
Lake Worth, FL, 147
Lake Worth Auxiliary Army Airfield, 138
Lalita (ship), 84
Land, Emory S., 27–28
Lantana Auxiliary Army Airfield, 138
La Paz (ship), 82
Leahy, William D., 24, 40
Ledo Road/Burma Road/Stilwell Road, 59, 116, 158, *159*
Leesburg Army Airfield, 41, 136, 137, *150*
Leesburg Army Service Center, 137
Leesburg prisoner of war camp, 126
LeMay, Curtis, 167n42
Lend-Lease: activities under, 45–46, *54*, 59–60, 121; Claude Pepper and, 32; Franklin D. Roosevelt and, 31–32; Great Britain and, 31, 32, 45–46, 121, 122; legislation authorizing, 32; PT crash boats for, 122; Russia/Soviet Union and, 113, 122
Leslie (ship), 82
Leslie, Desmond, 39
Leyte, Philippine Islands, 95
Liberia, 52, 53, *54*
Liberia Airport, 168n19
Lincoln, Abraham, 20, 75
Lincoln Army Flying School, 137
Lindbergh, Charles, 14, 43
Little Bahama Bank, 170n7
"Little Boy," 68
Lod airfield, 168n37
Lodwick, Albert I., 37
Lodwick School of Aeronautics, 37
Lombard, Carole, 111
Long Island, New York, 75
Lost Horizon, 168n13
Louisiana, 10, 41, 47, 79, 151, 161n7
Lower Matecumbe Key, 84
Lubrafol (ship), 82
Lucas, Ruth A., 130
Lumberton, NC, 64
Luzon, Philippine Islands, 62, 95. *See also* Philippine Islands

Lysefjord (ship), 86

Mabry, Dale, 41
MacArthur, Douglas, 56, 62, 144, 178n15
Macarthur Outlying Field, Naval Air Station Miami, 138
MacDill, Leslie, 41
MacDill Field/Southeast Air Base: and antisubmarine patrols, 155; Axis prisoners of war at, 126; bomber groups at, 41, 102, 104, *105*; characteristics of, 103; civilian trainers at, 55; dedication of, 41; establishment of, 39–40; expansion of, 106; hospital for, 133; Jimmy Doolittle at, 103; location of, 40, 103, 136; map of, *150*; Medal of Honor presentation at, 168n30; Project X and, 55–56; and racial unrest, 128, 129; size of, 106; training at, 41, 55–56
Macia, James H., 168n9
Madison Outlying Field, Naval Air Station Jacksonville, 135
Mahan, Alfred Thayer: on Caribbean's strategic importance, 3, 4, 5, 24, 70; colleagues of, 101; on definition of crossroads, 70; on Florida's strategic importance, 3, 69, 70, 157; on military importance of geography, 6; on need for small craft for defense, 79; as part of coal-powered era, 161n7; on US vulnerability and defense by sea, 2–4, 5, 22, 72
Maiduguri, Nigeria, 53, *56*
Maine, 3
Maj. Gen. Henry Gibbons (ship), 84
Makin Island, 180n56
Malabar Outlying Field, Naval Air Station Melbourne, 137
Malaya, 50, *57*
Malone Auxiliary Army Airfield, 134
Mambi (ship), 86
Managua (ship), 84
Manhattan Project, 68, 118, 141
Manila, Philippine Islands, vi, 62
Manzanillo (ship), 85
Maps (term), 71
Marathon Key Outlying Field, 139
Marianna Army Airfield, 134, *150*
Marianna prisoner of war camp, 126
Maritime Officer Candidate School, 27
Maritime Service Training Station, 27
Marshall, George C., 28, 40, 74, 98, 119

INDEX

Martinique, 3, 31, 42, 43, 171n40
Mary Esther Field, 134
Maryland, 97, 102
Maxwell Outlying Field, Naval Air Station Jacksonville, 135
Mayport, FL: 4th Fleet in, 157; location of, 24; military installations in, 25, 34, 35, 135, *150*, 157
McAllister Hotel, 139
McCampbell, David, 164n27
McCarty, Daniel Thomas, 180n51
McCloskey, Matthew H., Jr., 122
McCloskey Shipyards, 122
McGuire, Thomas B., Jr., 166n28
McTureous, Robert M., Jr., 178n6
Meacham Field, 79. *See also* Naval Air Station Key West
Meacham Outlying Field for Lighter Than Air, 139
Medals and awards: Distinguished Unit Commendation, 104, 108, 109; Medal of Honor, 61, 62–63, 91, 167n2, 168n30, 174n22, 178n6; Presidential Unit Citation, 175n48; Purple Heart, 177n87
Medical transports, 131–33
Mediterranean, 43, 48, *56*
Melbourne, FL, 34, *150*, 170n28
Melbourne prisoner of war camp, 126
Memphis (ship), 67
Mentor (ship), 83
Merchant Marine Act, 26
Merchant Mariners, 17
Mercury Sun (ship), 83
Merle Fogg airstrip, 26. *See also* Naval Air Station Fort Lauderdale
Merrill-Stevens Company, 120
Merrimack (ship), 84
Mexico, 3, 42, 44, 170n10
M.F. Elliott (ship), 84
Miami, FL: 1941 air fair in, 14; and air routes, 45, 113; and anti-submarine warfare, 85; and aviation, 26; aviation training at, 35, 37, 38, 46; civilian airlines in, 14, 44, 53, 113; and distance to Karachi, Pakistan, 113; and end of World War II, 144; Enola Gay Tibbets in, 68; Franklin D. Roosevelt in, 24, 31; Gulf Sea Frontier headquarters in, 80; Hap Arnold in, 116; harbor at, 1; Hepburn Board in, 22; hotels in, 133, 139; incarceration of *Arauca* officers and crew in, 32; location of, 15, 112; maps of, *54, 73*; military facilities at, 26, 29, 34, 35, 77, 133, 138, 139, *150*; military housing in, 15; number of military personnel in, 112; as part of US Coast Guard 7th District, 157; Paul Tibbets in, 178n12; population of, 14, 74, 112, 145, 146; post office induction station in, 48; *Potrero del Llano* survivors in, 75; prisoner of war camp in, 176n41; and railroads, 13, 64, 66, 115; as seaport, 14; Shenandoah neighborhood of, 68; and shipbuilding, 120; shopping center in, 125, 176n41; and SS *St. Louis*, 28; and U-boats, 73, 74, 81, 83, 84; vulnerability of, 26, 171n40
Miami 36 Street Airport, 138
Miami Army Air Depot, 138
Miami Army Airfield: and air cargo, 59; and civilian airlines, 59, 112–13, 174n33; establishment of, 42; Hap Arnold and, 117; landing of wounded soldiers at, 133; location of, 138; map of, *150*; post–World War II, 146; and preparations for invasion of Japan, 143; and South Atlantic, 59, 146
Miami Beach, FL: Adele Wainwright in, 179n17; Clark Gable in, 111; Elliott Roosevelt in, 154; hotels in, 109, 110, 133, 139, 143, 154; location of, 109; military facilities in, 139, 143; military housing in, 15; military training in, 109–10, 111, 154, 174n22; numbers of military personnel in, 109, 112; population of, 14, 74, 112, 146; returning GIs in, 180n55; sinking ship near, 74
Miami Beach Army Air Forces Basic Training Camps, 138
Miami Beach Army Air Forces Officers Training School, 138, 154
Miami Beach Army Air Force Training Base, 146
Miami Beach Golf Course, 111
Miami-Dade College, 138
Miami Daily Herald, 178n2
Miami Daily News, 178n2
Miami Gardens, FL, 138
Miami High School, 143
Miami Intermediate Air Depot No. 6, 112–13, 115–16
Miami International Airport, 146
Miami Municipal Airport, 26, 38
Miami River, 121
Miami Shipbuilding Company, 120, 121, 164n13

Middleburg Outlying Field, Naval Air Station Jacksonville, 135
Middle East, 45, 58, *115*
Midway, 166n22
Mile Branch Outlying Field, Naval Air Station Jacksonville, 135
Military Airlift Command (MAC), 154
Military Canine Corps, 76
Military draft/conscription, 30–31, 48–49
Military hospitals: beds in, 133, 177n85; facilities for, 110, 116, 133, 139; functions of, 133, 140; Hap Arnold at, 116, 117; locations of, 110, 116, 133
Military hospital ships, 96, 131
Military police (MPs), 112, 128, 129
Mills, James Henry, 172n28
Milton Outlying Field, Naval Air Station Pensacola, 134
Minneola Auxiliary Army Airfield, 136
Mississippi (state), 10, 37, 41, 47
Mississippi River: extent of, 4; maps of, *3;* military threats to, 31; mining of mouth of, 72, *73;* and Pensacola, FL, 24; as shipping route, 4; and Southeast Air Base/MacDill Field jurisdiction, 39; transport of LSTs via, 156; tributaries of, 4; U-boat battles near, 72, 73
Missouri (ship), 144, 178n15
Missouri River, 4
Mitchell, William "Billy": and air forces as independent military branch, 7, 8, 40, 153; B-29 as dream of, 117; court-martial and retirement of, 8; and Franklin D. Roosevelt, 9; on officers for aviation forces, 107–9; pilots serving under, 41; and proposal to replace US War Department, 9; and Royal Air Force, 9; and World War I, 7
Mona Passage, 2, *3*
Monroe County, FL, 145
Monroe Doctrine, 21, 28
Montana, 4
Montbrook, FL, 41
Montbrook Army Airfield, *150*
Montbrook Auxiliary Army Airfield, 135
Monte Cassino, Italy, 158
Monticello Auxiliary Army Airfield, 134
Montreal, Canada, 43
Moorman, Didi, 175n57

Morgenthau, Henry, Jr., 28
Morison, Samuel Eliot, 5
Morocco, 42, *56,* 66
Morrison Army Airfield/Air Base: and bombing of Japan, 52; establishment of, 42; facilities at, 58; HALPRO expedition at, 58; landing of wounded soldiers at, 133; location of, 42, 58, 65, 113, 138; maps of, *54, 150;* medical facility for, 133; and South Atlantic Route, 58; US Air Transport Command and, 65, 113
Mossy Head Field (Eglin auxiliary #1), 134
"Mother at Your Feet Is Kneeling," 65
Mounted Patrol, US Coast Guard, 76, 86
Mount Suribachi, 178n5
Mullet Key, FL, 136
Munger T. Ball (ship), 82
Murmansk Run, 113
Muskogee, FL, 134
Myrtle Beach Field, 137

Nagasaki, Japan, 143–44
Nagoya, Japan, 51
Nanking, China, 21, *57*
Naples, Italy, *56,* 89
Naples Army Airfield, 41, 137, *150*
NASA, 152
Natal, Brazil, 53, *54,* 67
National Airlines, 14, 59, 113
National Guard. *See* US National Guard
National Negro Council, 130
Nautilus Hotel, 110, 133, 139
Naval Air Navigation School, 26, 138
Naval Air Station Alameda, 51, 157
Naval Air Station Banana River: and antisubmarine warfare, *78,* 79, 151; and Atlantic Ocean, 26, 152; construction of, 26, 70; garrison strength at, 34; legislation authorizing, 26; location of, 70, 136, 151, 152; map of, *150;* post–World War II, 151–52; U-boat battle near, 70
Naval Air Station Daytona Beach, 34, 135, 136, *150*
Naval Air Station DeLand, 25, 34, 136, *150*
Naval Air Station Dinner Key, 34, 67
Naval Air Station Fort Lauderdale, 26, 34, 138, *150*
Naval Air Station Houma, 79
Naval Air Station Jacksonville, 34, 120, 134, 135, *150,* 165n60
Naval Air Station Key West, 34, 79, 139, *150*

Naval Air Station Lake City, 34, 135, *150*
Naval Air Station Melbourne, 34, 137, *150*
Naval Air Station Miami, 26, 34, 146, *150*
Naval Air Station Miami Mainside Field, 138
Naval Air Station Miami Masters Field, 138
Naval Air Station Miami Municipal Field, 138
Naval Air Station Pensacola: airfields of, 134; and base housing, 147; expansion of, 24–25; Franklin D. Roosevelt at, 164n20; garrison strength at, 34; instructors from, 155; location of, 133; map of, *150*. *See also* Pensacola, FL
Naval Air Station Richmond: airships at, 35, 77–79, 85, 151, 171n33; garrison strength at, 34; location of, 34, 35, 77; maps of, *78, 150*
Naval Air Station Richmond Lighter Than Air Navy blimp Station, 138
Naval Air Station Sanford, 34, 136
Naval Air Station Vero Beach, 34, 137, *150*
Naval Air Station Whiting Field, 133
Naval Amphibious Training Base Fort Pierce, 87, 97, 98–100, 137, 155
Naval Auxiliary Air Facility Barin Field, *150*
Naval Auxiliary Air Facility Boca Chica, 139
Naval Auxiliary Air Facility Bronson Field, *150*
Naval Auxiliary Air Facility Cecil Field, *150*
Naval Auxiliary Air Facility Dinner Key, 138, *150*
Naval Auxiliary Air Facility Ellison Field, *150*
Naval Auxiliary Air Facility Green Cove Springs, *150*
Naval Auxiliary Air Facility JAX Municipal #1, *150*
Naval Auxiliary Air Facility Mayport, *150*
Naval Auxiliary Air Facility North Pompano, 138
Naval Auxiliary Air Facility Saufley Field, *150*
Naval Auxiliary Air Facility West Prospect, 138
Naval Auxiliary Air Facility Whiting Field, *150*
Naval Auxiliary Air Station Barin, 34, 134
Naval Auxiliary Air Station Bronson Field, 34, 134
Naval Auxiliary Air Station Cecil Field, 34, 135
Naval Auxiliary Air Station Corry Field, 34, 133, 134, *150*
Naval Auxiliary Air Station Ellyson Field, 34, 134
Naval Auxiliary Air Station Green Cove Springs, 34, 135
Naval Auxiliary Air Station Jacksonville Municipal #1, 34

Naval Auxiliary Air Station Mayport, 34, 135
Naval Auxiliary Air Station Milton, 134
Naval Auxiliary Air Station Saufley Field, 34, 134
Naval Auxiliary Air Station Whiting Field, 34, 134
Naval Auxiliary Air Station Witham, 137
Naval Auxiliary Aviation Facility Bronson Field, 133
Naval Ball Gunner School, 138
Naval Base Key West, 139
Naval Beach Battalions, 99
Naval Ship Facility, 138
Naval Sound Training School Key West, 139
Naval Station Key West, 153
Naval Station Mayport, 23, 157
Naval Station Roosevelt Roads, 33
Naval Submarine Base Key West, 139
Navarre Outlying Field, Naval Air Station Pensacola, 134
Navy Combat Demolition Units, 99
Navy Reserve Aviation Training Base, 26
Nebraska, 37
Neubauer, Hermann Otto, 75
Neutrality Patrol, 28–29
Newark, NJ, 75
New Deal, 17, 24, 26, 37, 44, 152
New England Sector, 23
Newfoundland, Canada, 6, 43
New Guinea, 89, 94, 95, 174n31
New Jersey Shore, 77
New Orleans, LA, 24, 73, 97, 100, 156
Newport News, VA, 157
New River, 122, 167n2
New Smyrna Outlying Field, Naval Air Station Daytona Beach, 136
New York (state), 77
New York, NY, 14, 64, 75, 171n40, 180n53
New York Philadelphia Sector, 23
Niceville Field (Eglin auxiliary #2), 134
Nicholas Cuneo (ship), 84
Nickeliner (ship), 86
Nidarnes (ship), 84
Nigeria, 52, *56*
Nile River, 53
Nimitz, Chester W., 142
Nininger, Alexander R. "Sandy," 61–63, 161n14, 167n2, 168n30

Norfolk, VA, 25, 92
Norlindo (ship), 82
Normandy, France, 89, 95, 99, 108, 122
North Africa, 90, 104, 108, 125
North Atlantic, 8, 101
North Atlantic Route, 43
North Carolina, 41, 64, 167n42
Northeast Florida, 134–36
Northern France, 89, 95, 104
Northern Solomon Island, 89
North Florida, 19–20, 152
North Fort Myers, FL, 137
North Hutchinson Island, 98
North Miami, FL, 145, 147
North Perry Outlying Field, Naval Air Station Miami, 138
North Pompano Outlying Field, Naval Air Station Fort Lauderdale, 138
Northwest Florida, 133–39
Northwest Providence Channel, 71
NRTB Miami, *150*

Oahu, HI, 62
Oakland Park Outlying Field, Naval Air Station Fort Lauderdale, 138
Ocala, FL, 37, 106, 136, 147
Ocala Auxiliary Army Airfield, 136
Ocala CPS, *150*
Ocala National Forest, 13, 141
Ocala State Forest, 121
Ocean Venus (ship), 82
Office of Civilian Defense, 129
Officer candidate schools (OCS): Hap Arnold and, 154; US Army Air Corps/Air Forces and, 106–7, 109, 111, 112, 153–54; US Maritime Service and, 27, 97
Off We Go into the Wild Blue Yonder!, 105
Ogontz (ship), 83
Ohioan (ship), 82
Ohio River, 4, 75
Okaloosa County, FL, 145
Okeechobee Auxiliary Army Airfield, 137
Okeechobee County, FL, 106
Okinawa, Japan, 142, 178n6
Oklahoma, 4, 102
Olancho (ship), 86
Old Bahama Channel, 71

Omaha Beach, 99, 122
Onondaga (ship), 85
Ontario (ship), 82
Opa-locka, FL, 19, 26, 138
Operation Coronet, 142
Operation Downfall, 142
Operation Market Garden, 90
Operation Matterhorn, 118
Operation Paper Clip, 151
Operation Pastorius, 10
Orion (ship), 29
Orlando, FL, 15, 16, 121, 145
Orlando Army Air Base, 42, 136, 166n28
Orlando Army Air Forces School of Applied Tactics, 106
Orlando International Airport, 151
Orlando Municipal Airport, 42
Orlando prisoner of war camp, 126
Ormond Beach, FL, *vi*, 170n28
Ormond-by-the-Sea, FL, 170n28
Osage tribe, 41, 166n22
Osceola Outlying Field, Naval Air Station Sanford, 136

Pace Outlying Field, Naval Auxiliary Air Station Ellyson Field, 134
Pacific Fleet, 22
Pacific Ocean, *3*, 5, 8, 22, 43–44, 77
Pacific Sector, *23*
Pacific Theater of Operations, 94, 98, 142
Page Field, 137. *See also* Fort Myers Army Airfield
Page Field prisoner of war camp, 126
Pagh, William S., *vi*
Palatka, FL, 135, 168n23
Palatka Operational Training Base, 135
Palestine, 58
Palm Beach, FL: female Coast Guardsmen in, 129; hotels in, 110, 133, 139, 143, 174n20; military aviation at, 52; military facilities in, 110, 133, 139, 143; military housing in, 15, 129, 174n20
Palm Beach Coast Guard Training Station, 138
Palm Beach County, FL, 11
Palmer, Gus, *105*
Panair do Brasil, 45. *See also* Pan American Airways
Panama and Panama Canal: and air routes, 71; and anti-submarine warfare, 79; Florida and, 2, *3*, 4, 5; Franklin D. Roosevelt in, 20, 164n20,

165n50; Puerto Rican National Guard in, 29; and shipping routes, 4; threats to, 31, 42, 171n40; transport of Doolittle Raid aircraft via, 157; and US defenses, 6, 22, 42; US National Guard training in, 29
Panama City, FL: army airfield at, 41, 134; as coastal location, 15; female welders in, 123; population of, 16, 146, 147; and shipbuilding, 120, 121, 123, 146; as smaller municipality, 15, 16
Panama Coastal Frontier, 23
Panama Sea Frontier, 23
Pan American Airways: and air routes, 14, 44–45, 54, 66, 114; and cargo flights, 59, 113; and Chapman Field, 38; and Clipper Ship seaplanes, 44, 67; Franklin D. Roosevelt and, 67; and Great Britain, 45; headquarters of, 14, 44, 53, 113; and Liberia Airport, 168n19; and military aviation training, 26, 55–56, 168n9; pilots for, 44; subsidiaries of, 45, 53; and transport of newsreel footage, 21; wartime nationalization of, 113
Pan American and Miami Army Airfield, 38
Pan American Field, 112, 174n33
Panay (ship), 163n9
Pancoast Hotel, 133
Pan Massachusetts (ship), 69, 70, 82
Paratroopers, 90, 106
Passage Key Bombing Range, 137
Patrick Air Force Missile Test Center, 152
Patrick Henry (ship), 120
Patton, George, Jr., 90
Paul H. Harwood (ship), 84
Paxon Outlying Field, Naval Air Station Jacksonville, 135
Pearl Harbor, HI, 5, 22
Pearl Harbor attack: Chief of Naval Operations during, 40; events of, 49; impact of, 62; Japanese fleet travel to, 42; as point of demarcation, 11, 16, 19, 27, 30, 31, 47, 50, 69, 73, 99, 111, 120, 129
Peking, China, 50
Pennsylvania, 4
Pennsylvania Sun (ship), 84
Pensacola, FL: airport near, 133; as coastal location, 15; description of, 19; desire for US military presence at, 36; Franklin D. Roosevelt in, 165n50; growth of, 146; harbor at, 2; and Jacksonville, FL, 24; maps of, *3, 73;* and Mississippi River, 24; naval facilities at, 19, 34, 35; population of, 16, 147; and railroads, 14; as seaport, 14; shipbuilding in, 121; as smaller municipality, 15, 16; U-boat battles near, *73;* before World War II, 19. *See also* Naval Air Station Pensacola
Pensacola Fields, 134. *See also* Naval Air Station Pensacola
Pentagon, 116
Pepper, Claude D., 18, 30, 32, 41, 121, 152
Percival, Arthur, 144, 178n15
Perry Army Airfield, 134, *150*
Persian Gulf, 113
Peter O. Knight Field, 136
Petroleum, 4
Philip (ship), 29
Philippine Defense Force, 62
Philippine Islands: Bataan peninsula of, 50, 55, 62–63, 167n2; Douglas MacArthur and, 56, 62; fighting in, 62–63; and independence, 62; Japanese in, 50, 62; map of, *57;* provisional commonwealth government of, 62; US invasion of, 94; US Military Cemetery in, *vi;* as US territory, 62, 163n9; US troops in, 5, 62, 89, 95, 121, 144, 161n14
Philippine Scouts, 62, 161n14, 169n52
Pine barrens, 157
Pinecastle Army Airfield, 42, 136
Pinecrest, FL, 139
Pinellas Army Airfield, 136
Planes. *See* Aircraft
Plant City Auxiliary Army Airfield, 137
Ploesti, Romania, 108
Pointe du Hoc, France, 99, 158
Poland and Polish, 10, 28, 62
Polaroid Trainer, 27
Pomona Outlying Field, Naval Air Station Jacksonville, 135
Pompano Outlying Field, Naval Air Station Fort Lauderdale, 138
Ponce de Leon (ship), 120, 125
Ponce de Leon Hotel, 139
Ponte Vedra Beach, FL, *73,* 75
Poolaw, Horace, *105*
Port Antonio (ship), 84
Port Everglades, FL, 26, 29, 32, 138

Port Everglades Coast Guard Patrol Base, 138
Port Everglades Naval Facility, 122
Port of Miami, 80
Port St. Lucie, FL, 71, 82, 92
Portugal, 8, 48
Portuguese Guinea, *54, 56*
Potomac (ship), 32
Potrero del Llano (ship), 74–75, 83, 170n18
Pratt and Whitney twin engine propellers, 77
Prisoners of war: Axis, 10, 90, 119, 125–26, 176n34; British, 178n15; US, 50, 121, 178n15
Project X, 52, 55–57, 58, 59
PT (Patrol Torpedo) boats: building of, 120, 164n13; engines on, 164n13; as experimental craft, 22; fuel capacity of, 164n13; Hap Arnold and, 117; as inexpensive vessels, 164n13; John F. Kennedy and, 171n41; legislation authorizing, 22; materials constructed of, 13, 121, 124, 164n13; Rescue Patrol Craft (RPC) Type/aviation rescue boats/"crash boats," 121–22; speed of, 164n13; underwater demolition teams and, 100; US Army Air Corps and, 121–22. *See also* Watercraft
Puerto Rican-American 65th National Guard Infantry Regiment, 29–30
Puerto Rico: 10th Naval District in, 22; and air routes, 52, *54;* maps of, *3, 23, 44;* and US defenses, 6, 33, 45; war preparations in, 22
Puerto Rico Sector, *23*
Punta Gorda Army Airfield, 41, 137, *150*
Putnam Outlying Field, Naval Air Station Jacksonville, 135

Quezon, Manuel L., 62
Quincy Auxiliary Army Airfield, 134

Radar: on airships, 33, 77, 78, 85; Doolittle Raiders and, 51; training in, 49, 138, 158, 180n59; on warships, 81; workings of, 72–73
Raiford State Prison, 47
Railroads: and accidents, 64–65; Atlantic Coastline Train #91, 64; in Brazil, 33; FEC Railroad, 112, 115; and military supplies, 112; and racial segregation, 128; routes for, 13–14, 15, 101, 113, 115, 180n63; as sabotage targets, 75; Seaboard Line, 112; Tamiami East Coast Champion train, 64–65; Tamiami West Coast Champion train, 64–65; transport of ships via, 121

Ramat David airfield, 168n37
Rangers, 96, 98–99, 173n59
Rawleigh Warner (ship), 84
Rawlings, Marjorie Kinnan, 64, 77
Realm (term), 2
Ream General Hospital, 133
Recife, Brazil, 45, *54*
Reconstruction Finance Corporation, 27
Red Ball Express, 90
Red Cross, 17
Red River, 4
Republic (ship), 82
Rhineland, 89, 95
Richmond, FL. *See* Naval Air Station Richmond
Richmond, VA, 64
Richmond Heights, FL, 138
Riddle, John Paul, 37, 38, 46
Riddle Field, 137
Riddle-McKay Aero College, 46
Rio Grande, 3
R.M. Parker, Jr. (ship), 85
Robert, Georges, 31
Robert E. Lee (ship), 85
Roberts Airfield, *54*
Roebling, Donald, 100
Rogers, Edith Nourse, 129, 130
Roma (blimp), 41
Rome, Italy, 89
Rommel, Erwin, 58, 114
Roney Plaza Hotel, 110
Roosevelt, Eleanor, 37, 129
Roosevelt, Elliott, 154
Roosevelt, Franklin (son), 180n56
Roosevelt, Franklin D. (father): 1941 declaration of state of emergency by, 47–48; and airships, 33; and Albert H. Blanding, 47; and Arthur J. Hepburn, 22; assumption of presidency by, 20; on Axis threat, 48, 165n50; and Billy Mitchell, 9; and bombing of Japan, 50, 51; characteristics of, 67, 169n63, 169n64; christening of first Liberty ship by, 120; and citation for CBI Air Transport Command, 175n48; and Civilian Conservation Corps, 164n42; and Clark Gable and Carole Lombard, 111; as commander in chief, 40; and construction for Southeast Air Base/MacDill Field, 39; death of, 141; and Doolittle Raid, 52; and Douglas MacArthur, 62; and Emory S. Land, 27–28; and Florida,

20, 24, 31, 32, 66–67, 116, 163n6, 164n20, 165n50, 165n60; and George C. Marshall, 28, 40, 164n42; and Great Britain, 29, *30*, 31–32; health of, 163n6; and Japanese invasion of China, 21; and Joint Chiefs of Staff, 40; and Lend-Lease, 31–32, *54;* and military draft, 30; and Nazi saboteurs, 75–76; and Neutrality Patrol, 28; and outbreak of World War II, 28; and Panama Canal and Panama Canal Zone, 20, 164n20, 165n50; public persona of, 40; and seizure of German ships, 32; sons of, 154, 180n56; and travel to and from Casablanca conference, 66–67; and US Maritime Service, 26–27; and US Navy, 20, 33; and war preparations, 19, 20, 21, 22; and William D. Leahy, 40; and Winston Churchill, 31, 67; and Women's Army Auxiliary Corps, 129; as yachtsman, 20

Roseland Outlying Field, Naval Air Station Vero Beach, 137

Rosenborg (ship), 84

Royal Air Force (RAF): in Cuba, 167n49; as independent military branch, 8, 9; Middle East airfields of, 168n37; training for, 38, 39, 45–46, 167n49; and U-boat battles, 85

Royal Navy, 29, 33, 74, 99

Rudder, James E., 99

Ruiz, Simon Bolivar, 165n52

Russians, 10

Russia/Soviet Union: and air routes, 43, 113; as Axis ally, *44;* German invasion of, *44*, 166n32; maps of, *57;* post–World War II, 148; and railroads, 113; supplies for, 43, 69, 113, 122; as US ally, 88

R.W. Gallagher (ship), 84

Ryan Field, 136

Saboteurs, *73,* 75–76
Sahara, 56
Saint Lucie River, 92
Salerno, Italy, 156
Sama (ship), 82
Samuel Q. Brown (ship), 83
San Antonio Aviation Cadet Center, 154
San Blas (ship), 84
San Diego, CA, 5, 22
Sanford, FL, 15, 16, 25, 136
San Juan, Puerto Rico, 29
San Julian, Cuba, 79

Santa Cruz, Brazil, 171n33
Santa Lucia, *3*
Santiago de Cuba (ship), 85
São Paulo, Brazil, 39
Sarasota, FL, 15, 16, 147
Sarasota Army Airfield, 41, 68, 137
Saving Private Ryan, 173n59
School of Applied Tactics, 42
Scotland, 99
Scouts and Raiders, 98
Screen Actors Division, Hollywood Victory Committee, 111
Seaboard Air Line, 112
SEAL (Sea, Air, Land) Teams, 173n64
Sebastian Inlet, 98
Sebring, FL, 41, 137
Select Training and Service Act of 1940, 30
Shanghai, China, 19, 50, *57*
Shangri-La, 52, 168n13
Sheherazade (ship), 84
Shipbuilding: businesses engaged in, 27, 120, 121, 122, 164n13; federal government and, 123; financing of, 27, 120, 123; in Florida, 15, 27–28, 80, 97, 119, 120–23, 157, 164n13, 180n64; labor force for, 123; for Lend-Lease vessels, 121; materials used in, 120, 121, 124; New Deal and, 26; number of persons engaged in, 123; numbers of ships built, 120, 124; techniques for, 120, 122, 123; training for, 123–24; US Army and, 120, 121; US Maritime Commission and, 26, 27–28, 120, 121; US Navy and, 120, 123; War Shipping Administration and, 27–28; women and, 119, 123–24

Ships. *See* Watercraft
Shore Patrol, 112, 122
Sicily, 89, 94, 104, 108
Sierra Leone, 45, 53, *54, 56,* 65
Singapore, 50, *57,* 144
Smathers, George A., 152
Solomon Islands, 171n41
Sonar: airships and, 33, 77, *78;* training on, *30,* 49, 158; warships and, 81; workings of, 72–73
South America: and air routes, 8, 14; Allied airmen from, 39; defenses in, 29, 42–43, 45, 171n33; maps of, *3, 115;* threats to, 42–43, 48; U-boat battles in, 171n33
South Atlantic Route: and airlifts, 154; Aquila Force and, 52, 55; Casablanca conference

participants and, 66–67; casualties of, 116, 175n47; construction for, 113; embarkation point for, 58; and Flying the Hump, 116, 175n47; HALPRO expedition and, 52, 58; logistics of, 52, *54*, *115*; maps of, *54*, *56*, *115*; Miami and, 59; Pan American Airways and, 45, *54*, 66, 114; and preparations for invasion of Japan, 143; Project X and, 52, 55; stops along, 52–53, *54*; transport of wounded via, 132

South Atlantic Wing Command, 65

South Carolina, 10, 41

Southeast Air Base. *See* MacDill Field/Southeast Air Base

Southeastern Route. *See* South Atlantic Route

Southeast Florida, 138–39

Southern Defense Command, *23*, 44

Southern France, 89

South Florida: civilian aviation in, 26; Hap Arnold in, 116; military importance of, 26; military installations in, 19, 33, 42, 87; population of, 145, 152

South Hutchinson Island, 98

South Perry Outlying Field, 138

Southwest Florida, 137

Soviet Union. *See* Russia/Soviet Union

Spain, 48

Spanish Main, 72

SPARS program, 129, 131

Special Operations Command, 157

Spenser Outlying Field, Naval Auxiliary Air Station Milton, 134

Splinter Fleet, 80–81

Spruce Creek Outlying Field, Naval Air Station DeLand, 136

Stalin, Joseph, *44*

Stalingrad, Soviet Union, 113

Starke, FL, 47, 106, 135

Starke Army Airfield, 135

St. Augustine, FL, 15, 16, *73*, 139, 147

St. Augustine Coast Guard Training Station, 135

St. Augustine Outlying Field, Naval Air Station Jacksonville, 135

Stengel Field, 135

Stilwell, Joseph "Vinegar Joe," *54*, 59, 114, 168n23

Stilwell Road/Burma Road/Ledo Road, 59, 116, 158, *159*

St. Joe Paper Company, 92

St. Johns River, 20, *23*, 24, 157

St. Johns River Shipbuilding Company, 120

St. Louis (ship), 28

St. Lucia, *3*, 6

St. Mary's Outlying Field, Naval Air Station Jacksonville, 135

St. Paul's Catholic High School, 64, 65

St. Petersburg, FL: hotels in, 110, 133, 139, 143, 174n20; military facilities at, 26, 27, 41, 110, 133, 136, 137, 139, 143; military housing in, 174n20; population of, 15; railroads in, 64

St. Petersburg Coast Guard Station, 136

St. Petersburg Maritime Service Officer Candidate School, 97

St. Petersburg Merchant Marine Training Center, 97

St. Petersburg US Maritime Service Training Station, 27, 137

Straits of Florida, 3, 4

Straits of Gibraltar, 70, 171n34

Strategic Air Command (SAC), *115*, 154

Stuart, FL, 137, 170n28

Stuart Outlying Field, Naval Auxiliary Air Station Witham, 137

Stump Outlying Field, Naval Auxiliary Air Station Corry Field, 134

Subic Bay, 163n9

Submarine Chaser Training Center (SCTC), 80–81

Sudan, 53, *56*

Suez Canal, 58, 114

Sun (ship), 83

Surf Club Hotel, 139

Suriname, 4

Suwied (ship), 84

Swan Island, FL, 76

Sweeney, Charles W., 143

Switzerland Outlying Field, Naval Air Station Jacksonville, 135

Tactical Air Command (TAC), *115*, 154

Tallahassee, FL: African American population of, 128; African American soldiers in, 128; aviation training at, 39, 41; Frenchtown district in, 128; growth of, 146; location of, 15; military installations at and near, 87, 134; population of, 16, 128; post office induction station in, 49; racial

INDEX 213

unrest in, 128; as smaller municipality, 15, 16; state capitol in, 128; white police officers in, 128

Tallahassee International Airport, 151

Tampa, FL: and 1938 aviation war games, 39; African American population of, 128–29; female welders in, 123; maps of, *3, 73*; military installations at, 39, 128, 136; and military training, 106; population of, 15; post office induction station in, 48; race tracks in, 139; racial unrest in, 129; and railroads, 14; Scrub neighborhood of, 129; as seaport, 1, 14; shipbuilding in, 120, 122–23; Third Air Force at, 40–41; threats to, 171n40; U-boat battles near, *73*

Tampa Bay, 15, 39, 40, 103, 136

Tampa Bay, FL (city), 15, 112, 120, 144

Tampa Chamber of Commerce, 27, 39

Tampa Downs, 139

Tampa International Airport, 151

Tampa Marine and Bushnell Boatyards, 122

Tampa Shipbuilding and Engineering Company, 27

Tampa Shipbuilding Company (TASCO), 27, 122

Tarawa, Kiribati, 156

Taylor Auxiliary Army Airfield, 136

Tehran, Iran, *56,* 65, 113

Telogia prisoner of war camp, 126

Tennessee (state), 41

Tennessee River, 4

Tennille Auxiliary Army Airfield, 135

Texas: 265th Florida Coast Artillery Regiment in, 48; airships in, 35; and Doolittle Raiders training, 51; oil from, 4, *73,* 161n7; and rocket tests, 151

Thiel, Werner, 75

Thetis (ship), 81

Thomas, Ernest Ivey ("Boots"), Jr., 178n5

Thomas L. Haley (ship), 125

Tibbets, Enola Gay, 68, 143

Tibbets, Paul, 68, 117, 143, 178n12

Tibbets' Troubleshooters, 117

Tinian, 118, 143

Tinker, Clarence L., 41, 166n22

Titusville, FL, 106

Titusville Outlying Field, Naval Air Station Sanford, 136

Tokyo, Japan, 7, 51

Tokyo Bay, 142, 144

Tomoka Outlying Field, Naval Air Station Daytona Beach, 136

Torny (ship), 82

Touchet (ship), 86

Tower Hotel, 133

Trenchard, Hugh, 9

Trinidad: and air routes, 52, *54;* anti-submarine blimps in, *78;* as British territory, 6, 52; Casablanca conference participants in, 67; and US defenses, 6, 45, 53, 67

Trinidadians, 10

Tropical Park Racetrack, 139

Trout Creek Outlying Field, Naval Air Station Jacksonville, 135

Truman, Harry S.: assumption of presidency by, 142; and end of unlimited national emergency, 148; and Greenland, 166n36; in Key West, 153; and military leaders, 155; and post–World War II military reorganization, 155; as veteran, 144; on V-J Day, 178n16; warning of, to Japan, 144

Tunis, Tunisia, *56,* 158

Tunisia, *56,* 89, 108, 125

Tuscaloosa (ship), 31, 165n50

Tuskegee Airmen/322nd Fighter Group, 128

Tuskegee Army Airfield, 128

Two-Ocean War, The (Morison), 5

Tyndall Army Airfield, 134, 146, *150,* 174n27

U-boats: assignment of targets to, 72; battle tactics of, 72; in Bay of Campeche, 170n11; characteristics of, 72; concerns about US residents' collaboration with, 10; defenses against, 30, 72–73, 74, 77–85, 155; destruction of, 81, 85; and ease of entry into target areas, 71–72; and espionage, 75; along Florida, 30, 69–70; in Florida Straits, 71; in Gulf of Mexico, 170n11; at Martinique, 171n40; mission of, 72; navigation routes of, 170n11; near Bahamas Islands, 170n11; off Cape Canaveral, 69–70; off Florida Keys, 30; off Louisiana, 72; in Panama Canal Zone, 29; prisoners of war captured from, 125; *U-134,* 30, 85; *U-157,* 81; *U-176,* 85; *U-564,* 74, 170n18; along US Eastern Seaboard, 69; VIIC, 72; weapons on, 85

Umtata (ship), 84

Underwater Demolition Teams (UDTs), 99–100

Unified Combat Commands, 157

United Airlines, 113

United States: African American population of, 10, 127; and air routes, 43–45; Axis prisoners of war in, 176n34; Axis threats to, 42, 48; and Brazil, 43, 45; and Chiang Kai-shek, 114; and China, 88; desegregation of armed forces of, 153; East Coast of, 4, 91, 101; Eastern Seaboard of, 85; and Europe/Germany First strategy, 91, 101, 180n63; and French Guiana, 43; German declaration of war against, 50, 69; as global power, 155; and Great Britain, 29, 31, 32, 45–46, 88, 122; and Guadalupe, 43; and importance of land forces, 88; invasion of France by, 171n34, 171n40; invasion of Italy by, 171n34; and Lend-Lease, 31–32, 45–46, *54*, 59–60, 113, 121, 122; and Liberia, 53; maps of, *3, 44, 54;* and Martinique, 43, 171n40; military draft in, 30–31; military Oath of Allegiance of, 169n53; military population in, 112; and National Guard activation, 46–47; and Neutrality Patrol, 28; number of troops from, 16; population of, 9, 10, 127, 158; and post–World War II military reorganization, 153, 155; and preparations for invasion of Japan, 142; and Russia/Soviet Union, 88; Southeastern District of, 41; state of emergency in, 48, 148; troop ship embarkation from, 180n64; West Coast of, 4, 5, 101, 142

University of Florida, *vi*, 124, 136

University of Florida Medical School, 68

University of Miami, 37, 38–39, 139, 143, 162n44, 168n9

US Air Force, 103, *115*, 153, 154, 155, 167n42

US Air Transport Command (ATC), 112, 113, *115*, 143

US Army: African American draftees in, 127; and Axis prisoners of war, 126; and battle tactics, 93–94; and camouflage, 88; and Caribbean Sea Command, 29; commandos in, 97, 98; components of, 36; facilities for, 139; George C. Marshall as chief of staff of, 28, 40, 74; in Greenland, 166n36; as independent military branch, 7; infantry divisions of, 88, 89; landing craft skippers in, 97; Medal of Honor recipients in, 172n28; Military Police of, 112; number of troops in, 16, 20, 49, 127; officer training in, 97, 107; and Philippine Scouts, 62; and planes for Royal Air Force training, 46; and radio signaling, 49; Regular Army, 47, 87, 107; and ROTC, 136, 139; segregation in, 127; and shipbuilding, 120, 121; size of, 20; supplies for, 74; training of, 101, 130; and war preparations, 19; and watercraft, 123, 124; women in, 129, 130; before World War II, 20

US Army Air Corps/US Army Air Forces (AAF): and 1941 Miami Air Fair, 14; African Americans in, 111–12; and aircraft carriers, 51; and airlifts, 154; anthem of, 105; and anti-submarine activities, 77, 155; and Axis prisoners of war, 126; and bombing of Japan, 51; casualties of, 103; and Civilian Pilot Training Program, 46; Clark Gable and, 111, 174n27; Direct Appointees in, 110; as elite branch of US military, 112; Elliott Roosevelt and, 154; facilities for, 19–20, 38, 39–42, 110, 116, 117, 140; fighter pilot aces in, 103; in Florida, 36; and Gulf of Mexico, 37; gunner aces in, 103; and health, 110; as independent military branch, 106–7, 118; medical facilities for, 116, 117; and Miami Intermediate Air Depot No. 7, 112; and Neutrality Patrol, 28; numbers of troops in, 16, 117; and officer training, 106–7, 109, 110, 111, 112, 153–54; in Philippine Islands, 50; physical requirements for, 107; pilots for, 37; and preparations for invasion of Japan, 142–43; promotion of, 111; proposals to separate from Army, 8, 40; and PT boats, 121–22; and radar, 49; recreational programs for, 111; renaming of, 107; training for, 37, 38–42, 106–7, 109, 110, 111, 112, 121–22, 153–54; West Point graduates in, 153–54; before World War II, 19–20

US Army Air Ferrying Command. *See* US Army Transport Command (ATC)

US Army Air Forces Hospital No. 1, 110, 116, 117

US Army Air Service, 7, 18

US Army Amphibious Command, 91

US Army Amphibious Training Center, 155

US Army Basic Training Camps, 47

US Army Ground Forces, 87, 91, 110, 127, 171n3

US Army Harbor Craft Companies, 97

US Army of Occupation, 148

US Army Philippine Division, 62

US Army Rangers, 96, 98–99, 173n59

US Army Remount Service, 76

US Army Reserve, 37, 49
US Army Service Forces, 119, 127, 174n31
US Army Signal Corps, 169n62
US Army Third Air Force, 102
US Army Third Air Force Trainer Cadre, 104
US Army Third Bomber Command, 41
US Army Third Fighter Command, 41
US Army Transport Command (ATC), 45, 65, 115, 132, 156, 175n35
US Army Transport Service (ATS), 87, 96, 97
US Army Women's Army Corps (WAC), 129
US Asiatic Fleet, 163n9
US Census, 9
US Civil Aeronautics Administration, 44
US Coast Guard: 7th District of, 157; African American draftees in, 127; and anti-submarine warfare, 76, 79; and civilian small boaters, 79; facilities of, 136, 138, 139; and Maritime Service training, 27; and Neutrality Patrol, 29; and SS *St. Louis*, 28; training stations for, 138; women in, 129, 131; before World War II, 19
US Coast Guard Auxiliary, 17, 79
US Congress: and Army Air Forces as independent military branch, 118; and establishment of US Air Force, 153; and Four Base Plan, 39; Senate of, 152; and transfer of property to Eglin Military Reservation, 41; and veteran status for US Maritime Service members, 169n48; and veteran status for WASPs, 169n43; and war preparations, 21–22
US Congressional Research Office, 60
US Department of Defense, 153, 155
US Department of the Treasury, 123
US House of Representatives, 152
US Marine Corps: African American draftees in, 127; and Battle of Iwo Jima, 178n5; Franklin Roosevelt (son of FDR) in, 180n56; in Iceland, 166n36; and landing craft, 101; Medal of Honor winners from, 178n6; number of troops in, 16; in Pacific Theater of Operations, 101; pilot training in, 19; veterans of, 152
US Maritime Commission, 26, 27, 120, 121
US Maritime Service, 26–27, 37, 60, 101, 164n32, 169n48
US Maritime Service Training Station, 137
US Maritime Service Upgrade School, 97
US Middle East Air Force, 58, 168n37

US Military Academy, 61, 107, 116, 153, 169n52
US National Guard: activation of, 46–47; chiefs of, 47; divisions of, 172n8; from Florida, 18, 20, 47; Florida facilities of, 24, 47; infantry divisions of, 47, 48, 89; in Panama, 29; from Puerto Rico, 29–30; training of, 20, 29, 47, 48, 89
US Naval Academy, 99
US Navy: African American draftees in, 127; and aircraft, *30*, *33*; airfields of, *150*; and annexation of Miami Municipal Airport, 38; and anti-submarine warfare, 77–81; and aviation, 21, 22, 24, 28, 31, 33, 34, 35, 38; and Axis prisoners of war, 126; and bomb disposal, 99–100; cadets in, 49; and Caribbean Sea Command, 29; commandos in, 97, 98, 99, 101; corpsmen in, 64; and D-day invasion, 99; facilities of, 47, 138, 139–40; George C. Marshall and, 74; and gunnery, 33; and Imperial Japanese Navy, 51; as independent military branch, 7; landing craft skippers in, 97; Medal of Honor recipients from, 164n27; and merchant ships, 81; mission of, 5; and Navy Reserve, 163n73; and Neutrality Patrol, 28; officer training in, 139; and Pearl Harbor attack, 62; and Regular Navy, 163n73; and ROTC, 136; and Royal Air Force, 46; SEAL Teams in, 173n64; and shipbuilding, 120; shore patrol of, 112, 122; and sonar, 49; and submarine warfare, 73–74; training in, 19, 38, 101, 139; transfer of seized German ships to, 165n63; war games of, 24; and war preparations, 19, 21–22; and watercraft, 73, 80, 122, 123, 124; and WAVES, 64; during World War II, 16, 163n73
US Navy Department, 9, 155
US Navy Navigational School, 138
US Navy Reserve Women's Reserve (WAVES),
US Navy Subchaser Training Center, 85, 146
USO, 111
US Panama Canal Zone. *See* Panama and Panama Canal
US Philippine Islands Territory. *See* Philippine Islands
US Southern Command, 157
USS *Panay (PR-5)*, 21
US State Department, 9, 29, 52, 155
US Supreme Court, 75, 152

216 INDEX

US Virgin Islands, 6, *44*
US War Department: civilian employees of, 17; and defense of Western Hemisphere, 42; and Florida, 18; and hotels as troop housing, 174n20; and increased Army strength, 49; inefficiency of, 9; and land for Camp Gordon Johnston, 92; lands seized for, 11; and preparations for invasion of Japan, 177n87; proposals to replace, 9; and Southeast Air Base/MacDill Field, 39; and US Navy Department, 155; and US State Department, 155
US War Shipping Administration, 121
Utarom airfield, *vi*

Valkaria Outlying Field, Naval Air Station Melbourne, 137
Valparaiso, FL, 134
Van Kirk, Theodore "Dutch," 68
Velma Lykes (ship), 84
Venetian Pool, 110
Venezuela, *44, 45,* 161n7
Venice Army Airfield, 41, 137, *150*
Venice prisoner of war camp, 126
Veracruz, Mexico, *73*
Verdun, France, 64
Vero Beach, FL, 25, 34, *150*
Veterans Readjustment Act of 1944, 148
Vichy France, 31, 42, 171n40
Vichy-French Navy, 42
Vieques, Puerto Rico, 33, 165n64
Vietnam War, 158
Virginia, 39, 41
Virginia (ship), 83
Vitruvius (ship), 122
Volusia County, FL, 64
Vosges mountains, 165n52

WAAC (Women's Army Auxiliary Corps)/WACs (Women's Army Corps), 119, 129–31
Wainwright, Adele, 179n17
Wainwright, Jonathan, 121, 144, 178n15
Wainwright Shipyard/J.A. Jones Construction Company, 121, 123, 145
Wake Island, 50
Wakulla Springs, 95
Wallace Auxiliary Army Airfield, 136
Walt Disney Studio, 80, 115
War Bonds, 123

Warren Fish Boatyard, 121
Warrington, FL, 147
War Shipping Administration, 27, 74, 120, 124
War Training Service, 38
Washington, DC, 14, 64, 67, 75–76
WASPs, 49, 60, 175n57
Watercraft: aircraft carriers, 21, 22, *23,* 25, 31, 50–51, 171n40; ammunition barges and ships, 121, 122, 124; Army Barges, 124; aviation gas Liberty ships, 124; barges, 96, 97, 121; barracks barges, 122–23, 124; battleships, 21, 22, 49; boxed aircraft Liberty ships, 121, 124; cable-laying ships, 96; cargo ships, 96, 122; cement Liberty ships, 124; communications ships, 96; cranes, 97; cruisers, 21, 31, 49; cutters, 81; destroyer escorts, 122, 124; destroyers, 21, 28, 29, *30,* 31, 49, 67, 80, 85; destroyer tenders, 122; DUKW landing craft, 100; escort warships, 74, 171n40; floating, self-propelled warehouses, 96; freighters, 82, 83, 84, 85, 86, 121, 124; galleons, 72; Higgins Boats, 156; hospital ships, 96, 131; inter-island freighters, 96; landing craft, 87, 91–92, 93–94, 100–101; Landing Craft for Tanks, 100; Landing Craft Vehicle Personnel/Higgins Boats, 100, 173n66; Landing Vehicles, Tracked (LVTs/Alligators/Amtracs), 100–101, 173n68; for Lend-Lease, 122; Liberty ships, 120, 121, 122, 124–25; lighters, 97; liners, 85; LSTs, 156; materials constructed from, 13, 80, 121, 122, 124; Mechanized Landing Craft, 92; merchant ships, 85, 170n11; minesweepers, 13, 22, 120, 121, 122, 124; mini-subs, 100; oilers, 22; patrol craft, 80; picket boats, 51; railroad transport of, 121; repair of, 122; rubber boats, 99; sampans, 98; scows, 97; shrimp boats, 79; skiffs, 97; small craft, 79, 84, 85, 97, 121; subchasers, 13, 80, 85, 121, 124; submarines, 22, 153; tanker Liberty ships, 124; tankers, 69–70, *73,* 74, 81, 82, 83, 84, 85, 86, 96, 120, 170n13; tank transport Liberty ships, 121, 124; transports, 84, 100, 101; troopships, 96; tugs, 22, 96, 97, 121, 122–23, 124; warships, 29, 122, 153; yachts, 24, 79. *See also* PT (Patrol Torpedo) boats; U-boats
Watson Island, FL, 26
Wauchula Auxiliary Army Airfield, 137
W.D. Anderson (ship), 82
Weapons: .45 Caliber pistols, 88; bazookas, 88;

bolt-action rifles, 88; Browning Automatic Rifle (BAR), 88; cannons, 100; flame-throwers, 88; grenades, 88, 95; howitzers, 88–90, 106; M1 carbine, 88; M1 Garand rifles, 88, 173n66; machine guns, 88, 94, 100; mortars, 88; rocket launchers, 100; tanks, 121; Thompson submachine gun, 88
Welch Army Convalescent Center, 133
Wells Auxiliary Army Airfield, 137
West Africa, 8
Western Defense Command, *44*
West Palm Beach, FL, 15, 16, 42, 113, 138, 147
West Papua, New Guinea, *vi*
West Point, NY, 61, 169n52. *See also* US Military Academy
Whitehouse Airport, 135
White Springs prisoner of war camp, 126
Whiting Field prisoner of war camp, 126
William C. Bryant (ship), 85
William C. McTarnahan (ship), 83
William J. Salman (ship), 83
Williston, FL, 135
Wimauma Auxiliary Army Airfield, 137
Windermere, FL, 136
Windward Passage, 2, *3*
Winter Garden Army Airfield, 136
Winter Haven Auxiliary Army Airfield, 137
Winter Haven prisoner of war camp, 126
Withlacoochee Auxiliary Army Airfield, 136
Women: as Army nurses, *132;* and aviation training, 37; as flight instructors, 38; as government employees, 151; as Public Administration employees, 151; and shipbuilding, 119, 123–24; as soldiers, 129–30; and unemployment, 149; as Unpaid Family Workers, 151
Women Accepted for Volunteer Emergency Service (WAVES), 64, 80
Women's Air Service Pilots, 17

Women's Army Auxiliary Corps (WAAC)/Women's Army Corps (WACs), 119, 129–31
Women's Auxiliary Flying Squadron (WAFS), 169n43
Women's Flying Training Detachment (WFTD), 169n43
Worden (ship), 82
Works Progress Administration (WPA), 39, 47
World War I/Great War, *3, 7,* 18, 27, 38
World War II: in Asia, 5; enlistment period for US troops in, 91; in Europe, 5; military aviation during, 6; newspaper and radio reporting on, 178n2; outbreak of, 28; as point of demarcation, 19; scholarship on, 1, 5; US casualties in, 60–61, 169n50; US troop numbers in, 16; and V-J Day, 178n16
Wray, Joseph S., *vi*

Yamato Colony, 11, 162n44
Yangtze River, 19, 21
Yokohama, Japan, 51
Yucatán Channel/Passage: anti-submarine warfare in, 77; characteristics of, 70; flow of Caribbean waters into, 2; maps of, *3;* military importance of, 33; shipping in, 4; U-boat battles in, 70, 83, 84
Yucatán Peninsula, *73,* 83
Yucatán region, 79
Yuma, AZ, 93

Zelasko, Leonard E., *vi*
Zephyrhills Army Airfield, 41, *150*
Zephyrhills Auxiliary Army Airfield, 136
Zeppelin, Otto von, 33
Zeppelin Patrol (ZP) Squadrons, 77–79
Zeppelins. *See* Airships/blimps/zeppelins
Zone of the Interior, 133
Zoo Miami, *78*

Anthony D. Atwood, PhD, is the resident military historian at Florida International University. He is concurrently the founding executive director of the Miami-Dade Military Museum. A third-generation Floridian and a retired Navy Chief Warrant Officer 3, he lectures in military history and national security issues.

His work has restored the NAS Richmond, FL, headquarters building of the World War II Navy blimp base that fought the U-boat attacks on Florida. During the Cold War against Castro it was the CIA station for the gallant Cuban exile freedom fighters, and during Vietnam up to Desert Storm it was the local Army and Marine Corps Reserve Center. Repurposed into a museum, its grand opening was on Veterans Day 2023. This is his first book.

MICHAEL V. GANNON FUND

In honor of Michael Gannon's lasting legacy and his dedication to the scholarship of our state's history, the University Press of Florida has established the Michael V. Gannon Fund to provide continued support for first publications in Florida history. Royalties and gifts donated to this fund underwrite the costs of these monographs, helping to keep the price as affordable as possible.

Special thanks to Dr. Gary R. Mormino
for his very generous contribution to further publications
about the Sunshine State's long and fascinating history.